PRAISE FOR

YOU PLAY THE GIRL

"*You Play the Girl* by Carina Chocano blew my mind. Like a goldfish realizing that water existed, I instantly came alive to the air and the atmosphere of how my Otherness informed my girlhood. Each and every message of being asked to stand still so that I could be seen by the cultural product of male-made entertainment made me scream with recognition. In particular, the *Flashdance* chapter time-traveled me back to my youth, but holding hands with a clear-eyed, brilliant, hilarious friend. Re-looking at *Stepford Wives, I Dream of Jeannie, Bewitched,* and all of the other hypnotic suggestions about my supposed womanhood made me feel alive and energized and ready to topple the patriarchy. The world is changing for women and girls and here is one of the first steps — going back to do archaeology about what the heck happened to us, how we got colonized. If information is power, *You Play the Girl* is a superpower."

— JILL SOLOWAY, writer, director, creator

"Carina Chocano is a brilliant thinker, a dazzling stylist, and an intellectual in the truest sense of the word. An important critical work as well as an entertaining personal story, *You Play the Girl* looks at old archetypes in new and often astonishingly insightful ways and establishes Chocano as a unique talent and crucial voice in the cultural conversation."

— MEGHAN DAUM, author of
The Unspeakable: And Other Subjects of Discussion

"Carina Chocano unearths the little horrors of our culture's pervasive, insidious sexism in essays so brilliant and witty you'll wish her book would never end. Chocano is one of our sharpest, most original cultural observers, and *You Play the Girl* is as engrossing as it is unforgettable."

— HEATHER HAVRILESKY,
author of *How to Be a Person in the World*

YOU PLAY THE GIRL

YOU PLAY THE

GIRL

On Playboy Bunnies, Stepford Wives,
Train Wrecks, and Other Mixed Messages

Carina Chocano

A MARINER ORIGINAL
Houghton Mifflin Harcourt
Boston • New York
2017

For information about permission to reproduce selections from this book, write to trade.permissions@hmhco.com or to Permissions, Houghton Mifflin Harcourt Publishing Company, 3 Park Avenue, 19th Floor, New York, New York 10016.

www.hmhco.com

Library of Congress Cataloging-in-Publication Data is available.
ISBN 978-0-544-64894-4

Book design by Chrissy Kurpeski
Typeset in Miller Text and Benton Sans

Printed in the United States of America
DOC 10 9 8 7 6 5 4 3 2 1

"The Ingenue Chooses Marriage or Death," "Bad Girlfriend," "The Kick-Ass," "Surreal Housewives," "Celebrity Gothic," "A Modest Proposal for More Backstabbing in Preschool," and "Girls Love Math" first appeared in a different form in the *New York Times Magazine*. Portions of "Real Girls" and "Big Mouth Strikes Again" appeared in the *Los Angeles Times,* and a different version of "Thoroughly Modern Lily" was first published in *Salon*.

The author is grateful for permission to reprint lines from "Miley Cyrus Is Just Trying to Save the World" by Allison Glock (2015), courtesy of *Marie Claire,* Hearst Communications, Inc.

For Kira

In a society where values changed frequently, where fortunes rose and fell with frightening rapidity, where social and economic mobility provided instability as well as hope, one thing at least remained the same — a true woman was a true woman, wherever she was found. If anyone, male or female, dared to tamper with the complex of virtues that made up True Womanhood, he was damned immediately as an enemy of God, of civilization, and of the Republic. It was the fearful obligation, a solemn responsibility, which the nineteenth-century American woman had — to uphold the pillars of the temple with her frail white hand.

— BARBARA WELTER,
"THE CULT OF TRUE WOMANHOOD: 1820–1860"

The title women and fiction might mean, and you may have meant it to mean, women and what they are like; or it might mean women and the fiction that they write; or it might mean women and the fiction that is written about them; or it might mean that somehow all three are inextricably mixed together and you want me to consider them in that light.

— VIRGINIA WOOLF, *A ROOM OF ONE'S OWN*

From the time I was 11, it was, "You're a pop star! That means you have to be blonde, and you have to have long hair, and you have to put on some glittery tight thing." Meanwhile, I'm this fragile little girl playing a 16-year-old in a wig and a ton of makeup . . . When I wasn't on that show, it was like, Who the fuck am I? . . . My dream was never to sell lip gloss. My dream is to save the world.

— MILEY CYRUS,
ON PLAYING HANNAH MONTANA, IN *MARIE CLAIRE*

Contents

Introduction

MY DAUGHTER, KIRA, HAS HEARD BEDTIME STORIES AL-most every night since she was born. By the time she turned eight in 2016, she was surprisingly up to date on early *Peanuts* comics, the collected novels of Frances Hodgson Burnett, *Spider-Man* cartoons from the sixties, the existential adventures of Frog and Toad, the collected oeuvre of Roald Dahl, Star Wars through the ages, mother-and-daughter versions of the movie *Annie,* and *Ghostbusters* past and present. I didn't set out to lead her on a tour of my literary coming-of-age, nor did I anticipate, on revisiting them, that I would recall the stories I'd loved as a kid more vividly than actual events from my childhood. But that's exactly what happened. At times, I've questioned my motives. What did I think I was doing? What were my intentions, exactly? Was I introducing things to her, or introducing her to me? What if I was trying to introduce myself *in* her somehow, via her eyeballs and ear canals, like an airborne brain spore? Could that still be considered educational, or was it just creepy? Was I like every other parent, or like a parody of a hipster caregiver in a *Portlandia* sketch? Was that just how culture works?

Once, when Kira was five, I presented her with a beautiful, too-expensive illustrated copy of Lewis Carroll's *Alice's Adventures in Wonderland,* and I accidentally let it slip that I wasn't sure whether I'd read it before. She smelled a rat — probably because I was, in fact, proffering a rat. For one thing, we'd already established a system of recommendation rooted in unregenerate nostalgia, not pedagogy. For another, she'd already seen the animated Disney movie and read *Walt Disney's Alice in Wonderland,* the Little Golden Book based on the movie, and she hadn't liked them any more than I had at her age. But I was curious. I had the pressing feeling that the original had something urgent to tell me. So, I insisted, and

Kira relented, but a few pages in, she shut me down and demanded I read *Sleeping Beauty* instead.

The version of "Sleeping Beauty" we owned also happened to be the Little Golden Book version, *Walt Disney's Sleeping Beauty*, the one based on the movie featuring a Goth-Barbie Princess Aurora, the silly-goose fairies Flora, Fauna, and Merryweather, and the sophisticated supervillain, Maleficent. Kira was crazy about *Sleeping Beauty*. She could not get enough. We read the story every single night at bedtime, sometimes twice a night, for a year. She memorized it by heart from start to finish and insisted that I pause just before the part where Maleficent crashes the christening, so she could recite the lines. Every night, Kira gravely pronounced Maleficent's fatwa on the princess, followed by her parents' alarmed reactions.

"Before the sun sets on her sixteenth birthday, she shall prick her finger on the spindle of a spinning wheel, and d-i-i-i-e-e!" (she said in Maleficent's voice).

"Oh, no!" (she said in the queen's voice).

"Seize that creature!" (she said in the king's voice).

It was fun.

Her dad, Craig's, theory was that Kira loved *Sleeping Beauty* because it ends with the cursed princess Aurora reuniting with her parents after spending sixteen years in hiding with the fairies. Being welcomed home by her father, King Stefan, and her mother, the queen, who is nameless but alive (which is more than can be said for most princesses' mothers), was the real happy ending. This made sense to me; five-year-olds want nothing more than to be autonomous and free, but also safe, cherished, and loved — just like adults. Still, I wasn't satisfied. I kept fishing for some stunning preschool insight, some apocalyptic nugget of truth that would reveal all. Like, *why* did she like Sleeping Beauty so much? What about her did she rate so highly above the other princesses? I liked to imagine that it had something to do with her ultimately defying a death sentence, or maybe that Kira was unconsciously attracted to the power of the rebel fairy. But my daughter's answer was always the same: Sleeping Beauty was the prettiest. And it was true. She was. And really, what else was there to go by in a heroine? She had the longest, blondest, most flowing hair. Her dress had the fullest skirt and the most sharply drawn-in waist. Other than that, she was young, innocent, passive, naive, vulnerable, submissive, oppressed, kind to animals, handy with a broom, persecuted, and exploited — which is to say indistinguishable from the rest. An impotent pawn in a power struggle between the king and an "evil" fairy or "wicked" queen, who was always defeated in the end. She spoke very little, and when she did, she did so softly, never stridently. She sang sweetly, worked cheerfully, and suffered nobly and exquisitely. We're taught since birth to associate prettiness with goodness and worth. It's a hard lesson to unlearn. When I was little, I liked Sleeping Beauty best because she was the prettiest, too; because I recognized her as the feminine ideal. I understood that she was not descriptive so much as prescriptive, that she was not so much the hero of her own story as the grail.

After Kira fell asleep that night, I finished reading *Alice's Adventures in Wonderland* and was shocked by how familiar the story felt, how deeply it resonated. Alice was moody, snobbish, high-handed, judgmental, and quick to anger. She asked too many questions and had a real problem with authority. She was an emotional eater who anxiously scarfed whatever anyone put in front of her. She acted like she was entitled to things such as explanations, respect, and a nice house with plenty of toys to play with. She took offense easily and often felt sorry for herself. She was opinionated, argumentative, and self-absorbed. She was nothing like the heroines in fairy stories — nothing like the princess, or the girl. No wonder I didn't like her. Compared to Sleeping Beauty, Alice was a monster. She was just like me.

The story goes like this: Alice, age seven, is lounging by the river with her older sister on a warm spring day. Her sister is reading a book with no pictures, and Alice is bored and on the verge of dozing off, when suddenly a White Rabbit in a waistcoat runs by, checking his pocket watch and muttering about the time. Alice jumps up and follows the Rabbit under a hedge, accidentally tumbling down a rabbit hole. She lands in a nonsense land, where none of the rules of logic or physics apply. In Wonderland, depending on the ever-shifting, utterly nonsensical context, her body is always either too big or too small, her emotions are too much, and the creatures she meets are rude, bossy, dismissive, and hostile. They misapprehend and misunderstand her and mistake her for things she's not. The White Rabbit takes her for his maid. The Pigeon takes her for a serpent (her neck has stretched out like a flamingo's). The Mad Hatter and the March Hare tell her there's no room for her at the tea table, even though it's evident there's plenty. They offer her some nonexistent wine, then rebuke her for crashing a party she has not been invited to.

All this gaslighting eventually leads Alice to a full-blown identity crisis. She starts to doubt her sanity. ("We're all mad here. I'm mad. You're mad," the Cheshire Cat tells her. "How do you know I'm mad?" Alice asks. "You must be," says the Cat, "or you wouldn't have come here."[1]) She never believed in fairy tales when she was younger, and yet here she is, seemingly trapped in one. Someone should write a book about her, she thinks. Perhaps she'll write it herself when she grows up. Then it occurs to her that she *is* grown up — or as grown up as she's going to be allowed to get in this limiting, infantilizing place, where there's no room for a person like her to grow up in.

When Lewis Carroll published *Alice's Adventures in Wonderland,* in 1865, the world was in the midst of scientific, technological, economic, and social revolution. Industrialization, urbanization, mass communications, mass transportation, and free trade had given rise to market capitalism and the middle class. Darwinism, Marxism, and Freudian psychology had revolutionized the social world. Newly minted middle-class "ladies" found themselves in the awkward position of having to symbolically uphold the culture's values. What women were and how they fit into society became a kind of public obsession. The more educated upper-middle-class women organized around social causes like abolition, temperance, prison reform, education reform, marriage reform, and asylum reform, and the more they agitated for suffrage, property rights, custody rights, reproductive rights, legal rights, access to higher education and the professions, and dress reform, the more they were pressured to conform to a certain type. The "cult of true womanhood" was the capitalist answer to the "woman question" — as in, What was to be done about them and their infernal demands? It was the trope versus women of the Victorian era, the original backlash against liberal reforms that played out in the press, popular media, and advertising,[2] and it dominated the popular media in overt and covert, pandering and hectoring, polemical and service-oriented ways, as it does now. It sold papers and magazines, inspired sermons, launched letters to the editor, and moved a lot of soap. It provided a materialist answer to an existential question, filling the void left by the end of the old, "divine" feudal social order and replaced it with a "natural" social order based in "science." The "cult of true womanhood" split the symbolic world in two, sorting everything into categories. To men went the "public sphere" of commerce, politics, law, culture, reason, and science; and to women — "true women" — went the "private sphere" of the home, the children, morals, and feeling.

From here sprang the notion of wifehood and motherhood as a "job," and not just any job but a calling so noble and exalted that it could be done only for love, not for anything as corrupting as money or status. The "true woman" was tasked with creating a serene, restorative refuge for her husband, far removed from the filthy, corrupting world of capital where he went out to stalk his prey. In compensation for her complete civic and financial disenfranchisement, the upper-middle-class wife was given the run of the house — assuming she was fortunate enough to acquire one in marriage. The job included managing the servants, administering the household budget, overseeing the social, moral, and spiritual development of her husband and children, and devoting herself to accurately telegraphing her husband's status through "the ladylike consumption of luxury goods."[3] Safe at home in her "walled garden,"[4] she stoked and quelled her social and status anxieties at once by heeding the counsel of magazines such as *Godey's Lady's Book* (1830–1878), which offered fashion tips, hints on practical housekeeping, advice on social-etiquette questions, intimate glimpses into the lives of aristocrats and socialites, and advertisements featuring all the latest must-haves. The stuff that made a lady a lady.

That few could afford the lifestyles portrayed here, or keep to all the contradictory advice, was entirely beside the point. (Working-class women, with their labor for wages, were always too "real" to be "true.") "True womanhood" was nothing if not aspirational anyway, because there's nothing like trying to live up to an impossible standard to keep a woman in her place.

The "true woman," also called the "angel in the house," after a popular poem by Coventry Patmore, was an idea of "woman" endlessly promoted in advertising, newspapers, popular literature, and women's magazines.[5] This was the popular ideal every proper modern lady was expected to live up to.[6] The historian Barbara Welter narrowed the "true woman's" cardinal virtues to four: she was pious, submissive, domestic, and pure.[7] Her innocence was childlike, and her demeanor was modest and demure. She forgave her husband all his transgressions but committed none of her own. She absolved him of his sins. She aimed to please. Her manners were faultless, and her taste was unimpeachable. She was placed like a fragile doll atop a narrow pedestal from which, with one false move, she could fall from a very great height.

This was the world a girl like Alice was brought up to navigate. This was her pathway to successful adulthood. She was expected to marry, have children, and become a lady of the house, and she was educated for this purpose alone. A lady of the house became part of the house: under both British and American law, marriage divested her entirely of her property and personhood. A single woman was a *feme sole;* a married woman was a *feme covert,* or "covered woman," legally subsumed by the identity of her husband. Women began to acquire legal status as people with the Married Women's Property Acts of 1839, but they did not yet fully enjoy it in Alice's day.

In Peru, my own great-grandmother, Rosa María Montenegro, was married off when she was sixteen to a prosperous man twenty years her senior. "I still played with dolls," she told me once. "On my wedding night, I tried to climb out the window. Nobody had told me anything." Once she figured it out, she was happier. Her husband was nice to her and gave her more money and freedom than her mother had. Twice a year, she ordered clothes and furniture from Europe. They would arrive by ship and be transported from the end of the dock to the harbor by train. Everyone knew her husband had syphilis. He died when she was very young, leaving her widowed with three girls. They moved back in with her mother. Eventually, she married again and had a fourth daughter six months before her second daughter, my grandmother, had my mom. To remain a spinster was to be societally "redundant," but to marry, for a girl, was to be absorbed into the self of another, like a vanishing twin. A woman's education was designed to coax her to sleep at sixteen and keep her unchanged and unconscious forever. It was an undoing. It wasn't a start but a "finishing."

Why did I identify with this Victorian girl-child Alice? Alice's adventures in Wonderland were nothing like my life. So why were they so familiar? I'd never fallen down a rabbit hole into a strange, incomprehensible land, except, you know, when I had. I'd had an absurdly peripatetic childhood and experienced more culture shock by the time I was Alice's age than most people do in a lifetime. Then, as an adult, I'd spent almost a decade as a pop-culture critic. During the last four years, I spent most of my waking hours in darkened screening rooms. When I first started to work as a TV critic, in 2000, it was probably the best time to be writing about TV, and when I first started to work as a movie critic, in 2004, it was probably the worst time to be writing about movies. I found myself spending hours in the dark, consuming toxic doses of superhero movies, wedding-themed romantic comedies, cryptofascist paeans to war, and bromances about unattractive, immature young men and the gorgeous women desperate to marry them. Hardly any movies had female protagonists. Most actresses were cast to play "the girl."

"The girl" was the adult version of "the princess." As a kid, I'd believed the princess was the protagonist, because she'd seemed the most central to the story. The word *protagonist* comes from the Greek for "the leading actor in a contest or cause," and a protagonist is a person who wants something and does something to get it. "The girl" doesn't act, though — she behaves. She has no cause, but a plight. She doesn't want anything, she is wanted. She isn't a winner, she's won. She doesn't self-actualize but aids the hero in self-actualization. Sometimes, I'd sit in the theater and feel mounting despair and think, *Why do you keep telling me this? Why are you talking to me this way?*

Of course, there were good movies that reconnected me to myself and to the world, but most of the time I felt like some half-mad ethnographer lost in another dimension, frantically gathering field notes from inside this dark mirror in which I couldn't for the life of me locate myself. I began to feel unreal, peripheral in my own life, trapped in a dream not my own. I felt like a canary in a coal mine, bearing traumatized witness to the inhumanity of the tent-pole threequel, chirping my tiny, impotent protests into the dark void. I felt, I guess, like Alice in Wonderland. It helped to take notes, for some reason. I wrote things down to assuage the bricked-in, blood-ied-fingernail feeling of despair that sometimes came over me, to assert my existence, to remind myself to buy bananas on my way home. I filled notebook after notebook with loopy, illegible scrawls of outrage. I know everybody says their handwriting is loopy and illegible, but mine really was, because I wrote in the dark.

The writer Renata Adler once spent a year — the same year I was born, in fact — working as a movie critic for the *New York Times*. I know this because during my time as a movie critic, I felt so alienated from myself and my feelings that I went looking for evidence that I was not the first, or only, person in history ever to have felt this way. *A Year in the Dark* is a collection of Adler's reviews from 1968. In the introduction, she talks about how she left her job reviewing books at *The New Yorker* when she realized that she did not believe in "professional criticism as a way of life." When the *New York Times* offered her a movie job, however, she thought about how her favorite film critics used movies as a way into larger cultural conversations, "putting films idiosyncratically alongside things they cared about in other ways." Writing about movies was a way to write "about an event, about anything" — which spoke to me, because it was how I felt when I first started to write about TV. I wrote about what interested me and reacted to whatever seemed to be worth reacting to in the moment. With movies, though, I was beholden to release schedules and to divvied-up assignments. There were no more random connections, no more jumping into the conversation as it got good. Instead, I drove, I sat, I watched, I processed, I did it again. I started to shut down. Adler, too, reached the point when she felt the movies "completely blotted out the content of much of my life yet filled the days, like dreaming," so she quit.[8] I felt the same way, but I didn't quit. Craig would come upon me in a catatonic stupor, trying to find new ways to say the same things about the same things. "Just do it like a Mad Lib," he'd say. "Write up a few templates and fill in the blanks." I never took his advice, so he'd retaliate by reading my reviews aloud to me in a

Gene Shalit voice. Sometimes, he'd fix me with a dead-eyed stare and deadpan the movie-critic words I'd forbidden him ever to utter in my presence:

"Razzle-dazzle," he'd say. "Summer fare."

One day, in 2007, I read something that snapped me out of my torpor. It was a throwaway line in an Isla Fisher interview. Asked how playing the breakout role in *Wedding Crashers* changed her career, she replied that, much to her initial surprise, it hadn't. "I realized after *Wedding Crashers* there aren't that many comic opportunities for women in Hollywood," she said. "All the scripts are for men and you play 'the girl'" in the hot rod.[9] Following *Wedding Crashers,* Fisher was cast as the love interest in *Hot Rod,* an Andy Samberg vehicle about Andy Samberg in a vehicle. Her remark laid bare not only the reality — not enough comic opportunities for women in Hollywood — but also the ideology that created and perpetuated that reality. It was right there in the sentence structure, easily parsed: "All the scripts are for men and you play 'the girl'" suggests that the scripts were handed down by the clean, white hand of God. It banished "the girl" to the sidelines to perform her girly insignificance on command. It was right there in the dismissive way her comment was received as clickbait all over the Internet. "Borat's Babe Plans a Hollywood Sex Revolution,"[10] one headline announced, not only missing the point but mocking and dismissing it. Women's experience in its entirety seemed contained in that remark, not to mention several of the stages of feminist grief: the shock of waking up to the fact that the world does not also belong to you; the shame at having been so naive as to have thought it did; the indignation, depression, and despair that follow this realization; and, finally, the marshaling of the handy coping mechanisms, compartmentalization, pragmatism, and diminished expectations.

An old, familiar sense of unease started to take shape after that. It wasn't just the movies. It was everything, everywhere. It was the sublimated sexism that mutated every experience but that we weren't allowed to notice or acknowledge. It was the regressive subtext that seemed to undermine every progressive text. Between the time I was a curious little girl in the 1970s and the time I was an utterly confused and bewildered adult woman in the 2000s, I got lost in a nonsense world of double binds and mixed messages until I wasn't sure who I was or what I was supposed to do. Yet it was clear that I was supposed to do something, because there was always someone there to tell me that what I was doing was wrong. Women's ideas of themselves had changed, but the world's idea of women, somehow, had not. The cognitive dissonance was palpable at all times.

In 2012, about four years after I left the paper, I went to see a movie called *Ruby Sparks*, written by Zoe Kazan, who also starred. The film was about a nerdy prodigal novelist named Calvin who wrote a literary blockbuster in his youth but has been blocked and paralyzed by the anxiety of his own influence ever since. One day, he dreams a girl. Her name is Ruby. She is quirky and devoted, and he loves her. She's the kind of girl he'd love to meet — the girl of his dreams. He shows the manuscript to his brother Harry, who tells him, "Quirky, messy women whose problems only make them more endearing are not real . . . You haven't written a person, you've written a girl." But the next morning, he wakes up to find Ruby in his kitchen, eating breakfast. Somehow, not only has he manifested his dream girl, but it turns out he can write her any way he wants. He can literally control her story from his typewriter. (He uses a typewriter, because that's the kind of guy he is.) Calvin calls Harry to come over and confirm that he hasn't gone crazy. He hasn't. Not only is Ruby real, but also, as Harry observes, "You could, like, tweak things if you wanted." He begs Calvin, "for men everywhere," not to let the opportunity go to waste. But Calvin takes the high road. He puts away the manuscript and vows never, ever to attempt to control Ruby or in any way determine her fate through his writing ever again.

Ruby, of course, just thinks she's a person. She doesn't know she's been conjured from Calvin's imagination, that she is just an avatar. All she knows is that Calvin is squarely the center of her life, the only point of her existence, and she feels empty and rudderless. She's stuck at home all day, isolated, with nothing to do while he writes. She starts to get depressed and clingy, which drives Calvin crazy. Finally, he pulls out the manuscript and begins to subtly adjust her. What if she were just a little less needy, a little more independent? It works. Soon, Ruby enrolls in a class and makes new friends. She makes plans with them after class, and Calvin gets jealous. Ruby and Calvin visit his family, and much to his displeasure, she loves them and they love her back. Then one night, at a party, she jumps in the pool with a rival author, and Calvin freaks out. Back home, they fight, and Ruby accuses him of expecting her to live up to his "platonic ideal of a girlfriend." She says he doesn't control her, and he begs to differ. He sits down at the typewriter and starts to type, first making her bark like a dog, then crawl on all fours, and finally jump up and down like a cheerleader, yelling, "You're a genius! You're a genius!" over and over until she collapses, then scrambles to her feet and runs away.

I once read in an interview with Kazan that she was interested in writing about the violence inherent in reducing a person to an idea. Watching *Ruby Sparks,* it occurred to me that the movie was a perfect metaphor for how popular culture labors to reduce us to ideas every day, and how as girls we grow up in a kind of inverted media Wonderland that works diligently to erase and replace us with uncanny fantasy versions of ourselves. The character of Ruby is doubled. She's both a modern patriarchal ideal and an actual person struggling to emerge from under the oppressive veil of this ideal. *Ruby Sparks* is about what it feels like to grow up obscured by this phantom doppelganger, which is both the central conflict of the movie and the central thesis of this book. Also this: extreme power differentials are extremely bad for human relationships. And this: I'm not convinced that love is a job. And this: perspective matters; to the girl of your dreams, your dream is a nightmare if she's trapped in it.

Near the end of *Alice's Adventures in Wonderland*, Alice befriends a couple of misfits, the Gryphon and the Mock Turtle. They feel more or less the way she feels about the mad people of Wonderland, and come the closest to validating her feelings. The Mock Turtle tells her about his education, about the lessons he learned in school that "lessened" him every day. He helps Alice realize that she's neither mad nor alone. The validation gives her the confidence to return to the garden and challenge the authority of the Queen of Hearts, which, of course, makes the Queen turn purple with rage. "Hold your tongue!" she commands. And when Alice refuses, she yells, "Off with her head!" But Alice has stopped being afraid. She's started once again to grow back to her full size. She reaches out and waves the Queen away. "Who cares for you?" she says. "You're nothing but a pack of cards!" And at this, the Queen comes apart, and the cards scatter in all directions, and Alice wakes up from her dream and runs home.

Despite having refused to listen to the rest of *Alice*, Kira kept it in mind. She peeked at it here and there when I wasn't looking. One day, she spotted a vintage dress at the flea market. It was a smocked, light-blue flannel with a Peter Pan collar, puffed sleeves, and a bow in the back. It looked like Alice's dress. She asked me to buy it for her, and I did. She wore it often with her fancy headband with the huge gold-lamé bow on top that she picked out at H&M. On Read Across America day at school, she added a white pinafore and black patent-leather Mary Janes, and went as Alice. She was five then, and seven when I started writing this — the same age as Alice. At seven, a girl is on the cusp of falling down the rabbit hole into an artificial garden where she'll be taught to submit to the nonsense rules of an unwinnable game — croquet with hedgehogs for balls and flamingos for mallets — under constant threat of annihilation.

Kira has since outgrown the dress and lost the gold headband, but I hope she'll also outgrow all the limiting, oppressive, infantilizing stories — all the fairy tales designed to keep her small, and cowering, and afraid — long before I did. I hope that, like Alice, she wakes up and sees them for what they are: nothing but a pack of lies. I hope she swats them away without a second thought and writes her own fairy tale, one that reflects her own experience as her own person in this nonsensical world.

In the meantime, this book is for her.

PART ONE

Down the Rabbit Hole

If you drink from a bottle called poison, it is almost certain to disagree with you sooner or later.

— LEWIS CARROLL, *ALICE'S ADVENTURES IN WONDERLAND*

1

Bunnies

I LEARNED ABOUT SEX FROM *WHERE DID I COME FROM?*
but I learned about sexiness from my grandfather's *Playboy*s and
Bugs Bunny in drag. I gathered, from the book, that sex was an
awkward thing that happened when a lumpy man was feeling "very
loving" toward a lumpy lady and wanted to "get as close to her as
possible." From *Playboy*, I learned that sexiness was naked ladies
and weird, invisible men.

My grandparents' house was built in the mid-1950s and looked
like the set of a *Pink Panther* movie. The den, in particular, show-
cased the kind of rakish, cosmopolitan masculinity that was cool
at the time. Perhaps there was a time when my grandfather hosted
regular poker games with other guayabera-wearing, Brylcreemed,
sun-damaged men in white socks with sandals gathered around
the green-felted card table, but by the time I came along, he was
down to one. Tío César was a retired navy admiral whose gentle
mien, bulbous nose, and severe vision impairment recalled a be-
atific Mr. Magoo. Another interesting thing about him was that he
had lost his vocal cords to cancer and relearned to speak by gulping
down air and burping out words. (It's called esophageal speech. He
taught us to do it.) By the time I came along, the den was not a social space so much as a shrine to the persona my grandfather had
created for himself, with *Playboy* as his guide.

My grandfather collected *Playboy* magazines. I don't mean he
saved every issue; I mean he saved every issue, had them bound by
the dozen into leather-bound annuals with gold-embossed spines,

and arrayed them on a low shelf behind the poker table like a set of handsome encyclopedias. They imparted a pervy yet learned vibe to the room that offset the lowbrow ribaldry of the framed cartoons by the mirror-backed bar, featuring scenes of sexy nurses and sexy secretaries being sexually harassed. There was also — my former favorite — a cartoon of a man flushing himself down the toilet over a caption that read, "Goodbye, cruel world." The nurses and doctors in the framed cartoons in my grandfather's den looked like creatures from two different planets (Toad Mars and Bimbo Venus), but it was the pink, chubby, bald, and frizzy-haired illustrated couple in *Where Did I Come From?*, slotted together like a hippie yin-yang with little red hearts floating up from their naked embrace, that struck us kids as strange and unfamiliar; a little too fraternally similar for comfort.

This is how, in elementary school, I came to be sentimental about my grandfather's nudie magazines. Every year at Christmas, my family traveled to Lima to visit my grandparents. Because we lived so far away (first in São Paulo, then New York, then Chicago, then Madrid, then back to Chicago, then back to New York, then back to Madrid again) and our visits were brief and far between, I tried very hard to hold on to everything. I committed every detail to memory and heaped everything with significance. I adored my grandfather. A dashing, retired air-force colonel with an Errol Flynn mustache, he was a character straight out of a 1960s sitcom: uptight, high-strung, and hilarious; a Peruvian Major Nelson. (Flight was a recurring theme: his Irish great-grandfather, who was born in New York, went to Peru in the 1860s to work as a railroad engineer, likely for Henry Meiggs, the famous California railroad tycoon and fugitive from the law.) My love for him was metonymical, spilling over into the objects that represented him in my mind. He was whiskey, medals, cigarettes, racetracks, card tricks, toffee, Brylcreem, white socks with sandals, Saturday-night Mass, *Playboys*, gun.

When my cousin Christie and I were in first or second grade and my brother Gonzalo was in the grade behind us, we started stealing *Playboy*s while the adults were distracted with cocktails and arguments. We would sneak into the maid's room to check them out. This became our holiday prelunch tradition. Once, I laughed until I peed myself on Rosa's bed, which is how we got caught. A few days later, my mom produced a copy of *Where Did I Come From?* Written by adman Peter Mayle, of eventual *A Year in Provence* fame, it was a frank and friendly attempt to demystify sex for kids. The book was interesting but in no way related to my curiosity, because I wasn't in it for the mammalian science. I was in it for the mystification.

Playboy pictorials were all culture, no nature. All those gauzy photos of naked girls, alone in their kitschy rooms with their props and their yarn-ribbon pigtails (like mine!), had a strangely static and hermetic quality that made the girls' nakedness look somehow artificial. They made me think of the taxidermied animals at the natural-history museums in Chicago and New York. It was like they were specimens, more lifelike than alive. That they were stripped of their clothes didn't bother me as much as that they were stripped of all context. They were isolated and frozen in time. Even the outdoor shots seemed to be taken behind glass. The girls' accompanying biographical squibs only added to this impression, resembling the plaques next to museum dioramas detailing an extinct animal's name, geographic provenance, "statistics" (height, weight, bust, waist, and hip measurements), and dietary patterns and mating behaviors, or "turn-ons" and "turn-offs." The *Playboy* collection was a museum of girls, a taxonomy of girls. The pictures fascinated me and filled me with ontological terror at the same time. I knew, because everybody knew, that only girls were "sexy," that "sexiness" *was* girls — it was exclusively female. This confused me, so I kept going back to the magazines, trying to figure it out. It made me uncomfortable in ways I couldn't begin to express.

The models' aura of stuffed-bunny obliviousness, by the way, was precisely the vibe *Playboy* was going for. In 1967, Hugh Hefner told the Italian journalist Oriana Fallaci that he'd called the models Bunnies because

> the rabbit, the bunny, in America has a sexual meaning; and I chose it because it's a fresh animal, shy, vivacious, jumping —sexy. First it smells you, then it escapes, then it comes back, and you feel like caressing it, playing with it. A girl resembles a bunny. Joyful, joking. Consider the kind of girl we made popular: the Playmate of the Month. She is never sophisticated, a girl you cannot really have. She is a young, healthy, simple girl—the girl next door ... We are not interested in the mysterious, difficult woman, the femme fatale who wears elegant underwear, with lace, and she is sad, and somehow mentally filthy. The *Playboy* girl has no lace, no underwear, she is naked, well-washed with soap and water, and she is happy.[1]

I didn't read this as a kid, of course, but I still think the message got across. *Playboy*'s "idea of woman" was a naked fairy-tale princess: a young, dumb, defenseless, trusting, easily manipulated woodland creature. She gave herself entirely because she was too inexperienced to know any better. She was a fresh animal, well-washed with soap and water. She could not learn, grow, or change. She could not really exist in a temporal sense. All she could do was to try to preserve and display herself. Experience made her difficult. It got her banished to her witchy cottage in the forest. She had to remain a dumb bunny, an unconscious body, frozen in time and preserved in amber, for as long as she could in order to survive. The "sexy lady" is the only kind of lady that openly exists in the sunshine of the symbolic realm. She is the only kind of lady that warrants being looked at, paid attention to, or acknowledged. In order to be listened to, a lady should be nice to look at. There should be no doubt as to her sexual desirability, but this will undermine her argument,

no matter how sophisticated. We are not interested in sadness, so-
phistication, or experience. We secretly believe that female subjectivity is filth.

When you are a kid — when I was a kid, anyway — you believe in su-
perlatives and data, and find a great deal of comfort in this orderly
vision of the universe. So you set out to rank and rate and sort and
classify everything you can. When I was in first and second grade,
I thought that the Miss America, Miss World, and Miss Universe
pageants were actual statistical rankings of the prettiest women in
the country, the world, the universe. (I wasn't sure how Miss Universe could claim the title without competing against aliens from
other planets, but I was willing to suspend my disbelief.) I understood that being pretty wasn't the most important thing, as no
doubt some adult had dutifully informed me at some point, but it
was obviously the only thing that anybody cared about where girls
were concerned. You surmised this just by existing. Being the prettiest was the pinnacle of womanly achievement. It ranked you, if
you were pretty enough, as *the number one girl in the universe.* Yet
if prettiness made you visible, it also made you strangely invisible.
It made you recede into an undifferentiated, standardized mass.

Before Hugh Hefner came along, porn was furtive and hidden. After Hefner, it was everywhere; mainstream, pop, classy, cool. Hefner considered that his big innovation was realizing that *Playboy*
wasn't actual porn so much as lifestyle porn. He wasn't selling pictures of girls, he was selling a particular male identity via consumption of girls as consumer objects. This identity was similar in many
ways to the identity being sold to ladies in ladies' magazines, only
with naked ladies themselves as the expendable products whose
constant consumption would bring happiness. This is why Hefner
reportedly worried less about competitors like *Penthouse* and *Hus-
tler* than he did about "lad mags" like *Maxim* and *FHM*. For all

their surface differences, the Playmates didn't suggest individuality so much as variety, an endless cornucopia of consumer choices. As a second-grader, I could fully grasp the orgiastic appeal of beholding something like this. The pleasure of positioning oneself in front of a new sixty-four-color crayon set, complete with built-in sharpener, was impossible to overstate. Like casting a proprietary eye over the display at Baskin-Robbins, it was a heady feeling that quickly gave way to entitlement. I felt nothing short of outrage when the number of flavors fell short of the promised thirty-one. That I always chose the same flavor anyway, and wore out the same-color crayons while barely touching some of the others, was not the point. The possibility of infinite choice was the point. The too-muchness was the point. Knowing the Burnt Sienna was there at your fingertips. Empowering you was the point.

Of course, looking at naked girls in *Playboy* didn't make *me* feel powerful. On the contrary, it made me feel like I was getting a glimpse into a parallel universe where I was at once invisible and excruciatingly visible, negated and exposed. There was no inverse equivalent. I was unaware that just around that time, an academic named Laura Mulvey was coining the phrase "the male gaze." That language would remain unavailable to me for another two decades. At the time, all I had to help me make sense of it were things like the Frog and Toad story "Dragons and Giants," the one where Toad gets separated from Frog and runs into a giant snake at the mouth of a dark cave, and the snake sees him and says, "Hello, lunch."

In 2003, Hugh Hefner told CNN that it was only in retrospect that he realized that what he'd created was actually "the first successful magazine for young, single men" organized around a singular "artistic" idea. A naked girl was placed in a setting, and the suggestion of a male presence was introduced in the picture. "There would be a second glass, or a pipe, or a necktie," he explained, which would suggest "the possibility of seduction." For Hefner, presence of this item communicated the idea that "nice girls like sex, too."[2]

Playboy was instrumental in helping to combine the good girl and the bad girl into a single entity—what New York Radical Women cofounder Robin Morgan called "the unbeatable Madonna-whore combination." The culture bombarded women with mixed messages, putting them into impossible, crazy-making psychological double binds. "To win approval, we must be both sexy and wholesome, delicate but able to cope, demure yet titillatingly bitchy or should we say ill-tempered," wrote Morgan. Pageant queens and Playboy Bunnies sent to entertain troops in Vietnam were "death mascots" in an immoral war. "Where else," Morgan asked, "could one find such a perfect combination of American values—racism, militarism, capitalism—all packaged in one 'ideal' symbol, a woman?" As Morgan wrote in the group's manifesto, part of the reason for the 1968 Miss America protest was to call attention to the media's uncritical promotion of "the degrading mindless-boob-girlie symbol" and the "ludicrous 'beauty' standards we ourselves are conditioned to take seriously." Five years before the protest, in 1963, a young journalist named Gloria Steinem had spent almost two weeks undercover as a Bunny at the Playboy Club and had written an article about it for *Show* magazine, revealing the terrible working conditions of a job that could bill itself as "the top job in the country for a young girl" and could be taken seriously. I don't remember noticing any pipes in any photos, but even if the item left casually lying around had been, say, a pack of Bubble Yum or a little book of tiny, puffy Sanrio stickers, I still wouldn't have held myself at a cool remove as I cast a proprietary eye over the girlie. The question of where I fit into the picture was too existentially traumatizing. Was this what girls turned into? Would *I*? Did I want to? What if I did? What if I didn't? Which would be worse? The idea that nice girls like sex, too, never once crossed my mind while looking at a *Playboy* magazine. It had crossed my mind when playing with my Malibu Barbie and my brother's G.I. Joe, but there was nothing about the girls in the photographs that implied they were getting anything out of the experience. My cousin and I had been trained to redirect our subjectivity and to accept the mindless-boob-girlie symbol and her ludicrous standard of beauty as our standard of femininity long before we cracked our first *Playboy* magazine. We recognized the Bunnies from other images we'd seen. They were naked Barbies with princess personalities, just the pretty, passive, vulnerable, unconscious young girls we'd been trained to recognize as our personal ideal; the sleeping beauties. Christie and I thought it was funny that a magazine called *Playboy* had no boys in it. What a ridiculous oversight! Who was in charge? We were seven or eight or nine years old. We took everything literally. We were wrong, of course. What *Playboy* actually had was no girls in it.

As a little kid in the seventies, I was never not aware of how feminism defined itself against the ethos of *Playboy*, but until recently it never occurred to me to think about how *Playboy* defined itself against the ethos of feminism. I thought of the *Playboy* version of masculinity as eternal, as the status quo that scrappy feminism suddenly stood up against. I didn't know that they were parallel universes born of the sexual revolution, in one of which women demanded agency and control over their own bodies, as well as sexual and reproductive rights and freedoms, and in the other of which some men extended their sense of entitlement to the casual use of women's bodies as entertainment. The old, patriarchal, Victorian notions of protecting young girls' "virtue" and reputations fell away, and new, commercially exploitive patriarchal notions stepped into the void. Fashion modeling went from being a boring, low-paying workaday job for average-size women that showed customers how clothes fit, to a glam fantasy world full of underage girls made up to look like adults. *Playboy* helped by reinventing beautiful, naked, sexually available girls as the ultimate luxury item for the ultimate alpha man.

Playboy was in its heyday between 1966 and 1976, and the women's movement was in its heyday between 1968 and 1977. In 1969, *Playboy* assigned a story on women's lib to a freelancer named Susan Braudy who, after extensive reporting, wrote a sympathetic account of the movement. This infuriated Hefner. He responded in a memo: "These chicks are our natural enemy . . . We must destroy them before they destroy the *Playboy* way of life."[3] Braudy refused to alter her story to fit this point of view, so she pulled the piece, and *Playboy* ended up running an article called "Up Against the Wall, Male Chauvinist Pig" in its stead. A *Playboy* secretary leaked that story to the press and was fired after Hefner discovered who did it.

For me, trouble with *Playboy* was not that it had pictures of naked girls in it. It's that in its Looney Tunes universe, it had only predators and prey. Women who believed themselves to be equal were men's "natural enemy," as in all the binary dyads — Sylvester versus Tweety, Coyote versus Road Runner, Elmer Fudd versus Bugs Bunny.

In her 1967 interview, Fallaci asked Hefner to explain his real-life relationships with the Playmates he became romantically involved with. How did they work? Was he faithful to them? Did he expect fidelity from them? "The problem of being faithful does not even exist in such a situation," he replied. "I do not ignore other girls." He tried to explain that he usually had a special relationship that lasted for a few years and was supplemented by other less important relationships. He rattled off a string of names, girls he'd had primary relationships with for thirteen years. "I would like to make it clear that those never were pseudo-marriages, they were cohabitations, which, unfortunately, provoke jealousy in some women."

"And are you jealous, Mr. Hefner?" Fallaci asked.

"Sure I am," he said. "I wouldn't like Mary to be sexually involved with someone else. When this happened with some of my special girls, I was rather hurt. In my relationships, I do not look for equality between man and woman. I like innocent, affectionate, faithful girls who —"

"Do you mean you would never love a woman who has had as many men as you have had women, Mr. Hefner?" Fallaci broke in. "A woman who accepted and applied your philosophy?"

"Not in the least," he said. "I have never looked for a woman like me. I wouldn't know what to do with a Hugh Hefner in skirts."[4]

Judith Butler had only recently published *Gender Trouble* and introduced the idea of "gender performativity" into the culture when I started graduate school, in the early nineties; the idea was that masculinity and femininity were not something we *are* but something we repeatedly *do*.[5] Around the same time, in a piece in the *New York Times Magazine,* the critic Katha Pollitt coined the term "the Smurfette principle" to describe the weirdly gender-disproportionate world of cartoons. She had been surprised to notice as an adult that in cartoons it was common to see "a group of male buddies" that was "accented" by a single, stereotypical girl. This conveyed the message that "boys are the norm, girls the variation; boys are central, girls peripheral; boys are individuals, girls types. Boys define the group, its story and its code of values. Girls exist only in relation to boys." In other words, "the girl" was an intrusion, often unwelcome, in an all-male universe. She did not represent human consciousness but a psychosexual disturbance with a bow on top.[6] I found these ideas to be liberating. I also found them to be familiar. I'd encountered them before, not in college but in elementary school, and not through Playboy Bunnies but through Bugs Bunny.

When he is naked, which is most of the time, Bugs is an anthropomorphized caricature of a rabbit of indeterminate age and gender. He has a slim, androgynous body; big, lash-rimmed eyes; a perky tail; the sassiness of a teenager; and a knack for getting himself out of compromising situations. A bunny's existence is inherently precarious — there is no creature more defenseless — and Bugs Bunny lives all alone, unprotected. He cannot get through an episode without being preyed upon or bossed around by any number of bullies and blowhards, ranging from the merely irritating to the truly terrifying. Nobody respects his boundaries, and everyone underestimates him — which is how, on the bright side, he manages to outsmart them all. Bugs gives the slip to dumb hunters, sadistic sergeants, and pompous maestros alike, not just eluding capture but turning it into a game. He can transform himself utterly without anyone noticing. I deeply identified with the carrot-chomping Bugs Bunny, but he was also my first sexual crush. I liked his big eyes, his crooked grin, his mocking tone, the little cleft in his chest. He was my very first genderfucker.

I adored Bugs. He was my platonic ideal of a man. Yet I never liked him more than when he dressed up as a sexy girl-rabbit. Bugs "played the girl" in the most exaggerated, artificial, ridiculous ways imaginable. In a dress, he was a geisha, a mermaid, a ballerina, Lana Turner, a bobby-soxer, Carmen Miranda, the person giving the performance and the person the performance was for. Bugs in a dress was no helpless bunny all alone in the woods with her tits out. S/he as a girl was vast. S/he contained multitudes. S/he was playful, sexy, sublime. Of all cartoon animals, s/he was the one whose allegiance I never thought to doubt. I trusted Bugs implicitly. *I loved him/her.* Bugs was on my side. Which is why I never liked him/her less than when he ogled a sexy girl-rabbit and turned to the camera with a dirty wink. Later, in high school, I'd develop an obsessive crush but also a deep sense of identification with David Bowie. When Bowie died, decades later, and stories came out about his relationships in the 1970s with very young girls — girls younger than

I was when I first discovered him — I shut up that part of myself. It made me want to cry. *I loved him. I thought he was on my side.*

When Kira was three, we were driving home one afternoon and stopped behind a bus at a light. The bus was wrapped in an ad for a sexy vampire TV show. This was not a vampire show I'd heard of before, but it was hard to keep up — there were so many. The cast of this show was young, pretty, and stylish, like the cast of blood-sucking *Friends*. When Kira saw them, she piped up, excited, "Oh, Mommy! Look at those peoples! They're so beautiful. They're so 'dorable. They're so gorgeous!"

Her fervor surprised me. I'd never even heard her say some of those words before. Had I told her she was cute one too many times and accidentally triggered an unhealthy fixation on beauty, or was she just picking up on what the world was teaching her? There are billboards and buses and posters for movies, TV shows, cosmetics, and fashion all over the city. There are pictures of pretty people, but especially girls, everywhere. They communicate wordlessly. I thought about how, from the moment she'd opened her eyes, she'd been driven around town, absorbing things, picking up magazines at the doctor's office, saying, "I want to look at the princesses." (What else might Nicole Kidman be, after all, in a pink gown in a perfume ad?) The world reveals itself through images and gestures long before language intervenes. The bear is brown. The cow says moo. The lady in the bikini loves the hamburger very, very much. I was born in the same year as the Miss America protest; the first feminist political action in almost a century. Sometimes, I wonder what happened between 1968 and the year Kira was born, in 2008, the year Girls Gone Wild launched a magazine, a clothing line, and a compilation record, and founder Joe Francis's net worth reached $150 million. Was there progress? Did we move forward? in circles? Where did we go?

Sitting behind the vampire bus, waiting for the light to change, I thought about what to say to Kira that might help her remain more or less intact and discover who she really is in a world that literally never stops yelling at her that her primary value is sexual; that her identity is fungible (there is always a fresh crop of newer, younger, prettier girls); that her perspective is marginal, suspect, niche, and therefore not of real importance (unlike boys' experiences, which are human and therefore evergreen, universal, and innately valuable); that she's "entertainment for men," or else she's nothing. I wanted to give her something to help her resist this, but I also knew that to resist is to open yourself up to attack, to declare rabbit-hunting season on yourself.

The stories we tell ourselves are tricky and shape shifting. Much like Bugs, they will do what it takes to preserve themselves, to survive. They'll continuously, gleefully alter their appearance. They'll pretend to be whatever you say you want them to be. But deep down, they have a lot riding on these fixed ideas about opposites, about this great symbolic divide between male and female, black and white, old and young, gay and straight, that splits the world in half and sorts everything in it. I wanted to say to Kira, "Don't be fooled," but I couldn't, because to say that is to say, "The whole world is lying to you." I wanted to say, "The world wants to tell you that you don't exist, and that you don't belong, but don't believe it," but of course I didn't want to say it. I didn't want to break her heart. So, instead, I finally just said that anodyne thing, that worthless thing parents say. "Yes," I said, "they are very beautiful . . . but you know, beauty is not the most important thing."

And she thought about this for a second, and then she bellowed, with a fury that surprised me, "YES IT IS!" because nobody likes to have her perceptions challenged. And anyway, who was I to tell her that her eyes deceived her? That it was wrong to have deduced — empirically, as a new person in a tiny body in a strange world — that beauty does in fact appear to be the most important thing? Should I gaslight her? I mean, we still leave cookies for Santa Claus. We write notes to the tooth fairy. We dispel gnawing doubts about the Easter Bunny. And it's one thing to be asked to believe in the existence of something you can't see anywhere, but another thing altogether to be asked to disbelieve something you can see everywhere.

Who am I to argue with reality?

2

Can This Marriage Be Saved?

IN 1973, THE PHARMACEUTICAL COMPANY WHERE MY father worked transferred us from São Paulo, Brazil, where we'd lived for two years, to its New York headquarters. I was five years old, my brother was four, and my mom was about seven months pregnant with my sister. The company put us up in a hotel in the city, and a couple of months later my parents bought a house in New Jersey, which had a big yard and woods behind it. My dad was an executive in charge of marketing for Latin America, and he traveled for work about six months out of the year. We'd never lived in the suburbs before, and my mom wasn't used to being alone all the time in the quiet. One weekday morning, she was in the kitchen when she heard a loud noise and followed it outside. It was the neighbor, mowing her lawn. When she saw my mom waddling toward her, she cut off the mower, thinking she'd disturbed her. My mom begged her not to. She'd been so relieved to hear it. The silence had been so spectral that she'd started to wonder if she was dead and the last to know.

That story always makes me think of *The Stepford Wives*. *The Stepford Wives* was a best-selling 1972 novel by Ira Levin that was made into a movie a few years later. The main character, Joanna Eberhart, is an aspiring photographer whose husband, Walter, talks her into leaving New York for the (fictional) town of Stepford, Connecticut. Joanna, played by Katharine Ross, has the slightly bewildered air of a person who stepped off the path for a second and can't believe how quickly and irrecoverably she lost her way. Given the pressure she's under to fall in step as the pretty, young wife of an up-and-comer, her yearning to be recognized (she dreams that someday someone will pick up one of her photographs and know it as "an Ingalls," her maiden name) is especially poignant. She worries that her dreamy, bucolic images of children and everyday life aren't important enough to be taken seriously as art. And she is gently, encouragingly held back by her husband, the culture, other women, and her own insecurity, which is lovingly inculcated over a lifetime. With her two little kids, her wood-paneled station wagon, her long brown hair in Vera scarves, and her bewilderment at her sudden isolation, Joanna reminds me of my mom in those days. The movie was shot in a town much like ours, and the languid shots of hazy green lawns, prairie dresses, dark kitchens, and Muzak at the market trigger so many of my earliest sense memories that every time I see it, I feel a twinge of nostalgia, and I almost forget it's a story about a town where the husbands have colluded to murder their wives and replace them with housecleaning sex-bots.

In 1975, the producers of *The Stepford Wives* organized a special screening for feminist "opinion makers,"[1] notably Betty Friedan, in advance of the premiere. Friedan was the best-selling author of *The Feminine Mystique* and a cofounder of the National Organization for Women. *The Feminine Mystique* was a publishing phenomenon when it came out in 1963, reviving popular feminism after a long period of dormancy. Eleanor Perry, screenwriter of *Diary of a Mad Housewife*, introduced the film to the opinion makers as "finally, a movie that is not about two guys and their adventures."[2] The screening did not go well. Friedan called the movie a commercial "rip-off of the women's movement" and stomped out of the screening room.[3] I can see how she would have been disappointed when the alternative to "a movie that is not about two guys and their adventures" turned out to be a movie about two women getting murdered by a proto–men's rights cabal comprised of their husbands. Or maybe she resented being co-opted as a mainstream cultural reference, or disliked the way the women's movement was characterized as a fight between middle-class husbands and wives over domestic labor and hairdos, or was frustrated with the way people kept missing the point she was trying to make about equal rights and the kind of legal, institutional, and constitutional change she was focused on. Maybe everything pissed her off because she was contentious and a control freak. Or maybe it just looked a little too familiar. I don't know. But I don't think I'm going out on too much of a limb by describing *The Stepford Wives* as a campy, fictional re-imagining of Friedan's groundbreaking magnum opus, which had come out nine years earlier, and she didn't like seeing it turned into allegorical kitsch.

Like *The Stepford Wives, The Feminine Mystique* was tendered as the journey to consciousness of an ordinary, middle-class housewife who found herself adrift in what Susan Brownmiller once described as "a make-believe world of perfect casseroles and Jell-O delights," where "marriages failed because wives didn't try hard enough, single-parent households did not exist, and women worked outside the home not because they wanted to, or to make ends meet, but to 'earn extra income in your spare time.'"[4] *The Stepford Wives* movie, which came out three years after the novel, had the air of an underwater dream shot behind glass. Not long after arriving in Stepford, Joanna befriends another recent New York transplant, Bobbie Markowe, and together they marvel at the placid conformity all around them. Whereas in the city and in neighboring towns, women are increasingly involved in the women's movement, the Stepford wives are singularly devoted to their bodies, homes, husbands, and children. Their domesticity is cult-like in its utter self-abnegation. The wives exist only to nurture, please, and display their husbands' status. They go to the supermarket in full makeup. They decline invitations for coffee to stay home and wax the floor. In his review of the film, Roger Ebert remarked that the actors playing the robot women had "absorbed enough TV, or have such an instinctive feeling for those phony, perfect women in the ads, that they manage all by themselves to bring a certain comic edge to their cooking, their cleaning, their gossiping and their living deaths."[5] Ebert seemed to assume that the actresses were at once in on the joke and safely removed from it, just as he was. It didn't seem to occur to him that, both as women and actresses, they lived in Stepford, too. There was no ironic remove available to them. There was no escape.

It has long been fashionable to dismiss *The Feminine Mystique* as exclusionary for focusing exclusively on white, college-educated, middle-class housewives. Some of this criticism is deserved, but some of it misses the point. In the book, Friedan presents herself as an ordinary, alienated housewife nagged by a feeling of discontent she called "the problem with no name." She wonders whether she is alone in her feelings or whether her old college classmates are also suffering from this existential malaise. (They were.) But this self-portrayal wasn't exactly accurate. *The Feminine Mystique* wasn't focused on actual housewives as much as it was on the *housewifely ideal*, or the "cult of true womanhood" of the mid-twentieth century. "With a vision of the happy modern housewife as she is described by the magazines and television, by the functional sociologists, the sex-directed educators, and the manipulators dancing before my eyes," Friedan wrote, "I went in search of one of those mystical creatures."[6] What she discovered instead was a pervasive idea she called the "mystique," a complex, pervasive, self-perpetuating messaging system that told women that, for them, there is only one true path to happiness — and that the journey there is very, very brief. It told them that no matter what their particular circumstances, individual desires, financial situation, sexual orientation, and/or cultural background, marriage, motherhood, total economic dependence on a husband, and complete immersion in the domestic sphere were the only true, real, lasting, and "natural" route to contentment for women. Fulfillment was one-size-fits-all, and if it didn't fit you for whatever reason, then it was more than likely that you were the problem. The mystique dissuaded women from having goals beyond those dictated by 1950s gender roles. It said that "*only* a superwoman could choose to do *anything* with her life in addition to marriage and motherhood."[7] It encouraged women "to pity the neurotic, unfeminine, unhappy women who wanted to be poets or physicists or presidents," as well as women of previous generations with their pointless, doomed striving. A woman with aspirations had better make sure she was a genius, the *Ladies' Home Journal* warned. "If she ended up doing something only ordinary, or 'second-rate,' she would be wasting the chance to raise a 'first-rate' child." It made women feel guilty if they felt dissatisfied or frustrated or "didn't have an orgasm waxing the family-room floor," and explained why women were barraged by contradictory "expert" opinions about "how to catch a man and keep him, how to breastfeed children and handle their toilet training, how to cope with sibling rivalry and adolescent rebellion; how to buy a dishwasher, bake bread, cook gourmet snails, and build a swimming pool with their own hands; how to dress, look, and act more feminine and make marriage more exciting; how to keep their husbands from dying young and their sons from growing into delinquents," while being assured by the psychiatric profession that their inability to mold themselves into this fiction and to feel nothing but joy and contentment was their problem. Friedan's contemporaries, college-educated women in their forties and fifties, "still remembered painfully giving up those dreams, but most of the younger women no longer even thought about them."

All of this sounds painfully retrograde now, but it also sounds painfully familiar. There's a way in which girls are asked to account for their dreams and aspirations from the moment they start to form that hasn't changed very much since Friedan's time. In 2014, a sophomore in high school told me a story about how, when her friend got accepted to Stanford and announced her intention to start her own biotech firm, her mom had asked whether she'd given any thought to when she would fit having a family into that plan. The girl was seventeen.

Friedan felt this, too. As a 1940s career woman, she was appalled by the sudden domestic turn so relentlessly encouraged in advertising and so patronizingly validated by scientific experts. Decades before writing *The Feminine Mystique,* Friedan had worked as a labor activist and reporter for the *United Electrical Workers' News,* where she was inspired by union women's demands for equal pay, and she had covered the House Un-American Activities Committee. After getting pregnant with her second child, she was fired from the newspaper and became a freelance women's-magazine writer. She wrote articles about breastfeeding, natural childbirth, homes, and fashion but was discouraged by her male editors from writing about female artists or politics, because American women wouldn't identify with them. Not only could you not get an abortion at the time but even the word *abortion* could not be printed in newspapers.[8] Friedan reinvented herself as just another "mad housewife" in part to make herself palatable to the middle-class, women's-magazine and book-buying public, but also to avoid being labeled a Communist. But to read the book now and place it in the context of its time is to understand that *The Feminine Mystique* was anything but the whiny lament of a bored housewife. It was a Marxist takedown of patriarchal capitalism as rooted in the idea of the single-income nuclear family as the basic economic unit. But in Friedan's day, it was more socially acceptable to be thought a middle-class housewife than to be thought a socialist, so, in order for her to say what she wanted to say, it was safer for her to "play the girl" while she said it. What she wanted to say was that it was all bullshit, that the entire system had colluded to force women out of the workforce after World War II by selling them an ideology, and that she was sorry, as a women's-magazine writer, to have contributed to the problem. "I have watched American women for fifteen years try to conform to it," she wrote. "But I can no longer deny my own knowledge of its terrible implications."[9] Friedan demystified the fairy tale and traced it back to its roots. She named the unnamed problem. She told women they weren't crazy, that the culture was set up to drive them crazy and make them relinquish themselves and step into a mass-produced, ready-made identity, ready to please.

By the time *The Stepford Wives* rolled around, it really *had* been ages since *The Feminine Mystique* had come out. Maybe people Bobbie and Joanna's age believed those days were behind them, or almost. Maybe they thought their husbands agreed and that, as Joanna told her Realtor, they were interested in "women's lib," too. Second-wave feminism was much more diverse than we tend to give it credit for, ushering into the mainstream a wide-ranging political, institutional, and informal activism that had first come into being in the nineteenth century and never really gone away. It wasn't just about setting national agendas. Groups formed around personal identity, race, and class-based issues. Feminists took on cultural criticism and everyday experience.[10] Kate Millett kicked off modern feminist literary criticism with *Sexual Politics,* a work of political philosophy that argued that representation mattered, that words and images had the power to shape reality, for better and for worse. The book, which began as her dissertation at Columbia, argued that the relationship between the sexes was a master-slave relationship, "one of dominance and subservience." This power dynamic was at the basis of patriarchy: it was institutional and ideological. Stories functioned as a kind of "interior colonization . . . sturdier than any form of segregation, and more rigorous than class stratification," a colonization that socialized children in this unequal gender "caste system" that they agreed to long before they understood it. "However muted its appearance may be," Millett wrote, "sexual dominion obtains nevertheless as perhaps the most pervasive ideology of our culture and provides its most fundamental concept of power."[11]

The output was dizzyingly varied. Shulamith Firestone took on sex, reproduction, and child rearing in her brilliant, if insane, Marxist polemic *The Dialectic of Sex*. Rita Mae Brown published *Rubyfruit Jungle* and helped form the lesbian radical feminist group Lavender Menace, in part as a protest to Friedan's panicked exclusion of lesbian issues from the Second Congress to Unite Women in New York. (Friedan was afraid the movement's goals would be undermined if conservatives could dismiss them as "man-hating lesbians," which she needn't have worried about, because they'd do it regardless.) Gloria Steinem and Letty Cottin Pogrebin took on women's representation in the media by cofounding *Ms.* magazine. The Black Women's Alliance and Puerto Rican women activists joined to form the Third World Women's Alliance in the fight against racism, imperialism, and sexism. Liberal feminists were trying to help women gain equal rights and representation in mainstream society; radical feminists wanted to topple the patriarchy and start over again from scratch.

Friedan herself had moved on to other things, like setting a national agenda for women's rights and trying to get the Equal Rights Amendment passed. Suffragist Alice Paul had believed that an amendment was needed to ensure that the Constitution was applied equally to all citizens, so she wrote one in 1923 and rewrote it in 1943, when it was added to both the Republican and Democratic platforms. Social conservatives opposed it, though, and it wasn't until the 1960s that the civil rights movement inspired a renewed interest in the ERA. In early 1972, the amendment passed the Senate and the House and was sent to the states for ratification. In the first year, it received twenty-two out of the necessary thirty-eight states. Then, a conservative Christian by the name of Phyllis Schlafly began to organize a fear-mongering opposition campaign. As the leader of the right-wing Eagle Forum/Stop ERA, she convinced dependent housewives that they would lose the right to be supported by their husbands and would be sent into combat. The pace of ratification slowed dramatically. Only eight states ratified in 1973, three in 1974, one in 1975, and none in 1976. Meanwhile, the "feminine mystique" was adapting to the times. It was getting cooler and craftier, more pandering. It said, "You've come a long way, baby!" before baby had gotten very far at all. In 1980, just before Ronald Reagan was elected president, the Republican Party withdrew its support for the ERA from its platform. The amendment was defeated just three states short of ratification. In 1992, the year Bill Clinton was elected president, having campaigned on the quip "and you get two for the price of one," Pat Robertson wrote in an Iowa fund-raising letter opposing a state equal-rights amendment that feminism "encourages women to leave their husbands, kill their children, practice witchcraft, destroy capitalism, and become lesbians." As of 2016, the ERA has yet to pass.

Like most parents I knew, mine had a traditional marriage with a modern veneer. Or maybe it was a modern marriage built on a traditional foundation. Either way, my dad's career was the kind of career that required a wife and kids. And of course his wife and kids required that he have a particular kind of corporate career. Our identity was entirely predicated on it, as was our existence. On the face of it, my parents' marriage looked and functioned like a partnership. Unlike my grandfather, my father was not autocratic. Unlike my grandmother, my mother was not required to be outwardly submissive and secretly subversive. They had an egalitarian relationship, or an unequal relationship with an egalitarian vibe. Belief in the vibe of equality was crucial to the enterprise. Without it, the starship would have collapsed. Of course, my dad's salary underwrote the whole operation, and it was it, not he, that was the boss of all of us. Throughout my childhood, I don't remember once hearing the word *choice* applied to this arrangement, unless it was preceded by the word *no*. Between the time my mom got married and my younger sister turned three, she packed up the house and unpacked it again six times, across cities, countries, and continents. My dad would start a new job, and his family would magically re-form around him in situ. I couldn't picture myself living my mother's life, yet I couldn't picture what life I might live instead, either. I couldn't picture it because there were no pictures. Sometimes, my dad would joke around with me and say, "Never get married." And I'd laugh and feel anxious and wonder, *Is he talking about himself, my mother, or me?*

The trouble was that I wanted to get married, just not in the traditional sense. I wanted to get married in the sense that I wanted to enter into an ever-deepening, ever-evolving conversation with another; with a person who saw me for everything I was. Romantic love is a mirror in which you can see your whole self pleasantly reflected, if you're lucky. Or it's a dark mirror into which you can disappear. Traditionally, the only plot that has been available to the heroine is the "marriage plot." In stories, it has been her one thrilling, treacherous, booby-trapped obstacle course to transcendent happiness. Because marriage was the only culturally and socially sanctioned ("happy") outcome for a girl, her story could conclude only one way to be deemed a success. In *The Heroine's Text*, her seminal analysis of the marriage plot in eighteenth-century French and English novels, Nancy K. Miller argued that the novel as a form "would have never happened without a certain collective 'obsessing' about an idea called 'woman.'" More than a reflection of social reality, "literary femininity in the eighteenth century," Miller wrote, is "the inscription of a female destiny, the fictionalization of what is taken to be the feminine at a specific cultural moment."[12] If, traditionally, the hero's story was the story of a boy's transformation into himself, then the heroine's story, or text, was the story of a girl's transformation into a wife. The transition from her father's child to her husband's wife was understood to be her only adventure. Everything, therefore, was riding on this one, early adventure. Its outcome would be, as Miller put it, either euphoric or dysphoric. She would get it "all" (a rich, handsome, sexy, kind, smart husband attuned to her emotional needs) or she would get "nothing," and then she would probably die. Either way, the story ended. And there wasn't much she could do to steer it toward its successful conclusion. She could be as fetching as possible, compliant, and charming. She could go the route of virtue, or strategy, or might just get lucky. But she had very little decision-making power, no authority to make things happen. Her word was as ineffective as it was distrusted. The heroine and all who root for her yearned and yearned for a swift conclusion to her intolerable freedom and life of open-ended adventure. A happy ending was impossible without a successful coupling. Without marriage, a heroine was "unfinished." She had not quite yet become "herself."

So, what should a movie that wasn't about two guys and their adventures be about? This was the big question, the age-old question, the ongoing, perpetually trending "woman question." It was the raging question in 1865, 1890, 1920, 1940, 1963, and 1975. How did a modern girl become herself? What was a girl? Who got to say? What was spookiest about *The Stepford Wives* was the same thing that had seemed spooky and galvanizing about *The Feminine Mystique*. Had the husbands in the story been one-dimensional cartoon villains, they would have been easy to mock and dismiss. What was scary about them was that they weren't that. They were interested in the women's movement, as Joanna said of her husband to the Realtor. They did the dishes and took the kids to McDonald's and helped install darkrooms in basements for their photographer wives. Individually, they weren't bad at all. It was when they got together and let themselves be swayed by a charismatic leader that the trouble began. The husbands' ambivalence about replacing their wives with sexy wife-bots is apparent throughout the novel and the movie. They don't have an easy time of it. They need the constant affirmation of the guys at the Men's Association or they fall to pieces, as Bobbie's husband does after they swap her out for the new model. The husbands are following orders. They're not the ones making the rules. *The Stepford Wives* isn't really about men and women, or husbands and wives, but about how patriarchy and capitalism use "traditional" marriage — that is, the single-income, "family wage," upper-middle-class model that became dominant in the nineteenth century — to reinforce the existing global patriarchal power structure. And it's about how mass media helps perpetuate this power structure by forever spinning fairy tales about marriage that, on closer inspection, are revealed to be horror stories.

This was the idea *The Feminine Mystique* helped bring into the mainstream.

This was the idea that *The Stepford Wives* turned into campy gothic horror, that looked familiar and felt like home.

In real life, of course, the girl doesn't disappear after the story ends — I mean, she kind of does, narratively; her story just stops getting told, but as a person she sticks around. The plot ensures that whatever else she achieves or doesn't, receives or doesn't, this "becoming" a wife is what marks her successful passage into adulthood — only it's not the beginning of a lifelong adventure but the "happy ending." You could almost call it a plot against women. In an essay called "Stepford U.S.A.: Second-Wave Feminism, Domestic Labor, and the Representation of National Time," the scholar Jane Elliott observed that *The Stepford Wives* was notable not just because it was told from the point of view of the heroine but also because it took up where the heroine's story usually leaves off: from the successful conclusion of her risky, zero-sum journey to marriage, "after which nothing of interest — no meaningful change, in other words — was expected to happen."[13] Despite her youth — and the heroine is never not young — that is, despite how close she still is to the beginning, we cheer her toward this happy ending, this blissful state of suspended animation, this animatronic life — and who doesn't like to be cheered on?

What if, Elliott suggested, *The Stepford Wives* was more than just about housewifely ennui but also about the alienation and unending tedium of all modern work — of a moneymaking need that expands to fill the time available? Why else this constant repetition and reinforcement of a fiction that reality keeps refuting but that fiction keeps reimposing: the fiction of progress, the feeling that we are going somewhere, getting somewhere, that our lives have meaning, that we are not caught in a constant recursion, an infinite loop? Is there progress? What is progress? What if author Ira Levin was not ripping off Betty Friedan but was on her side? What if he was calling back to her, saying, "I feel you, sister! Fuck the patriarchy!" What if, as Elliott suggested, *The Stepford Wives* was an allegory for the lives not just of suburban housewives but of global corporate capitalism? of working ceaselessly with nothing to show for it at the end? What if it represented anxieties about lives of pointless repetition with no progress, no end result, and no possibility of transformation? If it wasn't just the housewives' problem, or a problem caused by housewives who ceased to perform their housewifely duties, but everyone's problem? What if "the problem that has no name turns out to be caused by the life that has no more plot?"[14] If so, Friedan and Levin weren't the first to notice.

The Stepford Wives opens in dead silence on a shot of some garish yellow wallpaper. It's a groovy, bilious, ornate seventies floral print with silhouettes of leopards and lions mixed in, reflected in the mirrored medicine cabinet of Joanna Eberhart's bathroom in her empty apartment in New York. It's moving day. The family is off to Stepford. She gazes wistfully at her reflection with the hideous wallpaper in the background. I saw this and thought, *You can't start a movie about a woman who is about to be murdered and replaced with a sexy robot with a shot of yellow wallpaper and not invite comparisons to* The Yellow Wallpaper.

The Yellow Wallpaper is a short work by the writer, sociologist, and feminist reformer Charlotte Perkins Gilman. Published in 1892, it's the story of a woman who suffers a "temporary nervous depression — a slight hysterical tendency" after the birth of her baby and is taken to a house in the country for a "rest cure" by her husband, a sympathetic but paternalistic doctor named John. The house is lovely but for the room where she and her husband move in. It's an upstairs nursery with bars on the windows; scarred, bolted-down furniture; and walls covered in the most hideous, crazy-making wallpaper the woman has ever seen — a horrible repeating pattern of snaking, twisted vines in a hideous shade of yellow. The narrator asks to be installed downstairs in a room with a view of the garden, but her husband refuses. Not only does the wallpaper assault her senses and pitch her further into a nervous (and aesthetic) crisis, but also she is forbidden to write, paint, read, talk to people, or do anything intellectually stimulating for more than two hours a day. She keeps a secret journal in which she records her growing fixation on the wallpaper as she slowly becomes convinced that there is a woman trapped behind it, creeping around. Determined to set the woman free, she starts to peel off the wallpaper in strips. Then she comes to believe the woman in the wallpaper is she herself. Having descended into psychosis, she locks herself up in the room. When her husband makes it inside, he finds her on the floor creeping around on her belly like a lizard or a ghost in a Japanese horror movie. "For outside you have to creep on the ground, and everything is green instead of yellow. But here I can creep smoothly on the floor, and my shoulder just fits in that long smooch around the wall, so I cannot lose my way," she says. The husband drops in a dead faint at the sight of the monster his angelic wife has become, and she just creeps over him, oblivious.

Gilman was inspired by her own experience following the birth of her only daughter, when she suffered a bout of severe postpartum depression and was taken to the country by her husband on the advice of her doctor, Silas Weir Mitchell, a neurologist known for treating women for "hysteria" with a "rest cure" that involved isolation from friends and family, bed rest, force-feeding of fatty foods, and no reading, writing, talking, or sewing. The idea was to break the patient's will and teach her to submit to male authority for the good of her health. Mitchell advised Gilman to "live as domestic a life as possible. Have your child with you all the time . . . Lie down an hour after each meal. Have but two hours' intellectual life a day. And never touch pen, brush or pencil as long as you live." She followed orders, her depression blossomed into psychosis, and she became suicidal. Eventually, she left her husband, moved to

California with her daughter, and became an internationally best-selling writer.

We think of women "leaving the house" and "entering the work-force" as being new at around the time *The Stepford Wives* appeared. But it wasn't really all that new. The postwar suburbs around which young couples were encouraged to structure their lives were new. The American middle class, such as it was, was fairly new. The notion that in America every man who was will-ing to work hard was all but guaranteed a house with a wife in it to work all the modern appliances and dust the faux-colonial fur-niture, and with his-and-her cars side by side in the garage — that was pretty new. And that brand-new world was sold as "traditional," maybe not the way things "used to be" so much as the way they were "supposed to be," the way people sometimes wished they'd been, as imagined by some people trying to sell soap from a soundstage in Burbank. It was a blip, though. And by the time *The Stepford Wives* came out, the postwar economic blip was already over. Peo-ple sensed it, perhaps, but they just weren't ready to admit it. I re-member getting up extra early so my mom could drive my dad to the train and then waiting in line at the gas station. I remember a weird kid named Teddy following me home from school, sitting down at the kitchen table as my mom served us a snack, and tell-ing her that she shouldn't smoke because she was killing the birds. "You're killing the birds," he'd say, and I'd look at him and think, *Why did you follow me here?* And my mom would say something like, "Thanks for letting me know, Teddy." The world was changing, you could tell. A kindergartner you didn't even like could get holier-than-thou with your mom, and your mom could just train him with a killer stare and keep right on smoking. So, it wasn't women work-ing that was new. What was (relatively) new was global corporate capitalism as the organizing principle, and what was still unclear was how women would fit in. It was global economies and ideo-logical wars that were new. It was the sense that we were citizens of our corporations more than our countries that was new. As Elliott writes, the image of the trapped, automated housewife symbolized a late-1960s collective anxiety over the stalling out of American progress, a fear of totalizing ideologies, and a paranoia about social control. I wouldn't have thought of it myself, but when I read it, I recognized something true.

Tales of housewifely desperation are still just as endlessly produced, endlessly popular, and contemptuously dismissed today. Jell-O delights have given way to gluten-free cupcakes, but the basic structure of the system that sustains us and keeps the economy going hasn't changed. We're just made to pretend it has, and we're punished for pointing out the ways in which it hasn't. We don't like to acknowledge this. We prefer that women blame each other or themselves. Mommy squabbles, feminist infighting, and generational antagonism are always encouraged. The media never stops concern-trolling us with essentialist ideologies couched in existential questions. Can women, as God and nature made us, really "have it all"? Or must we still choose between parts of ourselves, to preserve a Victorian idea of masculine wholeness?

It wasn't just the look of *The Stepford Wives,* the Vera scarves and the wood-paneled station wagons, that reminded me of my mom and her friends in those days. It was the sense of dissonance that arose from the disconnect between Joanna and Bobbie's understanding of the world they lived in and the actual world they lived in that was deeply familiar. I'd lived in that disconnect my whole life, though I couldn't have named it — not even after Betty Friedan did. I didn't know it, but the "woman question" was back with a vengeance — not that it had ever really gone away. As a girl, I was gathering that being a girl was a problem in the process of being solved, and that my generation — lucky me! — would be the first to benefit from the solution. The solution, I knew, would be related to fairness somehow, but I wouldn't have to worry about it very much. Joanna and Bobbie were so familiar. They were seventies housewives who were interested in women's lib and proud of their messy kitchens. They probably read Erma Bombeck and would soon graduate to Erica Jong. (*Fear of Flying* was published between *The Stepford Wives* book and the movie, but whatever.) They probably subscribed to *Ms.* magazine, or pretended they did, and hated Phyllis Schlafly. When they got together at each other's messy houses, they doubtless laughed at Barbie's parabolic boobs and Ken's smooth crotch-dome. They were cool, hip, post–*Feminine Mystique* housewives. They were in on the joke, which only made it harder to see that the joke was on them. The problem with the ironic postmodern stance, when you look back on it from our current, metamodern age, is that not everyone who indulged could really afford it — they paid for it on credit.

This is why the husbands in *The Stepford Wives* are so interesting and so conflicted. Diz, the former Disney Imagineer and founder of the Men's Association, is the bad guy. The others are torn between two sides: either they believe in the existing social and economic order, or they believe in women's equality. They can't have it both ways. They pretend to, for a while. But ultimately, they have to choose.

In *A Strange Stirring: "The Feminine Mystique" and American Women at the Dawn of the 1960s,* Stephanie Coontz writes, "Friedan captured a paradox that many women struggle with today. The elimination of the most blatant denials of one's rights can be very disorienting if you don't have the ability to exercise one right without giving up another."[15] "Disorienting" is putting it mildly. Blatant denials of their rights, of the kind the second-wavers had to deal with, had the curious upside of at least making it clear what women were fighting for. It's hard to fight a foe that pretends to be your friend. It's like Joanna in *The Stepford Wives* novel, not knowing whether to trust robot Bobbie or run for her life. The problem with traditional marriages and workplaces, says Coontz, is that "at their core they continue to gently guide women toward a choice that's not really a choice, to choose half of what they really want, and to blame themselves if that half fails to satisfy their needs."[16] This is gaslighting. It makes you wonder if you're crazy by denying your perceptions and encouraging you to think the problem is you. It makes you doubt yourself in the face of overwhelming evidence, even as the buxom robot that's supplanted your best friend comes at you with a knife, smiling, telling you to relax, calm down, and let your life be taken away from you.

A few years after publishing *The Yellow Wallpaper*, Charlotte Perkins Gilman wrote a treatise called *Women and Economics: A Study of the Economic Relation Between Men and Women as a Factor in Social Evolution*, in which she argued that it made no sense to think of wife- and motherhood in the same terms as work. For Gilman, women's lack of power in society was not inherent but the result "of certain arbitrary conditions of our own adoption." Her problem was with women's de facto economic dependence on men at the time; with "the commonly received opinion" that whereas "men make and distribute the wealth of the world . . . women earn their share of it as wives." This assumption made no sense to her, though. If it were really true that women were participating in the economy as wives, then a wife would be an employee or a partner in her husband's business, and entitled to share his income or profits. "But a manufacturer who marries, or a doctor, or a lawyer, does not take a partner in his business, when he takes a partner in parenthood, unless his wife is also a manufacturer, a doctor, or a lawyer." In reality, Gilman argued, a wife's work was regarded not as employment but as duty. The more money a husband made, the less hard a wife would be expected to "work."

To honestly take the position that wives "earned" their keep, Gilman argued, would require compensating wives for their work as cooks, housemaids, nursemaids, seamstresses, and housekeepers. "This would of course reduce the spending money of the wives of the rich," she wrote, but it would "put it out of the power of the poor man to 'support' a wife at all, unless, indeed, the poor man faced the situation fully, paid his wife her wages as house servant, and then she and he combined their funds in the support of their children. He would be keeping a servant: she would be helping keep the family." In this scenario, she argued, such a thing as a "rich wife" could not even exist, because domestic wages would never make anyone rich. "Even the highest class of private housekeeper, useful as her services are, does not accumulate a fortune," Gilman wrote. "She does not buy diamonds and sables and keep a carriage. Things like these are not earned by house service." Whatever women's unpaid domestic labor was worth on the open market, wives did not get it. Actually, Gilman argued, the wives who did the most domestic work got the least money, and the wives who had the most money did the least work. The same went for motherhood. It made no sense to think of motherhood as a job, because a job is payment for an exchangeable commodity (labor), and it would be impossible to establish a relation between "the quantity or quality of the motherhood and the quantity and quality of the pay." What she meant was that, if the argument for women's economic dependence on men was that motherhood is a job, then this would be reflected in the status of married women. Wives with no children would have no economic status at all, and the number of children a wife had would determine her status. "This is obviously absurd," wrote Gilman. "The childless wife has as much money as the mother of many, more; for the children of the latter consume what would otherwise be hers; and the inefficient mother is no less provided for than the efficient one."

But, of course, the number of children a woman has has no bearing on her economic status. And failure to produce a child is not grounds for "firing" a wife, at least not in Gilman's day, when a divorce was hard to get. "The claim of motherhood as a factor in economic exchange is false today," she wrote. "But suppose it were true. Are we willing to hold this ground, even in theory? Are we willing to consider motherhood as a business, a form of commercial exchange? Are the cares and duties of the mother, her travail and her love, commodities to be exchanged for bread? It is revolting so to consider them; and, if we dare face our own thoughts, and force them to their logical conclusion, we shall see that nothing could be more repugnant to human feeling, or more socially and individually injurious, than to make motherhood a trade."

Yet if motherhood *could* be defended as work in the usual sense, then it would be a strangely disempowered job. "We are the only animal species," she wrote, "in which the female depends on the male for food. The only animal species in which the sex relation is also an economic relation."[17]

I heard echoes of Gilman in Wednesday Martin, author of *Primates of Park Avenue*, in a *New York Times* op-ed. "Among primates," she wrote, "*Homo sapiens* practice the most intensive food and resource sharing, and females may depend entirely on males for shelter and sustenance . . . Access to your husband's money might feel good. But it can't buy you the power you get by being the one who earns, hunts or gathers it. The wives of the masters of the universe, I learned, are a lot like mistresses — dependent and comparatively disempowered."[18]

When Charlotte York, *Sex and the City*'s Victorian-lady character and aspiring "angel in the house," decided to quit her job at the art gallery to become a stay-at-home mom even before becoming a mom-to-be, she was disappointed when her friends met the news with something less than enthusiasm and support. How to justify and defend this choice? For Charlotte, the answer was to stand on the sidewalk, yelling, "I choose my choice!," which was not very convincing. We couldn't help but wonder: Was it really a choice? If so, why did it look so much like previous nonchoices? By the time my generation reached adulthood, nobody talked about adventure anymore. Nobody talked about anything but "the choice." The choice hovered over everything, flattening everything into an undifferentiated standard. You chose your choice, like Charlotte York or Charlotte Gilman. You could choose to be a person, or you could choose to be loved. This was framed as a choice between working and not working, but really it was a choice between the known and the unknown, between saving the institution and saving yourself.

Bewitched

After two years in New Jersey, we moved to Chicago, transferred by the pharmaceutical company that my father now worked for. A few months after we moved, my mom went to the hospital for minor surgery. As kids do, I believed all adult jobs to be equivalent, freely selected from a tantalizing portfolio of equally fulfilling choices. I also believed them to be inextricably bound up with the identity of the people who performed them. (One was a fireman just as one was a blond.) This idea, like all neat, categorical, deterministic ideas, appealed to me enormously — kids are natural-born fascists, big into essentialist, categorical ideas. I knew very few working women and almost no professional women as a child, so I concluded that being a lady was a woman's profession, which would then make women's magazines trade publications. I didn't want my mom to miss out on any important news, so I decided to make her a magazine out of old magazines and construction paper using a selection of clippings from old issues of the *Ladies' Home Journal*. My issue was a curated selection of recipes for Cool Whip and Jell-O–based things in fancy parfait glasses, a glittery makeup tutorial, a glam fashion spread, a parenting article biased in my favor, a funny Virginia Slims ad, a pudding ad featuring a droll Bill Cosby, and, of course, a column called Can This Marriage Be Saved?

Can This Marriage Be Saved? was a marriage-advice column that ran in the magazine from 1953 until it folded, in 2014. It was a triptych of subjectivity: first, the wife explained the problem, then the husband gave his side of the story, and finally the marriage counselor pronounced his or her verdict. If the spark had left the marriage, then the wife was advised to prepare a candlelit dinner and greet her husband at the door wrapped in Saran Wrap, for instance. Marriage saved! Decades later, I read in an *Aeon* essay by journalist and professor Rebecca Onion about the column that the counselor almost always favored the husband unless the problem was that the husband was trying to live some alternative lifestyle — say, he was a swinger resistant to "settling down" in the suburbs. The counselor would strongly recommend that he give up his "free love" lifestyle and live "a straight life."[19] The story might conclude with a happy report about how the couple got through it and wound up in "a distant suburb of San Francisco among a new circle of congenial friends who are more concerned with gardening, the Little League and PTA meetings than with the dubious virtues of drugs."[20] Your standard happy ending. Can This Marriage Be Saved? resonated because it presented marriage in a singular format, as a dialectic. You had your thesis, your antithesis, and your synthesis. Or, he says, she says, the expert decides. Another reason I liked Can This Marriage Be Saved? was that it had an aura of heroism about it. It was always a tale of rescue. The marriage counselor was the hero, and the marriage was the damsel. It had to be saved, even if that meant throwing the wife, the husband, the kids, or the whole family under the bus. In a fight for the greater good, you were going to be collateral damage. Marriage was a world with a population of two. It had to be saved because the world needs to be saved.

I thoroughly appreciated the *Rashomon*-like structure of Can This Marriage Be Saved? as a second-grader. The boys-versus-girls format really spoke to me. My brother and I were fewer than two years apart, close friends and mortal adversaries. Every single thing between us was a competition in which we took rigid, unyielding sides. I don't know if this was because our dad encouraged it (which he did: I was the brain, my brother was the jock) or if it was just the way we were. We split the world into spheres, took sides, and debated the relative merits of every "opposite" thing we could think of. The arguments were never gendered, that I recall.

They were never about "girl things" versus "boy things." They were more abstract, more philosophical, more "Spy vs. Spy." We argued the relative merits of pancakes versus waffles, hot dogs versus hamburgers, ketchup versus mustard, vanilla versus chocolate (all the natural food enemies), Ernie versus Bert, Superman versus Wonder Woman. (OK, that one.) We committed. We hunkered down. We fought to the death. No position was too inflexible. No blow was too low. There could be no compromise or middle ground. It was win or lose. That's how life was played. I saw the counselor in the Can This Marriage Be Saved? column as a kind of referee, whose fairness, scientific objectivity, and impartiality I did not question. I assumed fair play and a level playing field. I was confident that I lived in a free country, because "It's a free country" was a slogan that got bandied around the playground a lot. It was also my belief that we lived in a fair country, founded on the principles of turn taking and equal amounts of everything, at all times.

For years I thought my love of Can This Marriage Be Saved? was an obscure and offbeat personal quirk. I had no idea it was one of the most popular columns of all time, or that it was created by a eugenicist named Paul Popenoe, founder of an organization called the American Institute of Family Relations (AIFR). By 1960, AIFR was the best-known marriage-counseling institute in the world. Can This Marriage Be Saved? debuted in the *Ladies' Home Journal* in 1953 and gave Popenoe an extremely popular and influential platform from which to spout his right-wing views on the family and on how women should sacrifice themselves to uphold it. Popenoe, who acted as the advice-dispensing counselor for the column, had very definite opinions about the differences between men and women, which he made it his mission to point out at every possible opportunity. Popenoe believed that the average man "was more active, venturesome, aggressive, consistent, nomadic, businesslike, secular, rational, high-minded, and courageous," whereas the average woman was (surprise!) more "modest, submissive, romantic, sincere, religious, vindictive, 'catty,' drawn to trivia, and affectionately

demonstrative,"[21] and he advised couples accordingly. Even in cases of domestic violence, husbands' infidelity, and infertility, he tended to blame the wife for all the couples' problems. He tended to believe marriages failed because of a regrettable lack of wifely effort. In the 1950s, he sometimes advised battered wives to watch what they said in order to avoid further beatings. Wives' keeping their mouths shut was prescribed for husbands' alcoholism, gambling problems, and silent treatments. Silence was a cure-all.

To what degree Can This Marriage Be Saved? shaped my view of marriage, I can't say for sure. But the idea that marriage was so brutally sectarian that caring about it was the exclusive domain of the girl was confusing to me. How was this not exactly like the sound of one hand clapping? By dividing the world so inexorably into public and private spheres, into girl stuff and guy stuff, were we not just creating two alternate imaginary universes that served nobody, really, so much as our corporate masters? What was the point? In her essay, Onion noted that men's magazines don't write about marital trouble — they write about sex.[22] Promoting the idea that the responsibility for forming and maintaining committed relationships falls exclusively to women, even the power to decide whether relationships form in the first place, is a privilege that resides exclusively with men. The emotional labor is hers, the executive decisions are his.

By the time I started reading it, Popenoe's institute still supplied many of the cases for the column, but Popenoe was no longer dispensing the advice himself, and Can This Marriage Be Saved? was no longer doing things like advising battered women not to say things that made their husbands mad. Still, there was something spooky about it — very female gothic. I loved nothing better than to kick back with some Jell-O pudding and luxuriate in the titillating grotesquery of Can This Marriage Be Saved? If by reading the column I was learning how to be a submissive wife someday, I was not aware of it. I was eight. I thought pudding was delicious and Bill Cosby was hilarious and the magazines needed more arti-

cles on hair and makeup and fewer chicken recipes. I loved it when someone produced a Stephen King book or *Flowers in the Attic* at a slumber party. The seventies were awash in thrilling gothic tales of madness, female abjection, abuse, and domestic confinement, so maybe it just seemed normal. In the world of Can This Marriage Be Saved?, there were no problems that could not be covered up with a pretty tablecloth, a negligee, or bricked-in windows and doors. Still, as Onion wrote just a few years before it was discontinued, "There's a hermetic feeling to the present-day 'Can This Marriage Be Saved?' columns which persists in understanding marital issues as internal to a dyad," but "surely some of the 'work' that needs to be done is social and political, not personal." Not that those things don't get famously intertwined.

Still, it was always a surprise to stumble across these stories of radical action, more sincere, organized, and inspired than anything I'd ever seen, heard of, or participated in. When I read Susan Brownmiller's memoir, for instance, I was stunned to learn that in March 1970, before I was out of diapers, a coalition of feminist groups including Media Women, NOW, the Redstockings, and New York Radical Feminists (not to be confused with an earlier group, New York Radical Women) decided to occupy a women's magazine to protest its male bias, sexism, and racism. With their infinite tips and advice on how to be a girl, women's magazines conditioned girls and women to be subservient and insecure. Meanwhile, with the exception of *Cosmopolitan*, these magazines were almost entirely run and staffed by men. *Ladies' Home Journal* had been founded by a woman, but she ran it for less than a year, and it had been run by men ever since. The editor in chief was John Mack Carter, a member of the Sigma Delta Chi fraternity for distinguished journalists, which did not include women until 1969, but in that way it wasn't very different from the others. Popenoe's column was the main reason the coalition chose the *Ladies' Home Journal* for its sit-in. About a hundred protesters occupied the magazine's offices. They hung a banner that read WOMEN'S

LIBERATED JOURNAL from the window. They called for Carter's res-
ignation and demanded that a female editor in chief and an all-
female editorial staff be hired. They also demanded that the magazine hire women to write the columns and articles, hire nonwhite
women in proportion with the population, raise women's salaries,
and provide free day care on the premises. They demanded that the
magazine open its editorial meetings to all employees and elimi-
nate the traditional power hierarchy; that it stop running ads degrading to women and ads from companies that exploited women;
that it stop running articles tied to advertising; and that it kill Can
This Marriage Be Saved? They also gave Carter a list of suggestions
for articles that would benefit women over advertisers, things like
"How to Get a Divorce," "How to Have an Orgasm," "What to Tell
Your Draft-Age Son," and "How Detergents Harm Our Rivers and
Streams." Though at first Carter refused to negotiate, by 6:00 p.m.
a settlement had been reached. He promised to look into the feasi-
bility of an on-site day-care center. Carter did not resign, but within
a few years the magazine had installed its first-ever female editor in
chief since its founding, in 1889. He agreed to let the group guest-
edit a portion of an upcoming issue. The issue included a column
called Should This Marriage Be Saved?

Bewitched and *I Dream of Jeannie* were my favorite shows in 1975.
Twin sitcoms about a witch named Samantha who married an adman named Darrin and a genie named Jeannie who enslaved herself to an astronaut named Major Nelson, they both dealt nervously
with power and gender. Whereas Samantha and Jeannie could do
literally anything, the former by twitching her nose, the latter by
crossing her arms and nodding, they tried hard to "behave" themselves and suppress their powers out of love for their respective
husband and "master." Darrin and Major Nelson were perhaps two
of the most anxious, highly strung, insecure, and haplessly neurotic male characters ever to appear on TV. The humor was derived
from the contortions required of the women to make themselves

comparatively passive and weak. But it wasn't really Darrin or Major Nelson who required the display of "normal" domesticity or (in Jeannie's case) of total invisibility: it was their bosses. Samantha and Jeannie posed direct threats not to Darrin and Major Nelson but to the institutions they stood in for and depended on for food. Darrin's career was constantly threatened by Samantha and by her family: her disdainful mother, Endora, who thought her daughter had married beneath her; her silly goose of an Aunt Clara; and their daughter, Tabitha, who had inherited her powers. In episode after episode, Endora, Aunt Clara, Samantha, and Tabitha torpedoed Darrin's client dinners, enraged his boss, Larry, and got Darrin fired. It was almost always as a result of the fact that Darrin's career depended on his ability to uphold an image that his industry had created and was selling but that nobody could possibly live up to. Why anyone would want to — how anyone could even consider this slavish conformity to be in any way aspirational — is the question represented by Endora, who would have liked nothing more than to see Samantha liberated from the oppressive effects of Darrin's fragile ego. Darrin loved Samantha, and he was mostly sympathetic to her; he was just caught between a rock and a hard place. It was his boss, and ultimately his clients, who demanded compliance to an image that required Samantha to act a certain way.

There's an episode in which Samantha throws a dinner to impress a client who then makes a pass at her. When he doesn't stop, she turns him into a dog. When Darrin yells at her, Samantha locks them both out of the house. The next day, the client does it again, but this time Darrin punches him and quits. The client apologizes and asks Darrin to come back. In the next episode, Samantha comes up with a good idea for a campaign, but Darrin is jealous and accuses her of using witchcraft. Then he accuses her of using witchcraft to do housework, too. He pitches his own bad idea to the client, doesn't get the account, and Samantha leaves him. In the end, he pitches the bad idea to Larry, who loves it, and rushes home to make up with Samantha. Later, he returns to work, pitches

Samantha's idea to the client, and wins him back, and it's revealed that the whole thing was Samantha's plan all along — because she's crafty like that. In another episode, Samantha tells Endora she wishes Darrin would forget about business now and then, and Endora makes a bowl of popcorn appear. As soon as Darrin eats some, he announces he's taking the day off. Then the milkman has some and decides to join Darrin. Angry, Larry comes over to see what's happening, eats some popcorn, and joins Darrin and the milkman in a poker game. Then the client comes over to fire the agency, has some popcorn, and instantly loses interest in all business. Then a policeman comes — you get the picture.

I loved *I Dream of Jeannie*, but Jeannie's situation depressed me. Compared to the smart, capable, rational, ladylike, elegant, and highly respected Samantha, Jeannie was unpredictable, jealous, emotionally reactive, and openly sexual. She was Tonya Harding to Samantha's Nancy Kerrigan. Unfamiliar with the social codes Samantha knew by heart and followed to the letter, Jeannie was ostensibly shaped in a more benighted time with regard to women's roles. Here was a magical character who had all the freedom and power in the world, who could literally spirit herself around in time and space, but who still called a man "master." Nelson was always showing her ways in which she was more "free" in the modern world, and yet at the same time it was clear that Major Nelson was constantly terrified that she would commit some horrible social gaffe that would hurt his reputation or even ruin his career. It's obvious that freedom was a "choice" exercised at Jeannie's own peril. Major Nelson was always trying to coax Jeannie back in the bottle. Darrin was always trying to disempower Samantha.

My takeaways: (1) women who wield power openly are bad for business and wreck civilization; (2) women secretly control the world through magic, trickery, and witchcraft, and should therefore be controlled lest they ruin business and destroy civilization; (3) women who police and diminish themselves are good witches, and (old) women who say fuck it to all that and assert their power and authority are evil (I counted at least twenty such story lines in the first few seasons and then stopped counting); and (4) women should never get married.

The end, though. How we yearn for the happy ending. I always did. I remember being in college and feeling bereft one day, I'm not sure why. We'd moved so often. My parents always seemed on the verge of splitting up. Winter in Evanston, Illinois, was long and brutal. I was hungover. I saw some friends of mine, one of those couples who are attached at the hip, who seemed to carry an aura of home with them everywhere they went. I have no idea why I thought this. I'd heard him talk on the phone with a random girl he'd met in an elevator in Chicago. But there's something so irresistibly final about the idea of the happy ending that we settle for just an OK ending, or convince ourselves that "happiness" is something other than an emotion, and emotions are fleeting. The critic Frank Kermode said that fiction is inherently apocalyptic, because it forces readers and writers to move toward an imagined ending. The end creates "a satisfying consonance" with the beginning and the middle, and arranges time into a nice pattern. But time doesn't end, so the pattern keeps having to readjust. We understand that literary fictions are "consciously false," he said (the world doesn't end), but we don't care. We find this particular falseness comforting, because it beats open-endedness, not-knowing. If the end fails to materialize, the apocalyptic yearning remains. In other words, Kermode said, "the end is immanent, rather than imminent."[23] In *The Stepford Wives* and Can This Marriage Be Saved?, the end was immanent. In my favorite sitcoms about marriage, by contrast, similar themes were played for laughs. TV shows don't yearn for the end — on the contrary, they yearn for the never-ending now, for immortality or its TV equivalent, syndication. They home in on the moment-to-moment minutiae of an eternal present. They're not compelled toward a satisfying conclusion; stasis is far more economically favorable. No wonder TV was practically built on the comedy of marriage and family life. With its absurdist recursions and thwarted desires, marriage and family life is the ideal subject for comedy. Depending on how you frame it, it can be a clown show, or a horror show, or a static vision of a deadened, heavenly afterlife: a static dream of June Cleaver perfection with no beginning, no end, no age, no death, no upsetting turns of events that couldn't be resolved in an episode. TV — at least the TV of the fifties, sixties, and seventies, which I enjoyed all at once as a child through the ahistorical margin of reruns — was predicated on the same idea on which getting married and living happily ever after were predicated: on nothing changing, on an eternal, reassuring return to the status quo, on the heroine's circular journey to nowhere.

3

The Bronze Statue of the Virgin Slut Ice Queen Bitch Goddess

To be worshiped is not freedom.

— Shulamith Firestone

KATHARINE HEPBURN WAS A TALL, LEAN, ELECTRIC THIRTY-three-year-old when she played white-robed goddess, Main Line socialite, and divorcée Tracy Lord in *The Philadelphia Story*. I was ten or eleven when I saw her in it for the first time; a short, vaguely potato-shaped fourth- or fifth-grader, likely encased in gauchos and fancy kneesocks. I remember standing in front of the television in the family room on a Saturday afternoon, rooted in place like a tree, feeling thunderstruck. I felt how I imagined Omar Sharif must have felt near the end of *Dr. Zhivago,* glancing out the window of a crowded streetcar and suddenly clapping eyes on his long-ago-lost love, Julie Christie, on the sidewalk below. He banged on the window, but she didn't hear him. He tried to get off, but the crowd was oblivious. By the time he broke free, it was too late. He collapsed on the street and died of a coronary. Julie Christie never even knew he was there. My mom took me to see *Dr. Zhivago* one night when I was about eight, shortly before we moved to Madrid. We'd meant to see *Herbie Rides Again,* but it was sold out. *Dr. Zhivago* was being rereleased and was playing at the same multiplex. This was before there was Betamax, then VHS, then DVD, and then streaming. In theaters was how I got to see all my mom's childhood favorites — biblical epics with casts of thousands, Technicolor musicals, and Walt Disney's *Snow White, Cinderella,* and

Sleeping Beauty. I loved them all, but this *Dr. Zhivago*, with its epic snowy vistas, its fluttering fur hats, and its random, ruthless vicissitudes of history, politics, and circumstantial, wrong-place, wrong-time, roll-of-the-dice, cataclysmic bad luck pretty much killed me dead.

The Philadelphia Story opens with Tracy (draped in white, of course) imperiously kicking her husband, C. K. Dexter Haven (Cary Grant), out of the house — her father's house, we later learn — and then breaking his golf club over her knee, just to be extra clear. This is the gesture that crosses the line: it's one thing to stand up to your layabout society drunk of a husband, but it's another to say the hell with everything he stands for. Dexter makes this clear by marching back up the steps and pushing Tracy in the face. Tracy topples over backward, like a statue falling off a pedestal. I had mixed feelings about this scene. I recognized Tracy as the sassy heroine and Dexter as the rakish hero, which meant I understood that I was being made to understand that she was asking for it, that she had coming to her whatever she had coming. The "natural" order of things was about to be imposed.

I forgot this almost immediately, however, because in the next scene (two years later), Tracy is fully recovered and fluttering around the house on the eve of her second wedding. Having banished her father, Seth, from her wedding for publicly humiliating her mother by flaunting his affair with a dancer in New York, she has temporarily taken over the Lords' house and turned it into a giddy matriarchy. Tracy struts around, surveying the land, checking out her ludicrous wedding gifts, dashing off a few sardonic thank-you notes, and generally looking very pleased with herself. Never before had I seen a movie bride look so relaxed, or care less about the flowers or place settings, or express so few dress- or cake-related concerns. She spends the day before her wedding horseback riding, swimming, reading, playing jokes on her pervy uncle, and talking about her hopes and dreams for a life of adventure. She does go on, somewhat unconvincingly, about her fine, upstanding, self-made, man-of-the-people fiancé, George, to her mother, Margaret, and her little sister, Dinah (like Alice's cat!). But even before setting eyes on George, as Dinah seemed to know, I knew that Tracy would never stay with him. Dexter was charming in a suavely manipulative, narcissistic, emotionally abusive way. But George was a stuffy, middle-class striver with presidential aspirations. All he really wanted was power and access, and Tracy was his trophy and his ticket. And while she extolled his virtues to her mother and sister, she knew he was a fake. The first thing she did when she saw him by the stables was knock him down in the dirt. "You look like something out of a shop window," she says, rubbing the dirt into his pristine riding pants. And he complains the clothes were new.

Before watching *The Philadelphia Story*, it had never occurred to me that femininity and femaleness were not one and the same thing. I'd dutifully absorbed the lessons embedded in movies, TV shows, ads, magazines, commercials, and cartoons. The frillier, flightier, wilier, sweeter, gentler, kinder, bitchier, more nurturing, scarier, more insecure, and more insincere a character was, the more of a "girl" she was. I'd learned to rank female characters by prettiness. ("Who do you think is prettier, Irene or Minnie?" Kira asked me one Saturday morning while watching *Hello, Dolly!* — another symbolic heirloom, now on Amazon Prime, passed on from my mother to me to her.) Little girls like to claim their heroines' beauty as their own. It's like picking a team, though it's unclear what's being won. *The Philadelphia Story* marked the first time I remember encountering the idea that this ephemeral but familiar thing I'd recognized all my life as the feminine ideal might be not just distinct from but also possibly oppressive to women. It came as a shock. Here was Tracy, a heroine — a bride, no less — and she was different. She was experienced. She had learned from her youthful mistakes and was making deliberate choices. She had agency. She had a horse. (Not that this was germane, but I really loved horses.) She was comfortable in her own skin, secure, and she believed in herself. She radiated confidence of a kind I'd never seen before in a movie heroine. It wasn't the kind of confidence you usually saw in movie stars. It wasn't just that she was secure in her sexiness. On the contrary, she didn't seem to think about her sexiness at all. What made her attractive was that she acted like a person, not a girl. I did think it was strange to be encountering this for the first time in 1980, given that *The Philadelphia Story* was released in 1940. By the time I saw it, Hepburn had been described as "modern" for about five decades. After her film debut, in 1932, magazines called her "a new kind of star!" and "more modern than tomorrow!"[1] Which I guess she turned out to be, because Tracy's autonomy and independence were just the setup for setting her straight. It was the preface to her sudden adventure in the Wonderland of representation. The movie was a gauntlet. Tracy was put through the wringer. By the time her father, her ex-husband, her future husband, and the tabloid reporter were through telling her who she was and what she wasn't, she didn't know which way was up. This was part of what stunned me, I suppose. What kind of rabbit hole had we fallen into? How would we ever get out?

There are shades of *Alice* in *The Philadelphia Story*. When Dexter shows up unexpectedly, tabloid media in tow, Tracy steps unexpectedly through the looking glass. The movie is an allegory about Katharine Hepburn's experiences in Hollywood, but more abstractly it's about what it's like to be an independent woman pressured to conform to the culture's idea of woman. It's about Hepburn the person and Hepburn the star persona, and how (the fictional construct of) the latter came close to ruining the real life of the former until she realized that she couldn't be just herself, she had to be the version of herself that audiences were comfortable with, which had more to do with what passed for femininity at the time than anything else. At the start of the movie, Tracy leaves Dexter, but the structures stay the same. She returns to Seth's house and remains in a fairy-tale walled garden. As she is about to remarry, Dexter suddenly returns, ostensibly to save the day. He tells them all that he has made a deal with *Spy* magazine. In exchange for killing a story on Seth Lord's juicy, scandalous affair, he has agreed to sneak in a couple of tabloid journalists — a reporter named Mike (James Stewart) and a photographer named Liz (Ruth Hussey) — for an exclusive inside look at the society wedding of the year. Tracy is furious, but she goes along with it for her mother's sake.

I didn't know it then, but decades later I learned that Katharine Hepburn was raised by progressive parents who believed in raising girls the same way as boys. Her mother, Kit, was a leading suffragist and an early champion for birth control, causes she took up after getting married and having children and wondering why that was all that was expected of her. Her father was a prominent urologist and an advocate for public education about sexually transmitted diseases. When Hepburn was a little girl, she cut her hair, played sports, and made everyone call her Jimmy. The family discussed things like bisexuality and prostitution at the dinner table. Hartford society was not amused, so Hepburn was taught to stand up for what she believed was right. Her mother regularly took her and her brother to Greenwich Village to visit her lesbian "aunts," Kit's old classmates from Bryn Mawr Mary "Aunty" Towle and Bertha Rembaugh. Towle was a women's-rights activist and attorney. Her law partner, Rembaugh, was the first woman to run for municipal-court judge, one of the first reputable lawyers to defend prostitutes in night court, and one of the first single women to adopt a baby on her own. Hepburn went to meetings at the radical feminist Heterodoxy Club to hear Margaret Sanger and Emma Goldman speak. She wanted to do what she wanted to do. And what she wanted to do was act and be famous. She was married once, briefly, to her college boyfriend and lifelong friend, a Philadelphia industrialist named Ludlow "Luddy" Ogden Smith. Her family adored him. They called him "the prince." She convinced him to swap his middle and last names so that her name would not be Kate Smith, then divorced him to go back to Broadway. The family kept him on anyway, as a son.

Hepburn's mistake was the same mistake so many other ambitious, idealistic, earnest, guileless women make. It's the mistake of forgetting to "manage the optics," of forgetting to conform to the existing narrative, of thinking that you can not only get what you want but get it on your own terms, that you can change the story. Strategic girls manage perception; idealistic girls go up against the narrative, because it's at the root of the problem, and they get crushed every time. Throughout the 1930s, in her first decade of fame, Hepburn played unconventional, androgynous heroines: Jo March in *Little Women*, a home-wrecking aviator, a cross-dressing grifter, a deluded social climber, and a couple of madcap heiresses. Throughout the 1930s, Katharine Hepburn was framed by the press as a recognizable type: a threatening, refractory woman, heartless, stuck-up, bossy, entitled, and insufficiently grateful and humble. The tabloids confirmed what people suspected, what they were afraid of. Hers was a story they already knew. Stories decide what become of us; they remind us who's boss. Celebrity gossip is never surprising. It's familiar, reassuring, comforting — proof that nothing ever changes. That's why we love it.

Audiences liked Hepburn less and less. It's not just that Katharine Hepburn wouldn't flutter her eyelashes or shake her booty or wear a skirt. It's that she insisted on playing people instead of dream girls. In his review of the movie *Break of Hearts* for the *Spectator,* Graham Greene expressed this: "Miss Hepburn always makes her young women quite horrifyingly lifelike with their girlish intuitions, their intensity, their ideals which destroy the edge of human pleasure." Hepburn refused to sign autographs or answer fan mail or be nice to reporters, so *Life* magazine wrote, "People grew a little tired of Katharine facing the world, clear-eyed, forthright, arrogant and unafraid — in situations that merely called for relaxation."[2] Exhibitors put her on a list of actors they considered box-office poison. She desperately wanted the part of Scarlett

O'Hara in *Gone with the Wind,* but David O. Selznick wouldn't give it to her because he "couldn't see Rhett Butler chasing [her] for ten years." (Selznick never would have said what he said to her today, of course. He would have called her unfuckable in an e-mail.) He offered her one of the leads in *Mother Carey's Chickens* instead.

Hepburn declined the part in *Mother Carey's Chickens.* She bought out her contract at RKO and went back to the East Coast. She invited her friend the playwright Phillip Barry to spend a week with her at Fenwick, her parents' Connecticut summer house, and to talk about the play he would write for her. It was to be about who she was, who people thought she was, what happened to her because of it, and what she needed to do to fix it. Barry observed as Luddy hung around the house taking pictures of Kate's visiting boyfriends, like Howard Hughes and John Ford. Barry came up with the idea of a story about a socialite whose wedding gets turned into a tabloid story, thanks to her ex-husband, who uses the situation to win her back.

Hepburn put up a portion of the money to finance the play on Broadway, and Hughes bought the film rights and gave them to her as a gift. The play was a huge hit, and it made her rich. Then she sold the rights to Louis Mayer at MGM, chose the screenwriter (Barry's friend David Ogden Stewart) and the director (her dear friend George Cukor), and approved the costars. (She had wanted Spencer Tracy and Clark Gable, but they weren't available, so she was offered Cary Grant and James Stewart instead. She said yes.) The movie was also a huge hit and made her even richer. As the critic Andrew Sarris later put it, *The Philadelphia Story* was about Hepburn "getting her comeuppance at long last, and accepting it like the good sport she was."

Sarris was right about the comeuppance, but I think it is more than that. What Hepburn did in her most popular movies with her real-life (married) lover (one of many) Spencer Tracy was to show one independent, high-achieving, highly threatening woman after another subsuming herself, at the very last minute, in a traditional marriage. Time and again, she "gave it all up for love." Which is how she got it all back. She traded fairy tales about love for the freedom to never get married. She got what she wanted by playing "the girl" she refused to become.

Technically, Hepburn belonged to the first postfeminist generation. She didn't take up the mantle of her mother's causes but was grateful for them and expected to enjoy them. But as she found out the hard way, she was a new kind of woman in the old kind of system. Which is what *The Philadelphia Story*, the story of a girl in the city of brotherly love, is actually about. At the start of the movie, Tracy thinks that leaving Dexter and banning Seth from her wedding is all she needs to do to take control of her life. But Dexter's sudden appearance lays bare the way male authority functions in patriarchy: it trumps logic. His arrival pulls Tracy into an alternate reality where male authority is laid bare, and she is made to see that it has the power to cancel out reality and replace it with nonsense. The Tracy we've seen until now is Tracy as she sees herself. The Tracy we see after Dexter arrives with the mass media in tow is Tracy — the girl — as she is seen when not playing "the girl." The movie's second act is a gauntlet of scrutiny. Depending on who's judging, she's idolized and devalued, mocked and excoriated, undermined and shamed. Dexter tells her she's too cold, too unforgiving, too demanding. She sets too high a standard for herself and others, and she is no "helpmeet." He also thinks she is distant, vain, and spoiled. To George, she is a symbol of unattainability; a prize, a trophy, a goal. She should be locked up in a tower, worshiped, punished. It's her fault Dexter drank. It's her fault her father cheated. It's her fault George is jealous and possessive. It's her fault Mike is resentful and feels cheated by life. One by one, Mike, Dexter, Seth, and George hoist Tracy up on a pedestal and knock her back down again until she has no idea who or where she is.

The Philadelphia Story is a story about a story. Specifically, it's a story about a tabloid story that, thanks to Dexter's clever, behind-the-scenes puppeteering, changes the outcome of the event it's supposed to be chronicling and that causes Tracy to break up with George and remarry a reframed, recontextualized Dexter instead. But it ends on an ambivalent note: Sydney Kidd, *Spy* magazine's publisher, crashes the wedding and catches the moment on camera. Will they make it or won't they? It's hard to say. It's hard to sustain an equal relationship in an unequal world, where the stories aren't true or real, where the stories have agendas. That's what the movie is about: it's a true story about fake stories, about how they shape reality and perception. It's about how stories guide our empathy and identification. *The Philadelphia Story* lampoons this while simultaneously capitulating. Tracy thumbed her nose at convention and then gave in. Hepburn's solution was the solution that smart and ambitious women have always sought. She found a way around the system, but the system remained in place.

As the philosopher Stanley Cavell wrote in his book, *Pursuits of Happiness: The Hollywood Comedy of Remarriage, The Philadelphia Story* is a story about transformation through marriage in the Shakespearean tradition: the woman is remade as a wife at the hands of lecturing men. But it's also a story about the corrective power of reframing. The movie suggests it's not women or men who need to be remade, but marriage itself that needs to change from a condescending patriarchal indoctrination to a mutual conversation between equals. The gauntlet that Tracy runs lays bare the hypocrisy that the system is built on, and calls out the men who insist on upholding it and subjecting others to its double standards for injustice and inhumanity. Via Tracy, Hepburn reframed her experience as a star from her point of view. As a star playing the part of a happy bride, she put the audience in her shoes. She made herself the underdog and spoke truth to power and emerged dazed, bruised, clear-eyed, herself. Only then did she decide to set off once again on the ship *True Love* with Dexter — charming, manipulative, sexy, problematic Dexter — with no expectations and no guarantees, on an open-ended adventure of becoming.

"The dire or merely domestic outcomes of so many of her movies can be easily dismissed as the requirements of a less enlightened age," Claudia Roth Pierpont wrote in *The New Yorker* after Hepburn died, "or as a sign of the ongoing bewilderment about how a truly 'modern' woman's story might conclude." What is marriage anymore, anyway? How is the institution structured? What assumptions do we bring to it? Is it an irreducible economic unit, in which production and labor remain distributed along traditional lines (the model of husband as protector and breadwinner and wife as "angel in the house," domestic goddess, and nurturer)? Or is it a spiritual, intellectual, artistic, and social partnership — a lifelong collaboration, a project, a constant becoming? Is it what patriarchal society said it is, or what Hollywood pretended it was? What does it mean to be a modern woman? Where does a woman's "modern-ness" reside? In what she looks like, how she acts, what she does, wears, or says? Or is it somewhere else entirely outside of her, in a larger system that allows her to be a whole, free person? that represents her as such? that allows her to represent herself? that recognizes her individuality and subjectivity? Is it about things like voting and birth control, the issues that Katharine Hepburn's mother devoted her life to fighting for? Is it about wearing pants, not aiming to please, sleeping around, and not getting married, like Katharine Hepburn did? Is it about smoking Virginia Slims? Is it not perhaps all and none of these things but the fact that we keep having to make a case for our personhood? Is it not the story that needs to be reframed? the heroine who needs to be allowed to create herself, from scratch? These were the questions I think Hepburn was really posing. These are the questions we are still asking today, more than seventy-five years later. This is the elephant in the room.

What worked for Hepburn in the end, what allowed her to become the person she was, was her tactical decision to play the girl on-screen. Playing the girl on-screen liberated her from having to play her in life. "I put on pants fifty years ago and declared a sort of middle road. I have not lived as a woman. I have lived as a man. I've just done what I damn well wanted to and I've made enough money to support myself and I ain't afraid of being alone," she told Barbara Walters in a 1981 interview, when she was seventy-two. Not that she was ever alone much. Still, if you had told her 1940 self that, more than three-quarters of a century later, the question of how a truly modern woman's story might conclude would still be bewildering, I think she would have been surprised.

4

--- --- --- ---

What a Feeling

I'M FIFTEEN AND NEW IN TOWN, A FRESHMAN AT A CATHO-
lic school. Why I'm at a Catholic school, I have no idea. My parents
panicked. They got me to a nunnery. I have one friend. She seems
a little bewildered, too. And miserable. We are both miserable. We
are so miserable.

We go see *Flashdance* over Christmas break. Then we see it
again. And again. And again. Our moms drive us to the mall without comment, and I'm grateful. The movie is our *Star Wars*. We
watch like we're trying to absorb it, merge with it, organize our lives
and build our identities around it. If my friend and I ever discuss
this, I have no recollection of what we say. It's not the sort of thing
you talk about. It's not even the kind of movie you talk about. There
isn't anything to discuss. We just commune with it in silence. One
gray and freezing Sunday afternoon, my mom drops us off at the
crappy mall, where the movie has washed up after ending its run
at the fancy mall. My naked longing to see this movie again makes
me feel self-conscious. Standing in the empty parking lot on this
dreary and windy day, I'm not quite Jane Eyre; maybe more like
Cathy in the Pat Benatar version of Kate Bush's tribute to *Wuther-
ing Heights*. All at once, I'm overcome with a shame so bilious I
think I'll dissolve into the asphalt. I'm fifteen, but I'm not stupid.
I know this is a terrible movie. I know it's a lie from start to finish.
But it's a lie I very badly want to believe in. Because what other lie
is there for me to believe in — I mean, that I can get really behind?

Puberty is a disturbance. You change, like a werewolf. It causes
upheaval, perturbation — in your own body, yes, but also (mostly,

when you are a girl) in others' bodies and words and attitudes. It transmutes the world. It's not that you lose control of your body so much as that you lose control over the way your body is interpreted. Your body becomes an alien body, a question rather than a statement. The same culture that once hijacked it as a symbol of its own inviolable purity and innocence now finds this transformation unbearable, and blames you for defiling it, for allowing it to happen. Who else? The girl is always burdened with impossible standards. She is made to pay for the loss of innocence with more loss — of love, respect, protection. In the story, she is given one way out, a single path to validation. The story says: Don't get dirty. Don't break. Don't think you can escape the narrative. To think you can escape the narrative is the definition of crazy.

In the male coming-of-age story, the boy creates himself. In the female coming-of-age story, the girl is created by forces around her. In the feminist coming-of-age story, the girl resists the forces and becomes herself. Movies about teenage girls in edgy, aestheticized peril are everywhere. Brooke Shields, Jodie Foster, and Tatum O'Neal grow up so fast it threatens to kill or ruin them, or kill or ruin those around them. In *Foxes* (directed by Adrian Lyne, who would go on to direct *Flashdance* three years later), *The Blue Lagoon*, *Pretty Baby*, *Endless Love*, *Taxi Driver*, *Carrie*, *The Exorcist*, and *Christiane F.*, girls don't get into trouble, they turn into trouble. The danger comes from inside. It's mutative, transgressive. It made them uncontrollable. "At 12, it was angel dust," read the tagline for *Christiane F.* "At 13, it was heroin. Then she took to the streets." Maturity and experience were gateways to the most dangerous substance of all: unsupervised freedom. Why is a girl's leaving childhood and venturing out into the world always the go-to symbol for everything that can, and absolutely will, go wrong?

Jennifer Beals in *Flashdance* is not very many years older than we are. She's a freshman at Yale, which is in the general ballpark of where we also hope to be at her age. She graduated from the Francis W. Parker School in Chicago—Anna knows people who know people who know her. It's almost like she could be us. We could never be her. Jennifer Beals is ideal feminine beauty circa 1983. She is the standard. We can bask in the proximal thrill of it all.

Her character's name is Alexandra Owens, but she goes by Alex. The boy's name implies she's cool and you can trust her. Alex works as an arc welder in a steel mill by day, but at night she gets on stage at a bar called Mawby's and dances. To say her dancing is flashy does not come close to describing it. It's like strip-club kabuki theater staged, costumed, set-designed, and shot for a 1980s music video. Actually, it's not *like* that; that is precisely what it *is*. At Mawby's, the salt-of-the-earth clientele has a surprisingly high tolerance for experimental performance art, so Alex can really express who she is—with her clothes mostly on.

Ultimately, though, it is not Alex's dream to dump bucketfuls of water over herself every night in front of a bunch of steelworkers. She wants to be a ballerina and dreams of training at a prestigious dance conservatory. It's part of the story of how she's not an average girl. Alex is exceptional. She's so exceptional that she can start training as a ballerina at the age of eighteen. She's so exceptional that she has a boy's name, and a man's job, and holds her own in an all-male environment. She lives all alone in a cavernous warehouse space off a dark alley with only her pit bull—the preferred breed of toxic masculinity—Grunt, for company. She has the temperament of an angsty suburban teenager but the life of a landed eighteenth-century poet or bohemian, garret-dwelling genius in 1920s Paris. Her warehouse is decorated in a kind of high-bordello style—*Pretty Baby* meets *Blade Runner*. She is so free, so unself-conscious, so impervious to norms and conventions and her effect on others, namely, men, that she'll remove her bra from under her shirt in front of her boss while maintaining a kind of inquisitive Bambi look on her face the whole time. In Alex, all the things that should be "girl things" are reversed except the ones that count. She is the antithesis of a lady, a portrait of a non-lady. She's a twelve-year-old boy in a young woman's body.

Nominally based on a true story, or a composite of true stories, *Flashdance* is as divorced from reality as it is possible to be without being of a different planet. Inexplicably free of the gender, social, and financial constraints that fetter the rest of humanity, Alex is free to be a genius. And we know she's a genius because, like (the idealized image of) most geniuses (who are male), she is moody, impulsive, reckless, entitled, and rude, and it makes people fall in love with her and realize the error of their stuffy, mannerly, and classically trained ways. She is represented not like a girl in a romance so much as like a romantic hero. She's Byronic in her tempestuousness and effrontery. She tosses her hair over her shoulder like a cape before stalking off in search of sublime Alpine vistas — or the Pittsburgh equivalent. One night, Nick, the owner of the steel mill, notices her dancing at Mawby's and asks his buddy who she is. His buddy laughs and yells him her social security number — she works for him. The next day, at the mill, Nick invites Alex to dinner at a fancy restaurant. There, he tries gamely to make conversation while she performs oral sex on her entrée and simultaneously rubs his groin with her stockinged foot. Her appetites are lusty, and she chews with her mouth open — I can't decide which is more rebellious. Nick's ex-wife happens to be there, and she approaches their table. She looks down her nose at Alex and sneers. Did Nick take her to his favorite spot by the tracks, the same place he takes all the girls? Alex peels off her tuxedo jacket in response, revealing only a dickey, possibly made of paper, underneath. She informs Nick's ex that she did in fact fuck Nick's brains out, as Nick smiles sheepishly. This is how she signals to the ex-wife that she's won. We think this is amazing. We think, *You tell that stuck-up bitch.*

But what sort of gauntlet-throwing one-upmanship is this, really? What does it mean to me, a girl whose father spends mealtimes relentlessly correcting her manners? It looks like freedom, I guess. Like self-assertion, or punk rebellion, or some kind of corrective power. Also, and this is important, it's the first time I've seen a girl whose artistic genius does not get her frog-marched directly to a course of electroshock treatments and long-term institutionalization.

Of course, the blissful, naughty transgression can't last, and worlds will collide. Alex is a feral princess: she'll resist domestication until after she's proven she can make it on her own. Driving home from dinner one night, Nick lets slip that he made a call and helped Alex get her audition at the prestigious dance conservatory. Alex freaks out. She desperately needs to believe in a level playing field. She *wants* to do it all on her own. It's *meaningless* otherwise. She wants to be recognized and validated by the establishment in the most punk-rock, antiestablishment way possible. If not, she'll take her ball and go home. In fact, she jumps out of Nick's moving Porsche in a tunnel, dismissing the high potentiality that a pileup could quickly turn into a blazing death trap for hundreds of people.

We get it. We're fifteen, and we have big, vague dreams. We need to believe in a level playing field, too. We think Nick indulges her outbursts because he totally "gets" how passionate she is — not because he's paternalistic, not because he owns her. For a girl whose destiny is determined entirely by her body — as a dancer and the future wife of the rich prince — she is blissfully oblivious to her material conditions. With her blue-collar job, her tough-girl dog, her uncontrollable emotions, and her atrocious manners, Alex is an archetype that I've never encountered before. She's a teen-girl übermensch, an übermädchen, a maniac. She's utterly, implausibly, ahistorically free. Alex's confidence and unflappability are disconcerting, bordering on delusional, but it is rather fascinating to watch this girl not much older than us enact this particular romantic fantasy. "Man becomes that which he wills to become, his willing precedes his existence," Nietzsche says, and I guess Alex says so, too. Her rebellion is like a superpower, an invisible shield against reality. The limitations of her embodied existence are no match for her grit, her determination, her bizarre ability to enjoy all the perks of living in the body of a teenage girl with none of the drawbacks. Because there are both, but media tends to misrepresent the perks and rarely talks about the drawbacks.

Decades later, in an interview, the screenwriter, Tom Hedley (with Joe Ezsterhas), explained his decision to spin a Cinderella fantasy from a grim true story, saying, "I was touched by her dream of what she was. I made a decision early on in the piece to stick with her fantasy, not her reality."[1] We don't care how this young girl in a depressed steel town got a union job. We don't care how she manages not to get slighted, diminished, harassed, or bullied at work. We don't care how she affords her enormous warehouse space, and heats it, while saving money to attend a prestigious dance academy. We don't care that she is too old to be a ballerina and too young to be a steelworker because by then the steel mills had stopped hiring, and wouldn't have hired her in the first place. We don't notice how creepy the love story is, that her boyfriend is twenty years older than she is, that she works for him, that he *owns the means of production, for Karl Marx's sake*. We don't think it's weird that she has at least two full-blown tantrums in his presence, that she jumps out of his car and throws a rock through his window, and that he looks on indulgently at her adorable, childlike impotence and it only makes him want to fuck her more. We don't ask how she manages to single-handedly produce, choreograph, costume, art-direct, and stage a high-end cabaret every night after her shift at the steel mill. *Flashdance* doesn't ask us to ask these questions, so we don't. After the movie came out, it was revealed that Alex's big audition scene had been performed by not one but three different uncredited body doubles — a dancer, a gymnast, and a break-dancer, who was a guy.

So this is what *Flashdance* tells us about (young, sexy) female aspiration: that it is a fantasy; that a girl's dreams are a gift only a prince can make happen for her, if he loves her and chooses her for her unique, not-at-all-feminine specialness. Alex is the lucky winner of the patriarchal lottery: different from all the rest. And in case that message is not clear, her best friend, Jeannie, aspiring figure skater, takes her one shot and fails. Auditioning for the Ice Capades, she falls and doesn't get up. Alex tells Nick that she practiced for two years. (Two whole years!) Next time we see Jeannie, she is naked on the stage at the Zanzibar, the strip-club alternative to Mawby's, where a girl is not valued for her talent, so the only thing left is to roll around on the floor without any clothes on.

Only now, decades later, do I see *Flashdance* for what it was: a fantasy of self-creation ungrounded in political, material, or economic reality. It was a feature-length music video hawking the individualist, bootstrapping Reagan-era fantasy. It said you can do anything (in your imagination). All it takes to lift yourself off the lowliest social rung and be borne aloft on wings of stardom and true love is a big dream, a flashy style, a psychotic belief in yourself, and a willingness to sleep with your boss. You just have to want it. You can do it! Girl power! Dream on, sister! And hey, if it doesn't work out, remember you have only yourself to blame. Maybe you weren't good enough, did you ever consider that? Here are some tips for self-improvement. *Flashdance* taught us that stripping was cool and a great way to put yourself through school. It taught us that the window to success is open for a very short time. Without Nick, Alex would have curdled into something monstrous in no time.

*

I was in college when Adrian Lyne next gave us his next Alex, a curly-haired, loft-dwelling, single career woman, played by Glenn Close, with whom a happily married lawyer named Dan Gallagher (Michael Douglas) has ill-advised sex one night when his wife and daughter are out of town in *Fatal Attraction*. Alex persuades him to stay with her for a second night, which she caps with an attempted suicide. Dan, who has already put his apartment up for sale, hustles his family to a rambling white house in Bedford (one of the inspirations for Stepford), Connecticut, but Alex is only getting started.

As an impressionable young college student, I was terrified of

Glenn Close's portrayal of Alex. At forty, she was a cautionary tale — everything a girl like me had been conditioned to fear turning into; the embodiment of the 1986 pop-art greeting card by Roy Lichtenstein featuring a weeping woman below the thought bubble "I can't believe I forgot to have children!" At the same time, I was a comp lit major in the eighties. I got the message and it annoyed me. It especially annoyed me because it was so cloyingly underscored by Anne Archer's portrayal of the idealized wife, Beth, with her bovine eyes and her smug smile, gazing beatifically in the vanity mirror first at herself, then up at her cheating-turned-heroic-avenger husband. "She's so beautiful," my boyfriend whispered. It occurred to me that perhaps this was intended as some kind of compliment, because we both had brown hair and brown eyes, and I thought, *No, thanks.*

Not that Alex was a viable alternative, as somebody to aspire to. The alternative to the cow-eyed wife was an obsessed, psychotic, child-endangering bunny boiler who *wouldn't fucking die no matter how many times you killed her.*

Most of the time, watching stuff like this made me feel as if my eyes were attached to another brain inside another body. I understood what I was being told, it just felt all wrong. The cognitive dissonance was palpable. I could only recognize it in contrast to the rare experience of seeing something that saw the world through a perspective I recognized. That felt like a revelation every time. In a piece on the thirtieth anniversary of its release, the film critic Carrie Rickey called *Desperately Seeking Susan* "both a New Wave *Feminine Mystique* and an urban fantasia featuring New York as a graffiti-tagged Emerald City." She wrote about how she worked for the *Boston Herald* at the time it was shot, and how she visited the set. She wrote that Leora Barish, the writer, had been influenced by the 1974 Jacques Rivette film *Celine and Julie Go Boating*, which in turn was inspired by *Alice's Adventures in Wonderland*. Barish had told Rickey that she liked the way Rivette "play[ed] with reality in an offhanded, barely perceptible way," showing how "the two women from different realms are curious about each other" in a nonsexual way. Two girls on open-ended adventures. The movie was a revelation, she said, because it was about liberation and "exploring the person you want to be."

Rosanna Arquette plays Roberta, a New Jersey housewife unhappily married to a hot-tub salesman. Madonna plays Susan, a con artist and drifter on the run from the mob. Roberta has everything she is supposed to want, whereas Susan washes her armpits in the bathrooms at Port Authority and then blows them dry with hand dryers. Roberta knows about Susan because she reads about her in the newspaper personal ads, where Susan's boyfriend places ads in desperate search of her. "I wish I was desperate," Roberta tells her friend at the hair salon one day. She wishes she cared about something enough to be desperate, that she had a singular focus. If she did, it would inevitably lead her into adventure — and it does. Susan represents both the feminine object of desire and the feminine subject of desire.[2] The desire isn't sexual, it's identificatory; Roberta longs for the animating, liberating, empowering "desire to desire"[3] that has somehow escaped repression in Susan. Roberta starts out wishing she could be like Susan, and ends up believing she *is* her. As Molly Haskell wrote in her 1974 book, *From Reverence to Rape: The Treatment of Women in the Movies*, "Too often we interpret the roles of the past in the light of the liberated positions that have only recently become thinkable. We can, for example, deplore the fact that in every movie where a woman excelled as a professional she had to be brought to heel at the end, but only as long as we acknowledge the corollary: that at least women *worked* in the films of the thirties and forties." Not only that, but even if their stories ended in tears, she argued, we remembered them for their grit, their intelligence, their courage, and their intermediate victories. We remembered them for being heroes and badasses. Meanwhile, by contrast, "here we are today with an unparalleled freedom of expression and a record number of women performing, achieving, choosing to fulfill themselves, and we are insulted with the worst — the most abused, neglected, and dehumanized — screen heroines in film history."[4] She probably wouldn't have guessed then that it would only get worse.

The adventure in a nutshell: Susan swipes a pair of earrings from a guy she has just slept with, which turn out to be priceless artifacts. Later, she goes to a thrift store and sells her distinctive leather jacket with a pyramid on the back. Roberta follows her to the store and buys the jacket, and is mistaken for Susan by a mobster trying to recover the earrings. Meanwhile, Susan's boyfriend, Jim (the desperate personal-ad writer), has asked his friend Dez to pick Susan up, and when he sees Roberta, he thinks she is Susan, too. As Dez approaches, the mobster snatches Roberta's bag, and she falls and hits her head. When she comes to, she can't remember anything. Dez thinks she is Susan, so she goes with it. Eventually, she recovers her memory, has sex with Dez, and tries to reveal her true identity. "I'm a housewife from Fort Lee, New Jersey," she tells him. "I've been married for four years. My husband, Gary, he sells bathroom spas . . . saunas." Dez laughs. Of all the unlikely things she could be, this is the most unlikely one of all. "That's what I like about you," he says. "I never know what you'll say next."

After reading Carrie Rickey's piece about *Desperately Seeking Susan,* I called her to ask her what it was like to visit the set, to talk to the filmmakers, and then to see the movie. Why did it feel like such a revelation when I first saw it, at the age of seventeen? What about it was so inspiring? *Desperately Seeking Susan* was written by a woman (Leora Barish), directed by a woman (Susan Seidelman), produced by two women (Sarah Pillsbury and Midge Sanford, who started a production company to make the movie), and starred two women, Rosanna Arquette, who was an indie-movie star, and Madonna, who wasn't really famous outside of New York yet. Aidan Quinn played the insanely handsome Dez, whom Roberta ends up falling in love with, but it wasn't only that. Or rather, the fact that the story was told from a girl's point of view so reframed what might otherwise have been a fairly unremarkable goofy-heist, mistaken-identity movie that it felt like something profound had happened. There's something so practiced, so polished about the image of the male rebel hero, but the rebellious girl, the girl who truly doesn't care what people think, is a very rare bird. What people think has traditionally been a girl's only currency.

When I was in high school, I thought we girls were entering a new era — that this would be the way things were from now on. Once perception had shifted, it could never shift back — right? Until around this moment in film, there were very few representations of the happy conclusions of female adventures that didn't end with marriage. All conflicts — social, familial, financial — were resolved by marriage. But then, between about 1975 and 1980, movies made by women came in a fast and furious clot. Carrie told me she was twenty, at UC San Diego, when she saw Agnes Varda's *Cléo from 5 to 7*. Shortly after that, she drove up to UCLA for a Dorothy Arzner retrospective. By the time she was at NYU, in 1978, she was aware of many female filmmakers, from Lois Weber to Elaine May. For her, it was the release of movies like Gillian Armstrong's *My Brilliant Career*, Diane Kurys's *Entre Nous*, Nancy Myers's *Private Benjamin*, and Amy Heckerling's *Fast Times at Ridgemont High*, along with *Desperately Seeking Susan*, that made her aware of a new, female gaze.

Desperately Seeking Susan eroticized Aidan Quinn in a way she'd never seen an actor eroticized before. The idea that a straight female director might look at a man differently, frame him differently, was just dawning for her. When she said that, I realized why my friends and I had fallen so deeply in love with Quinn as Dez: we'd seen him through Roberta's eyes. Rickey said she'd never really come across that kind of rueful black humor by women before, but suddenly there it was in movies like *Private Benjamin*. Written by Nancy Myers and Charles Shyer, *Private Benjamin* was the hilarious story of the gradual awakening, or self-deprogramming, of a young self-made Stepford Wife. Judy Benjamin, played by a hilariously wide-eyed Goldie Hawn, knows her whole life that all she wants "is a big house ... nice clothes, two closets, a live-in maid, and a professional man for a husband." She gets it all — and then the husband dies of a heart attack on their wedding night. So she does what people do when they run out of ideas: she joins the army. Against all odds, she makes it through basic training, then meets a French doctor played by Armand Assante and has an affair. "Now I know what I've been faking all those years!" she says of sex with her second partner. She also says, "I didn't understand *An Unmarried Woman*. I would have gone away with Alan Bates." But she doesn't go away with Armand Assante at the end. There were echoes of this humor in *When Harry Met Sally* and *Thelma and Louise* — the feeling that we knew ourselves from somewhere, that we'd met us before.

Carrie also told me that, in the original screenplay, Susan was a hippie, but director Susan Seidelman wanted to make her more downtown. Nobody had heard of Madonna outside of New York. Then her single "Into the Groove" dropped in the middle of production and made her into an instant international star, and people mobbed her on the street. I was in high school then. I sensed something "new" but assumed this was just the way things would be from now on. We appeared to be done with the marriage plot. ("What's the alternative to the marriage plot?" She said: "The alternative is adventure.") My generation (I thought) was the first postfeminist generation. The first to be allowed to see love in terms of adventure and quest, not salvation and redemption. I didn't know (couldn't have known) that this moment was the tail end of a brief period in American cinema, between 1978 and 1985, when heroine's stories didn't end in marriage but started with adventure, as in *An Unmarried Woman*, *9 to 5*, *Alien*, *Norma Rae*, and the like. Mike Medavoy, the head of the studio, was reportedly persuaded by his stepdaughter to make *Desperately Seeking Susan*. Nobody expected it to do well.

It's an old story with a recurring theme; this idea that there is no audience for films about women, unless the women are abstracted to the point that they no longer resemble people. *Desperately Seeking Susan* was a revelation for many reasons, not least of which was the fact that it was told from a woman's point of view, a woman who had everything a woman was supposed to want, and yet was miserable. "I remember getting excited and talking to Molly," Carrie told me, referring to her colleague and fellow moviegoer, the critic and feminist film theorist, Molly Haskell, about what a revelation it was to start to see films directed by women in the 1970s. She recalls talking to her "about how there were no women in *The Godfather*." Or rather, that the women only served to reaffirm that it was a man's space, that they were only there to serve drinks and be shut out. In classic Hollywood cinema, a woman walks on-screen: She is there to be looked at. She interrupts the action. Diane Keaton in *The Godfather* is a foil for Al Pacino: She whines, she interrupts, and at the end she's put in her place. She makes drinks and gets the door shut in her face.

It reminded me of a story a friend told me about a job she had at a production company where she was the only female development executive. Every Friday at five, all the others would meet in their boss's office for drinks without her. One Friday, she decided to invite herself. A few minutes before five, she walked into her boss's office and sat down. He looked at her like she was insane. "Don't you have work to do?" he asked. She got up and left as the others filed in. This was in the twenty-first century.

This idea of who was looking, of how directors create reality from a point of view, came gradually. Rickey was a graduate student at NYU when she first heard of Dorothy Azner, for example, when Francis Ford Coppola mentioned that she had been a teacher of his in film school. Dorothy Arzner was a prolific and highly successful director within the studio system throughout the 1930s. In Linda Seger's *When Women Call the Shots: The Developing Power and Influence of Women in Television and Film,* I read about how she was the first female member of the Directors Guild until Ida Lupino joined seven years after she had shot her last film,[5] though she was far from the first famous female movie director. The list of forgotten female pioneers in Hollywood is long: In 1895, Alice Guy, a young secretarial employee of Gaumont, a film company in France, had the idea to film a story, and she asked her boss for permission to write a scene or two for friends to perform in. He agreed to let her, as long as she did not neglect her secretarial duties. In 1896, Guy made a film called *The Cabbage Fairy,* about babies who grew in cabbage patches. Gaumont loved it and set up a studio for her. She became the first female writer, producer, director, and studio head of production in the business, before there was a business. Then he sent her to America, where she did it again in New Jersey. Lois Weber, an American actress who acted in Guy's films, would go on to be the only other woman to write, direct, produce, and control a studio. "By 1915, she was as famous as D. W. Griffith or Cecil B. DeMille," Linda Seger wrote, and "a year later Lois Weber was reputed to be the most important and highest-paid director at Universal Studios, making $5,000 a week."

Guy, who made hundreds of films in every genre, was very influential and set the tone for how women were portrayed. "At a time when male filmmakers were objectifying the woman," Seger wrote, "Guy focused on strong female protagonists who took charge of their lives and their destinies. In 1912, she directed *In the Year 2000,* a film about a time when women rule the world."[6] Julia Crawford Ivers, who was the first female general manager of a studio, brought Guy over from Universal Studios to Bosworth Studios, where she became the first to hire screenwriter Frances Marion. Marion, who would go on to become one of the major writers in film history, wrote 130 produced screenplays. Nell Shipman made wilderness adventure stories with nudity, wild animals, and feminist themes. She pioneered animal safety on the set. "From the early 1900s to the early 1920s, there were hundreds of successful and prolific women in film," Seger wrote. "Anything seemed possible. The film industry was open to anyone with talent and determination and a dream. And it was open to women primarily because women already in the industry either directly supported other women or influenced them as role models. Under these conditions, women excelled."

As Seger recounted, the film industry, which had been fairly spread out, consolidated and moved to Los Angeles. Alice Guy's "Blaché Solax Studio was taken over by her husband, Herbert, who renamed it Blaché Features, drove it into bankruptcy, and then ran off to Hollywood with his mistress . . . Alice Guy Blaché's career was ended . . . As a woman now in her fifties, she was not wanted. She tried to freelance but was unable to get work in either the United States or Paris. Credit for the first fiction film . . . was given to George Méliès . . . Nell Shipman experienced the same fate." Seger quoted an early script supervisor named Meta Wilde, who wrote a book about her eighteen-year relationship with William Faulkner and was a script supervisor on more than two hundred films, including *Who's Afraid of Virginia Woolf?*,[7] saying the pioneering days of Hollywood were far more open before the studio system compartmentalized everything and created hierarchies. As Seger quoted Wilde, "By the 1930s, the only women on the set were the wardrobe women." And so, if you were a girl in Hollywood, it was back to fucking and shopping for you.

By the time Arzner began her career, in the late 1920s, women directors were no more. Arzner started as a writer, quickly became an innovative and sought-after editor, and then became one of the top ten directors in the studio system. She directed sixteen feature films in her career, more than any other woman has to this day.

How much does perspective matter? How much does it shape the fiction we think of as reality? It wasn't until the first time I went to Craig's apartment that I realized I'd been looking at portraits of him for about five years before we met. And not just any pictures, but portraits by one of my favorite contemporary artists. The first time I ever saw a painting by the artist Elizabeth Peyton, it was 1997, and I had just turned twenty-nine. I'd been living in San Francisco for almost seven years before I came across it at the San Francisco Museum of Modern Art. The portrait looked like something a twelve-year-old would draw on the back of her notebook, only incredibly luminous and jewel-like. The portrait reflected my perspective, which I'd never seen legitimized in quite that way before. It was fan-girlish and besotted. It was the most radical thing I'd ever seen. My first thought was that it had to be a joke. Then I got angry. Was this allowed now? Since when? And why had I not been informed? There was no way that this small, precious, unabashedly romantic likeness of Kurt Cobain could be for real. It couldn't be sincere, and yet it appeared to be. Validated. Legitimized. Institutionalized.

It wasn't until years later that I discovered that my fascination with Peyton's work began not very long after Craig had become one of her regular subjects. By the time I met him, I'd seen her idealized version of him many times. Craig and I met in Los Angeles, at a party at the house of some mutual friends. A couple of weeks later, I was shocked to discover one of Peyton's paintings hanging on the wall of his shabby Hollywood studio. He was shocked that I was shocked. Nobody he knew in Los Angeles had ever recognized it before.

Peyton once replied to the observation that there seemed to be a lot of melancholy in her work by saying, "It's not so much sentimental, it's just really overwhelming to me that time passes. I'm constantly thinking about it and kind of obsessing about it. How things change, how I change, how there's no stopping it." If this chapter has a theme, it would have to do with this comment. Ever since Craig and I met, I've wished we could have met when we were younger. It's not that, in our thirties, we were so old. It's that as we got to know each other and told each other stories about ourselves before we met, the same things got to me that had gotten to me when I first discovered her work: emotion as aesthetic experience; romanticism; imagination; bohemia; nostalgia; the fleeting nature of beauty, youth, fame, time, life; the ardent revolt I felt against the pragmatism and triumphal materialism that eventually ate us all.

It also had something to do with this: Peyton, whose 2008 retrospective was called *Live Forever*, has said that her career began to take off when she began to meet people who could see what she was doing. In an interview with her, Steve Lafreniere remarked, "You once told me that you're fascinated by that moment when a person's worth and destiny are revealed." When I met Craig, I had the feeling he could see what I was doing. I wish we could have known each other when we were very young, that we could somehow go back to the moment of pure potential and do it all over again, together; it's predicated on the fantasy that we could have guided each other through the perils of growing up. Somehow, when I imagine us having met when we were very young, I can believe in the idea that we might have lived forever.

We sold the painting that I had recognized as Peyton's shortly after our wedding, about a year before Kira was born. It was a completely pragmatic, totally heartbreaking decision that I often still regret. Maybe the romantic decision should have won out in the end. Maybe, in some way, in some parallel reality, it still will.

5

The Eternal Allure of
the Basket Case

I have gone to pieces, which is a thing I've wanted to do
for years.

— MRS. COPPERFIELD, FROM *TWO SERIOUS LADIES*,
BY JANE BOWLES

I LOVED STORIES ABOUT FEMALE ARTISTS WHO WENT OFF
the deep end when I was young — tragic tales of beautiful, passionate girls who escaped the plot by losing the plot. Madness was refusal and rebellion. It was punk. It was a tale I loved in fiction, in nonfiction, and at the movies, where the crazy artist was likely to be played emblematically by the hauntingly beautiful, prodigiously emotive French actress Isabelle Adjani. Nobody made a nervous breakdown in pre-Prozac times look so sexy. François Truffaut, who directed Adjani in *The Story of Adele H.* when she was nineteen, called her a genius — though there are those who impute his effusion to his shock at her refusal to sleep with him. We'll never know.

When *Camille Claudel* came out, in 1988, I was a student in Paris trying to imagine how a girl became an artist when the world insisted on defining artists as the opposite of a girl. I lived a few blocks away from an Italian restaurant called Villa Borghese, just like the place where Henry Miller rented rooms in *Tropic of Cancer*. I'd borrowed the novel from a friend who'd found it in her room, left there by some other American student on a year abroad program. I'd started reading it on the Metro on the way home and didn't put it down until I'd devoured it whole, like a python swallowing a rat. It was ingested in a moment. It took longer to digest. I'd never loved and hated a book so much in equal proportion. Every time I walked by the Villa Borghese sign, the first lines of the book popped into my head: "I am living at the Villa Borghese. There is not a crumb of dirt anywhere, nor a chair misplaced. We are all alone here and we are dead." I wondered if it was the same place, if there were rooms above the restaurant, if the lice still lived there. I was a junior-year-abroad girl in Paris. I was a sucker for modernism, despite its glaring woman problem, which I did my very best to overlook. In my class on postwar European cinema, my professor refused to learn the names of all but two or three of his female students, even though (or maybe because) there were only three boys in the class. He renamed the rest of us mnemonically, or perhaps onanistically. My friend Heather with the long, curly, side-parted auburn hair was *"Vous,* Rita Hayworth-*là."* You-Rita-Hayworth-there. You-Rita-Hayworth-there, say something about *L'Eclisse.*

Camille Claudel was the true story of a nineteenth-century bourgeois girl who became an artist and then went gorgeously, flamboyantly, furiously off her rocker. I knew about Camille because she was one of the flags you could wave when someone said there were no famous women artists. You could point the big side-of-the-road arrow sign at her: Camille Claudel — five miles! I collected them like action figures, the famous female artists, long before I knew it wasn't their existence that was rare but their inclusion in history. I also knew her by association with Rodin, which is the real reason anyone knew her. She is a footnote in art history, a note under his foot. Claudel was Rodin's student, apprentice, assistant, muse, and mistress for more than a decade. Twenty-four years younger than him, she was born the same year he met his lifelong companion and the mother of his child, Rose Beuret. Rodin and Claudel were madly in love, but Rodin refused to leave Rose and marry Camille, which made Camille crazy. She and Rodin were intellectual equals and partners. They had an artistic, spiritual, and sexual connection. Rose, in her view, was a glorified housekeeper and nursemaid. Camille made Rodin sign a contract saying he would stop sleeping with other students, take her on a trip to Italy, and then marry her. He signed it but didn't honor it. Eventually, Camille left him to devote herself entirely to her career and to develop her own separate artistic identity. She developed a new style of "narrative sculpture" around small moments of everyday life. Rodin continued to publicly support her work, but she was socially ostracized and neglected by the art world. She was broke and paranoid, convinced that Rodin was trying to sabotage her career and poison her. A week after her father died, her brother had her committed to an asylum. She stopped sculpting and became a mental patient until she died, thirty years later. "The events of my life would fill more than a novel," she wrote to Eugène Blot from the Montdevergues Asylum. "It would take an epic, *The Iliad* and *The Odyssey*, and a Homer to tell my story. I won't recount it today. I don't want to sadden you. I have fallen into an abyss. I live in a world so curious, so strange. Of the dream that was my life, this is the nightmare."

Camille Claudel was my first Isabelle Adjani movie about an artist tipped into madness by a bad boyfriend, but it wasn't her first. In cinema class, we watched François Truffaut's *The Story of Adèle H*. Adèle was the daughter of Victor Hugo, and herself a writer and a composer. The screenplay was adapted from Adèle's journals and focused on the story of her demented pursuit of a British army lieutenant named Albert Pinson. Pinson had proposed to Adèle, but she turned him down. Later, she changed her mind, but by then he had moved on, literally, with his regiment to Halifax, Nova Scotia. Adèle told her parents she was going to London, and set off to Canada to win him back.

Adèle is widely understood to have suffered from erotomania, also known as de Clérambault's syndrome, and schizophrenia. After spending several years in Canada stalking Pinson, she followed his regiment to Barbados. A Barbadian woman found her wandering the streets talking to herself, wrote to her family, then accompanied her back to France. Victor Hugo then had his daughter committed to an asylum for the rest of her life. We know better now than to romanticize mental illness, but Adèle's insanity has a way of exposing the double standards and hypocrisy of the era—those of her father, the Great Man, especially.

Whatever her actual diagnosis, in her mind (Adjani/Truffaut's) Adèle was a Byronic hero who needed her life to be a story with meaning; a passionate adventure. She set out, quite literally, on a voyage of discovery, or recovery, to get the boy back. The boy was platonically beautiful, distant, remote, indifferent. The boy was a symbol just out of reach. The boy was perfect, ideal. Her decision to follow Pinson and to persevere in her devotion to him was doubtless a crazy decision, but—at least as portrayed by Truffaut—it was also an aesthetic decision, an ethical decision, in keeping with the romantic spirit of the age. She was in it for the feels, for the "unappeasable yearning for unattainable goals," to quote the philosopher Isaiah Berlin. Which totally spoke to me, because I was in it for the feels, too. I was in *everything* for the feels—for the sublimity, the transcendence, for the aesthetic transport, for the truth and beauty that drove my every fleetingly sublime, absurd, doomed decision. Adèle, *c'était moi*. Obsessive, hysteric, seeker-of-the-sublime type, weirdo. My very favorite scene in the movie, the part that spoke to me the most, was near the very end, in Barbados, when Pinson decides to finally deal with Adèle. She is walking down a dusty street in a black cape, her eyes staring blankly ahead and hair wildly disheveled. He walks up to her and does what she's been longing for him to do for years—he says her name. She walks right past him, unseeing. She doesn't even recognize him. He's completely blotted out by the image in her head.

In the movies, as in the popular narrative in general, a boy who does this is a hero and a girl who does this is a stalker. She is a bunny boiler. Standing on the edge of a windy bluff in Guernsey overlooking the turbulent ocean, clutching her journal, Adèle immortalizes herself in her own mind, as literary heroes have always done; she declares to herself and the camera, "This incredible thing, that a young girl should step over the ocean, leave the old world for the new world to rejoin her lover; this thing will I accomplish."

It's a remarkable statement and sentiment, even if she ultimately doesn't accomplish it — though not for lack of trying. In *The Madwoman in the Attic,* Sandra Gilbert and Susan Gubar make the case for madness as feminist protest, subversion, and resistance. The madwoman, they say, serves as "the *author's* double, and image of her own anxiety and rage" toward a culture that oppresses her. But Adèle is the nineteen-year-old daughter of the greatest of Great Men in the nineteenth century. The fact that she believes that she can accomplish this incredible thing, that she thinks this narrative is available to her at all, is how you know she is crazy.

Camille and Adèle were artists in an era of high gender anxiety. The fear of "unnatural" women was high, as it was in the 1980s, as it is as I write this, in 2016. Women's behavior was strictly delimited and policed. To react to the limits in frustration or anger was to get labeled hysterical — female madness comes from the womb. It was believed to be a reproductive ailment. Adèle was thirty-four years older than Camille, but they were contemporaries and could conceivably have met. Bruno Nuytten, who directed *Camille Claudel,* once told the *New York Times,* "At one point, we considered having a scene where Camille would meet Adèle H. at a party, and say, 'I think she's going crazy.' Luckily, we came to our senses." I think it would have been glorious, actually. They could have both used a friend who understood them, who could relate. Adèle could have mentored Camille. Camille could have used a mentor who wasn't also her lover and a national symbol and the most famous sculptor in France.

There's a decadent glamour to falling apart, but not everyone can afford it. At the time of *Camille Claudel,* McLean Hospital was already known as the most aristocratic of all the psychiatric hospitals, and it was beginning to acquire a reputation as the most literary as well. It was the nuthouse to the poetry stars. The poet Robert

Lowell, with whom Sylvia Plath and Anne Sexton both studied, had done several stints there, and Sexton was jealous of Plath's stay. "If only I could get a scholarship to McLean," she confessed to a friend. Plath was well aware of the appeal. "I *must* write [something] about a college girl suicide," she wrote in her journal after reading some mental-health articles in *Cosmopolitan* magazine. "There is an increasing market for mental-hospital stuff," she wrote. "I'm a fool if I don't relive, recreate it."[1]

That line of Plath's makes me cringe, probably because I recognize it as the kind of thing I might have written in a journal, or a variation on the kind of thing I did write. The girl writer and her relationship to the marketplace are complex. What identity is hot now, which hallway should you choose? The fixation on crazy-girl artists makes me uncomfortable, too. It is such a cliché, after all, so mopey and indulgent, so irritatingly *girly*. When have feminine genius and madness *not* been linked?

This may explain why, near the beginning of *Girl, Interrupted*, Susanna Kaysen's memoir of the two years she spent as a teenage mental patient, she describes her compliance with the doctor's decision that she should be institutionalized as though it were nothing at all. She'd recently tried to kill herself with aspirin but changed her mind. She'd been picking at a pimple on her chin. The doctor, whom she'd never met before, said she looked like she needed a rest. Within fifteen minutes she was in a cab on her way to McLean. "What about me was so deranged that in less than half an hour a doctor would pack me off to the nuthouse?" Kaysen asks, and you wonder. Such is her detachment that she muses on possible justifications: It was 1967. Kids were acting crazy. Maybe the doctor was trying to protect her, or to spare her parents some tragic outcome. Still. "I wasn't a danger to society. Was I a danger to myself?" Maybe she was just a victim of society's low tolerance for deviant behavior, she thinks. Maybe she was sane in an insane world. Maybe it felt in some way like an honor, or an opportunity. What's striking is the sense of inevitability. She moves through the scene as if in a trance, a hypnotized heroine sleepwalking toward her doom, a spindle-sedated Sleeping Beauty, a vacant-eyed anorexic model on a catwalk. In 1967, a girl who was made miserable by the gender role she was expected to play was a girl who was crazy, sick, glamorous, cool.

On the other hand, maybe what attracts us aren't the stories of falling apart so much as the stories of self-creation. The falling apart stuff is just a byproduct, a hazard of the trade. Maybe what I loved about *Camille Claudel* was what she created out of what she smashed to bits. How did a bourgeois girl become an artist and a woman? What was the female equivalent of the Great Man? If it didn't exist, why not? Who said it didn't? Who said it couldn't? What were the conditions that made it so hard? Rodin was the image Claudel identified with and against which she defined herself. Scott was this image for Zelda. A woman could not be a great artist and have a traditional marriage — not unless her husband was a Leonard Woolf. One boyfriend I had in college used to joke, "Only one artist in the family," meaning not me. I didn't get it then, but I get it now. There was always something self-annihilating in the act of loving, for a girl with creative aspirations — always — but far more then than now. The message, invariably, was that youthful passions lead to middle-age breakdowns, so choose your institution wisely. Marriage or the nuthouse. One or the other. It started to dawn on me that it wasn't that I was attracted to stories about girls who went mad, I was attracted to stories about girls with ambitions who wound up institutionalized. Getting locked up was not the result of adventure, it was the price you paid for adventure, it was your punishment. I had mistaken correlation for causation. Rookie mistake.

In 2014, I stumbled across an article in the *Guardian* by James Dearden, the screenwriter of *Fatal Attraction*. He was talking about how Glenn Close's character, Alex, started as a sympathetic character and ended up as a psychopath. Dearden said he originally wrote Alex as "an essentially tragic, lonely figure." "Yes, she does go a bit far, but I think we can all recognize how close to obsessive behavior we can be driven by love — or the illusion of love."[2] The movie was in development for four years, the rewrites continuing even after Michael Douglas and Adrian Lyne were attached, but Paramount remained resistant. "'How do we root for this guy?' they keep asking. 'He cheats on his wife!' Hollywood likes its leading men unequivocally heroic, and it seems there are far too many shades of grey to Dan Gallagher, Douglas's character," Dearden wrote. "So gradually, remorselessly, Dan is made more and more blameless, while Alex turns inevitably more and more into the villain of the piece. The changes are subtle, almost imperceptible, but they accumulate, so that she has become — without us fully realizing — this predatory and eventually deranged character." A monster nobody can identify with.

In 2011, and apparently not without trepidation, Nancy Joe Sales profiled Courtney Love in *Vanity Fair*. Everything that could be said about Love had already been said so she wrote about what it was like to try to portray someone whose story precedes her. She wrote about how we interpret people, and what the responsibilities are to the people we portray. What emerged was a fascinating portrait of a person in conflict with her persona as observed by someone ambivalent about shaping the story. Everybody "knows" Love. Should she part from this assumption? address it? confirm it? ignore it? try to dispel it? To defend the public figure known as Courtney Love is to risk an identification you probably don't want. To defend Love against the charge that she's crazy is to take on her alleged crazy yourself. It's to martyr yourself to the crazy. You think twice.

In the story, you learn that Love is obsessed with the idea that she's broke. She says she's been defrauded of hundreds of millions of dollars. Sales and Love spend the weekend at the country house of the Earl of March and Kinrara, and Love says she fits in among "the toffs." They get her. Sales skates on the edge between credulity and disbelief. It was a fascinating study in ambivalence. The story seemed to dare to you empathize with the vilified woman, to own the consequences of hating her, and, at the same time, the chill of sticking your neck out. At one point, Love tells Sales that when she was little, she dreamed of growing up and getting famous so people would finally love her. But a girl as ambitious, as reckless, as needy as she is is never loved in the way she probably dreamed of, uncritically, by millions. To be loved in that way, you can be a mess or you can be a girl, but you can't be both. A girl like her is never loved that way — which is why girls love her. The story was called "Love in a Cold Climate," and the subhead was "Human train wreck or victimized genius?"[3]

In her book *The Female Malady: Women, Madness, and English Culture, 1830–1980,* Elaine Showalter talks about how in the Victorian era madness became a gendered condition. Until then insanity had been represented as male, but was reinvented as a sexier, swoonier "female malady." The newly built asylums of the nineteenth century were mostly filled with women, whose "delicate constitutions," it was believed, whose hysterical tendencies, and whose logical deficits made them especially susceptible to the diagnosis. Victorians ushered in crazy girl chic, by reframing insanity as a disease of sensibility, of refinement. A Great Man could be expected to weather the nerve-jangling force of genius, but the finely strung lady nerves of a woman artist, the thinking went, would eventually succumb — usually in middle age, when her eccentricity stopped being cute. This is why nobody romanticizes Alex Forrest in *Fatal Attraction,* or identifies with Laura Dern's character, Amy Jellicoe, on Mike White's HBO show *Enlightened,* and why Tina Fey jokes that "the definition of 'crazy' in show business is a woman who keeps talking after nobody wants to fuck her anymore."

Enlightened begins with Amy's nervous breakdown: she's holed up in a bathroom stall, wailing and moaning as black streaks of mascara run down her contorted Melpomene-mask face. The scene is a front-row seat to her unraveling. Amy is a forty-year-old sales executive at Abaddon Industries. Her younger, married boss has just transferred her from her beloved Health and Beauty Department to the Siberia of Cleaning Products, because he doesn't want to sleep with her anymore. (Health and Beauty to Cleaning Products! The sequel to the marriage plot in a nutshell!) When two of her coworkers enter the bathroom and start gossiping about her, Amy bursts out of the stall, calls one a backstabbing cunt, and storms out to confront her boss, who is on his way out to lunch with vendors. Her assistant tries to stop her. "Amy," she hisses. "You look insane." And she does, but she's beyond caring. When a forty-year-old woman is transferred from Health and Beauty to Cleaning Products, she's expected to go quietly. If, by the time a woman reaches Amy's age, she has not sublimated her passion, ambition, and ego to others' needs, then she is "an essentially tragic, lonely figure," worthy of our sympathy.

Amy loses her mind in front of everyone and gets shipped off to a mental-health retreat, where she swims with dolphins and wears flowy garments and has the epiphany that she is one with the universe. She returns home transformed and full of hope for transforming her evil corporate overlord, her drug-addicted ex-husband, her depressed, shut-down mom. She wants to change the world with positive affirmations. She believes she can. When Amy learns that Abaddon is hiding something big, she decides to become a whistle-blower. A sexy reporter, played by Dermot Mulroney, talks her into it. He really wants that story. She really wants something to believe in.

I once interviewed Mike White for a *New York Times Magazine* profile, and we spent the first twenty minutes talking about Kim Richards's meltdown on *The Real Housewives of Beverly Hills*, which had aired the previous night. Richards, a former child star who long ago eclipsed her dowdier sisters, is now the broke, twice-divorced, alcoholic family head case, at once pitied and despised by her well-married sisters. Her elder sister, Cathy, is married to a Hilton, with whom she produced Paris. Her younger sister, Kyle, is married to a sexy, high-end Realtor who dotes on her and their daughters. Now in her fifties, Kim has the kind of life that makes her sisters feel smug and lucky. The pathos of Kim Richards — of "the Kims of the world" in general, as White called them — flows from an admixture of bad choices and bad luck, overexposure and neglect. Kim has no apparent defenses. She is a raw nerve vibrating with hope, anxiety, and need. She tells truths that nobody wants to hear; they don't want their own feelings exposed. We understand Kim and Amy to be crazy in the way of all disruptive, uncontained women; women who simply cannot hold themselves together, who spill out grotesquely in all directions.

Not long after seeing *Camille Claudel* with You-Rita-Hayworth-there, I was walking down Montparnasse on my way home. I'd just passed the Villa Borghese and was waiting to cross the street when a tall, lanky man with wild, curly hair and glasses, a kind of French Jeff Goldblum, made a reference to the villa, which I caught. Then he fell in step with me without asking. It was broad daylight on a crowded street close to home, and he seemed harmless. He asked me if I was a writer. I was the kind of girl who believed in signs and portents. I enjoyed flattery as much as the next person. I'd been waiting for a sign from the universe to give me the go-ahead, to anoint me in some way. At the same time, I felt a hard twinge of annoyance. I thought: *This dude thinks I'm an American college girl. Read: Dumb. Read: Easy. Read: A bunny to be seduced with a carrot. He reads me as a sign with referents going back to Jean Seberg in* Breathless. To him, I communicated, "I will fuck you and then you will have sixty seconds to vacate the premises before I detonate the crazy or the insufferable kitsch." I was twenty-one. French Goldblum was about forty. I thought, *I'm going to get this fucker.* I thought, *I am not harmless.*

The feeling that my identity could be so easily negated and

swapped out for another bothered me. Jean-Paul Belmondo swapping out Jean Seberg for the femme fatale in his imagination had annoyed me, and reading Henry Miller had made me feel defensive, ambivalent, pricklier than usual about power relations. Miller's style was so exhilarating, and his contempt so eviscerating. If I kept walking, whatever Jeff Goldblum's assumptions about me were would remain intact. If I engaged with him, he would assume that I was an impressionable, easily manipulated ingenue with Eiffel Towers in my eyes. Even if I walked away, someone would eventually come along and confirm those assumptions. So I agreed to get coffee with him, intending not to sleep with him but to change him.

This is kind of an embarrassing story. I tried for years to write it and get past the cringe-inducing surface of it. I failed a million times.

We talked about my future as a writer.

He said that (T/F?) I would have a tragic life, because a woman can't be a writer and be happy both.

He said it's not because they can't be artists but because society won't let them. Women are expected to stay within the bounds of acceptability and to limit their experiences and their expression in ways that are counterproductive to art. T/F?

I said I could do anything I wanted to do, because I was afraid of nothing. T/F?

He said it was obvious that I was a well-brought-up little bourgeois and that I would most likely lose my nerve. T/F?

I said I was not. T/F?

He said, "Prove it."

"How?" I said.

"Come with me to a hotel and spend the afternoon . . ." I think there was some pornographic description of activity, but I can't remember it and my French was deficient in that area. This sort of stuff didn't get talked about in my *nouveau roman* seminar. *Bonjour, tristesse.* I neither went with him nor left on my own. Instead, I ordered another *café crème* and willingly stepped into a "communicational matrix." I tried to show him that — what? that I was a person? that I could change things with words? that I was a hero who would one day demystify the story he took for reality, revealing it for the authoritarian nightmare that it was? I was not successful. Neither was he. We arrived, at the end of our third coffee, at an exhausted stalemate. We said goodbye politely, completely drained of piss and vinegar on my part and sexual interest on his. I wandered out blinking into the street, dazed and jacked up on caffeine, depleted and depressed. I felt ashamed for some reason, like I really hated myself. The guy was a dick, but he was right about the double standard. Stories about men tend to have a certain swashbuckling quality; they read like open-ended adventures full of setbacks and brushes with disaster leading inexorably to a satisfying conclusion. Stories about women rebelling and deviating from the conventional path tend to end in disappointment, arsenic, laudanum, or brief encounters with oncoming trains. My attempt to tell him a story about me that would overwrite his story about me (he didn't even know me!) had failed. His story was the official story, the weight of history, of repetition, of authority, of might. His version was the official version, and mine was a rank conspiracy theory. I was just a stupid American college girl. You know the type. A year later, I went to Jamaica on spring break, and my friend Whitney tried telling a guy who was harassing us on the beach about how he was actually harassing a cultural construct. I was like, *Let's maybe just keep walking.* Except I'd done that the previous spring break in Greece with my friend Rita Hayworth, and the guy had ended up following us for two blocks calling us bitches. It was never not a hard call. You did what you could.

Why would he give up this position, when all fictions are oriented toward his subjectivity? Would I, if I were in his shoes? If the world were made for me? Then again, who knows, maybe I got through to him just a little. Maybe he saw me and changed. I doubt it. Either way, I'm sure he forgot about me a long time ago.

PART TWO

The Pool of Tears

Dear, dear! How queer everything is today! And yesterday things went on just as usual. I wonder if I've been changed in the night? Let me think: Was I the same when I got up this morning? I almost think I can remember feeling a little different. But if I'm not the same, the next question is, Who in the world am I? Ah, *that's* the great puzzle!

— LEWIS CARROLL, *ALICE'S ADVENTURES IN WONDERLAND*

6

The Ingenue Chooses
Marriage or Death

Fairy tales are about money, marriage, and men. They are
the maps and manuals that are passed down from mothers
and grandmothers to help them survive.

— MARINA WARNER

IMMERSING YOURSELF IN LITERARY THEORY AS AN IM-
pressionable young person is a little like squinting at a piece of toast
until the face of Jesus materializes. It's a slight perceptual shift (all
you have to do is unfocus your eyes) but risky, because there's no going back to plain toast after Jesus. Similarly, once you've engaged in
enough feminist readings of *The Iliad,* or performed close textual
analyses of *Alf,* or written papers limning the intertextual relationship between *Videodrome* and *Madame Bovary* — once, in other
words, you've glimpsed the social, political, historical, and ideo-
logical underpinnings of every text ever constructed — you'll never
again see stories in the same way. They'll shed their innocence and
expose their dirty secrets and reveal the world as a darker, more
dangerous place than it once seemed. You might find yourself longing, at this point, for a return to a simpler relationship with your
toast/stories, for a return to the way you saw things before your innocence was lost to some icy French bastard like Foucault or Bau-
drillard. But that innocence will be lost to you forever, as will your
formerly effortless communion with the vast, transformative commercial enterprise known as "pop culture," and you'll feel the way

Thelma did when she told Louise that something had crossed over within her and she couldn't go back.

When I look back on my first postcollege year, I imagine *Pretty Woman* and *Thelma and Louise* flanking it like a pair of quick-draw gunfighters in a showdown, or dueling metanarratives at dawn, or a fork in the postfeminist road, or some other desolate but decisive Wild West scene. In any case, dust, tumbleweed, and plaintive Ennio Morricone music are in the background. The culture wasn't big enough for the both of them. *Pretty Woman* appeared a couple of months before my college graduation, and I went to see it with my boyfriend, whom my father had nicknamed "the Landowner," not because he owned land but because he looked like he'd just stepped off the set of a Merchant-Ivory movie. He was Julian Sands in *A Room with a View,* and I, on a very, very good day (and exclusively in my own mind), was Helena Bonham Carter.

The first line of *Pretty Woman* is "No matter what they say, it's all about money." The line is uttered by a hired magician performing coin tricks at a party in Beverly Hills. Philip, a sleazy lawyer played by Jason Alexander, is the host, and his guest of honor is his fat-cat client Edward (Richard Gere). Edward is an eighties-era corporate raider on the brink of a raid. He's a snake recoiled for a bite. We first see him on the phone with his girlfriend in New York, who is letting him know that she won't be flying out to Los Angeles to be his plus-one at the plunder. "I speak to your secretary more than I speak to you," she complains, and you understand that this line is intended to communicate her entitled bitchiness and self-delusion. Edward, you understand, has no time for women like these — women who expect to be treated like people.

"I see," he says.

"I have my own life, too, you know, Edward," she says, but it doesn't sound convincing.

Edward looks at his reflection in the big plate-glass window. It's a reflective moment with a reflective surface. He tells her what's what. It's "a very important week" for him, and he needs her there with him.

"But you never give me any notice!" she says. "You expect me to be at your beck and call!"

"I do not believe that you are at my beck and call," Edward says. And, like that, it's over between them. The bossman does not tolerate dissent, and will not suffer girly conversations.

Edward borrows his lawyer's fancy sports car and sputters off into the sunset (he can't drive a stick shift), and as he heads off on his journey of discovery (he has no idea where he's going), the movie begins to crosscut with the have-not life of Vivian, baby streetwalker, played by a then nineteen-year-old Julia Roberts. The very first shot of her is of her ass in black lacy underwear. She flips over and we get a front view, then a shot of her boobs in a tank top, then of her legs as she zips them into boots, then of her arms as she piles plastic bracelets on them, and then of one eye as she cakes on mascara on the lashes. The parts finally add up to Vivian, sneaking out of her fleabag motel because her roommate has taken all the rent money for drugs again. She climbs out the fire escape down to the street, where a cop is pulling a dead hooker out of a Dumpster.

Pretty Woman was a confusing movie. It did something I'd never even thought possible. It took "the unbeatable Madonna-whore combination" and inverted the Madonna and the whore. It made the whore virtuous by turning her into a princess on the inside, and holding her up to the smudgy mirror of her cynical, gum-snapping roommate, who did drugs and did not believe in fairy tales. Vivian didn't do drugs or have a pimp or kiss on the mouth. She controlled her own destiny. She kept business separate from pleasure. She got monthly AIDS tests and flossed religiously. Mostly, she believed in the power of her perfect body parts to win her the life of privilege that could be traded for on the open market, but never, ever acknowledged this. She maintained an aura of blithe, childlike innocence at all times. She was the most wholesome, intemerate hooker ever to walk Hollywood Boulevard. Vivian and Edward meet when Edward stops to get directions to the Regency Beverly Wilshire, and Vivian charges him for a personal escort. By the end of the night, she has accepted $3,000 to spend the week with him as his girlfriend. The hotel's concierge tries to kick her out, but he is soon won over by her princess-like charm and doe-like innocence. He appoints himself her own personal Tim Gunn. Later, after doing it on the grand piano in the hotel lounge, and after Edward instructs Vivian not to chug champagne but to swish it delicately around a ripe strawberry, he gives her a credit card and deputizes her to go to town. There is scarcely a moment in this great romance that is not transactional, instructional, or otherwise deeply condescending.

An ingenue is a dramatic and literary archetype. She is defined not only by her age — that crepuscular moment between childhood and adolescence — but also by her doe-eyed innocence. Naive in a complex, urbane, foreign world, she is usually portrayed as a newcomer and a fish out of water. She moves through this world unaware of the hypocrisy, duplicity, and exploitation all around her. She is credulous and vulnerable and dependent on a protective paternal figure, and lives in constant peril of being exploited or corrupted by some lurking cad or villain. This threat is the central tension of her life. What makes her interesting is the question of how she will navigate this world, who she will become, and what will become of her.

"The ingénue symbolizes the mutable character par excellence, the blank slate in search of an identity," the scholar Julia V. Douthwaite writes about the role of the ingenue in French literature.[1] She sets out in the world as pure potential — changeable, malleable, and moldable. She's an empty stage upon which to enact whatever it is that's troubling us at the moment. For E. M. Forster, the ingenue was a transitional figure between the Victorian era and the modern one.

Girls of my generation were transitional, too. We were raised to inhabit a world that was at that very moment being willed into being by another generation; to step into the unknown. Not long after going to see *Thelma and Louise*, I went to a party with the Land-owner, where I mentioned to a friend of his, visiting from home, that I'd just seen *Thelma and Louise* and loved it. What a great movie it was, I said. What a world-altering movie. He smiled at me. It was a stupid movie, he said. It was an embarrassingly sincere, irrelevant throwback of a movie. Nobody with any discernment thought it was anything but a cringe-inducing turd of a movie. And where had I been? Didn't I know that even Betty Friedan had disavowed Betty Friedan? (I had no idea, of course. I'd heard of Betty Friedan, and had gleaned from the culture that I was supposed to have contempt for her, but beyond that, I didn't know much. Who would have taught me?) Whatever I'd felt on seeing the movie, I was wrong to like it, to relate to it, to identify. I was especially wrong to find it revolutionary, world-changing. He knew it was wrong because his mother was active in the women's movement. He had it on authority. He was also very rich. I stalked out of the party and walked home alone. I was furious, but also confident that soon, encounters of this sort would be a thing of the past. The movie itself was evidence that things were changing, and soon we could all dust ourselves off, shake hands, and live happily ever after. I had no doubt that we were entering a new, more enlightened age.

Julia Roberts was credited with bringing back the character of the ingenue, but Geena Davis in *Thelma and Louise* played one, too. Both Vivian (Roberts) and Thelma (Davis) start out childlike and cloistered—Thelma by her repressive marriage to the chauvinistic Daryl, Vivian by her rather alarming denial—and both embark on a journey of transformation. Thelma transitions into herself, whereas Vivian finds a way to be a wide-eyed child bride forever. What is remarkable about *Pretty Woman* is how it manages not just to erase the distinctions between the naive, innocent ingenue and the cynical, jaded streetwalker but also to merge them. It gets around the fact that its ingenue is also a whore by making everyone else in the movie an even bigger whore — by leveling the whore playing field. Sure, Vivian is for sale, but so is everyone else. At least she is friendly about it. At least she is grateful and maintains a cheerful, professional attitude about it, unlike Edward's bitchy ex-girlfriend or the snooty Rodeo Drive salesgirls. At least she is comfortable in her role as a commodity. At one point, Vivian tells Edward flat out, "I want the fairy tale," and, violating all narrative logic, she gets it. She goes back to the Rodeo Drive boutique that snubbed her and lets them know they made a "big mistake" in snubbing her. Because she's expensive now. She got the highest bidder and didn't even have to hold out. Everyone cheered for the once-shamed prostitute who got her chance to revenge-shame the sales associates. It was so ludicrous and absurd and brainlessly life-negating and deeply sad.

In high school, I decided that I would be a writer with a day job in advertising, because this seemed like a path to both art and money. My dad approved. He later gave me a copy of *Bill Bernbach's Book: A History of Advertising That Changed the History of Advertising*, and David Ogilvy's *Ogilvy on Advertising*. My senior year in college, I took a copywriting class at J. Walter Thompson in Chicago. A few months before I graduated, my uncle helped get me an interview at McCann Erickson in New York. It was 1990 and we were in a recession. The guy who interviewed me said, "I have guys who just graduated from NYU film school who can't get an internship." He did not add, "Why would I hire you?" but I did, in my head.

I'd tell my dad that when I walked into interviews, I could see the guy — it was always a guy — cock his head ever so slightly to the side and mentally pat me on the head. My dad would get angry. He'd say, "Bring it out in the open. Say, 'I know what you're thinking.' Turn it around." What he meant was "Let them know you're not a *girl*," which was both helpful and not. What he meant was,

I should consider myself that enduring fictional type — the exceptional girl.

I moved to San Francisco and got a temp job stuffing envelopes and then a full-time job folding sweaters, and then when the store closed (the recession), a part-time job steaming milk at a café where my boss suggested that the scheduling conflicts I'd been having with the other twenty-year-old barista were the result of "women not having been in the workplace that long." I remember thinking that the eighteen-year-old boy we worked with had also not been in the workforce that long. A year or two later, a TV writer friend opined that maybe the reason there weren't many girls on TV writing staffs was that men still weren't comfortable with the idea of women in the workplace. I thought, *Wait. Weren't we just in college together? What did I miss?* Obviously, I'd missed something. I'd been absent on some very important day. What I remember about conversations like these was how stupid they made me feel. After my shift, I'd go home to eat burritos and watch the Clarence Thomas–Anita Hill hearings on TV.

I started film school and made a friend. I was twenty-three and he was thirty, and he'd worked in advertising for years. He made a lot of money and thought it was funny that I couldn't afford a vacuum cleaner. But I really couldn't afford a vacuum cleaner. I helped him write his short film, and I asked him to help me get an interview at an ad agency, and he told me I was too cool for advertising. Also, girls didn't make good copywriters unless it was for feminine products. He didn't mean only feminine-hygiene products, though he did mean those, but also girly stuff in general, the kind that was popular then, shortly after the discovery of the "women's market." Suddenly, the marketplace was full of products that "celebrated" women, offering us pink, indulgent, usually creamy respite from the cross to bear of being a princess and a goddess, domestic and otherwise. Eventually, I wrote to a creative director at the same agency, where my friend used to work, and got an interview. The guy who interviewed me complimented my work but had no job to offer. When I told my friend about the interview, he laughed and said that the guy was infamous for using informational interviews as a way to meet girls.

Nowadays, when people describe something as "a Cinderella story," they are almost always referring to a story about a girl lifted from obscurity, mediocrity, or worse by a rich and powerful man who re-creates her to make her worthy of his love — forgetting that Cinderella, in the original story, was robbed. The modern-day Cinderella is raw material from which the highly discerning woman connoisseur may fashion his ideal. The man — and we've seen him a lot, from Richard Gere's corporate raider to Jamie Dornan's avid spanker in *50 Shades of Grey* — is not satisfied with the women he knows. His tastes are peculiar. He needs someone he can mold and control. We call this "rescue." What's interesting about this is how different this story is from the actual *Cinderella*, in which a young bourgeois girl, following the death of her father, is cheated out of her rightful inheritance and forced to work as her stepmother's maid. Marrying the prince is a political move — it's a way to reclaim her property and restore her position and, of course, get revenge.

The Cinderella story that interested me was the one I heard about a year after *Pretty Woman* came out — the one about the waitress whose feminist script was made into a major motion picture by Ridley Scott. Both *Pretty Woman* and *Thelma and Louise* tapped into something current and served up fantasies of escape from the condition of being broke, powerless, underestimated, and objectified. As far as I could tell, it was Vivian, not Thelma and Louise, who ceased to exist at the close of each of their stories. For the few years that followed *Thelma and Louise*, the culture would be unusually and strangely receptive to the howls of a generation of girls who felt exiled from a culture. The Riot Grrrl scene would explode, and once again, just as I'd felt in the early eighties, around the time that *Desperately Seeking Susan* came out, I'd think, *This is it. From now on, progress will move forward.* Yet within a few more years, the whole thing would be played out and supplanted by a far more chipper, far more palatable, far more marketable version of itself. It was a pretty quick traverse from "revolution grrrl-style now" to "girl power," from Riot Grrrls to Spice Girls. The commodification of "girl power" would be swift and total. Ultimately, *Pretty Woman* wasn't a love story; it was a money story.

When *Thelma and Louise* came out, I'd been living in San Francisco for a year, with a boyfriend about whom, when making the case for my sanity and clearheadedness, I found myself saying things like, "Well, it's not like I'm going to marry him." The prospect of finding a job that didn't involve foaming milk seemed about as likely as discovering a magical portal to Narnia inside one of the envelopes I was stuffing (temporarily) for a large financial institution. Not only did I feel powerless and lost but I kept having to read about how powerlessness and lost my generation was in the *New York Times*.

In 1992, Rebecca Walker coined the term *third wave* in an essay in *Ms.* magazine that she wrote when she was twenty-two and I read when I was twenty-three. She was inspired by the 1991 Senate hearings before Clarence Thomas's Supreme Court confirmation, after a report of an FBI interview with Anita Hill was leaked to the press. Hill had testified that Thomas had repeatedly asked her out, told her about movies he'd watched about women having sex with animals, with group-sex and rape scenes, that he'd measured his penis and told her its name, that he'd picked up a can of Coke on his desk and asked who had put a pubic hair on it. The more she was grilled by the Senate Judiciary Committee, the more obvious it became that Hill's character had been put on trial. Like Walker and every other person I knew, I was riveted by the spectacle of Hill being humiliated by an all-male Judiciary Committee. We believed Anita Hill. And yet, there it was. Reading Walker's essay, I felt as if she'd reached into my soul, scooped out my rage, and sprayed it in lacerating shards in every direction. She had articulated the relationship between women and the establishment culture perfectly, and exposed the workings of a system that pretended to include us but didn't; that pretended to care about us, but only so long as we stuck to its guidelines of behavior; that pretended to hear us unless we spoke out against it, at which point it would turn on us with no mercy. In a contest between Hill's reputation and Thomas's, there was no contest. No matter how credible, how exemplary in any other context, in the framework of the confirmation hearings Anita Hill was a threat to the power structure, and she was shot down with prejudice. You couldn't watch this as a young woman and not come away with this lesson. For Walker, the takeaway was the panicked reaction to the threat of Hill's word undermining Thomas's career. If she stood up to him and was vindicated, would the system crumble? Hill's testimony was more than a threat to Thomas's confirmation, it was a threat to the patriarchal order. To watch as a young woman was to anxiously await a verdict on whether we were equal or whether male privilege always won out. She wrote:

> While some may laud the whole spectacle for the consciousness it raised around sexual harassment, its very real outcome is more informative. He was promoted. She was repudiated. Men were assured of the inviolability of their penis/power. Women were admonished to keep their experiences to themselves. The backlash against U.S. women is real. As the misconception of equality between the sexes becomes more ubiquitous, so does the attempt to restrict the boundaries of women's personal and political power. Thomas' confirmation, the ultimate rally of support for the male paradigm of harassment, sends a clear message to women: "Shut up! Even if you speak, we will not listen."[2]

Walker asked her boyfriend what he thought of the hearings, and she was shocked that his main concern was Thomas's dismal record on civil rights and opportunities for people of color. "I launch into a tirade," she wrote. "When will progressive black men prioritize my rights and well-being? When will they stop talking so damn much about 'the race' as if it revolved exclusively around them? He tells me I wear my emotions on my sleeve. I scream 'I need to know, are you with me or are you going to help them try to destroy me?'"

When Walker declared herself part of the "third wave," what she was saying was that she no longer considered herself part of the so-called postfeminist generation. She was repudiating the idea that the "second wave" had both succeeded (so move on) and failed (so shut up), which was just one of the many crazy-making paradoxes our generation was raised on. What Walker was articulating made perfect sense to me. Nothing in my experience contradicted it. She was taking up the mantle after a long period of backlash and dormancy. Things would be different now.

Several years later, I was working at a start-up in Silicon Valley. My job consisted mostly of managing hundreds upon thousands of tiny digital files, which I rotoscoped, compressed, named, logged, stored, and cataloged in dozens of one-gigabyte drives the size of cinder blocks. (It's true. That's how big they were in the late nineties.) I worked from 9:00 a.m. to 9:00 p.m. on weekdays, and at least one full day per weekend. I made so little money that I went into debt buying sandwiches from the café in the lobby. I did it because when I first interviewed for the job, somebody told me that the previous year, they'd all gotten $30,000 in bonuses at Christmas.

When the day of the salary-review meeting finally arrived, my manager escorted me to my boss's office and we sat down.

"So, you want a raise," my boss said with a grin. I said I did. He asked me what kind of guys I dated. I knew he thought he was being funny. When a certain type of guy (like, say, your fun boss) in a certain type of situation (like, say, your much-delayed salary review) thinks he's being funny, there's not much you can do to disabuse him of this notion, and even if you could, even if you did take it to the human-resources lady (isn't she always a lady?), your victory would be Pyrrhic and it would probably cost you more than it netted you. So, I did what I always did in these situations. I shut down and let my eyes go dead. I smirked and cocked my head and went into my go-to "I see what you are doing and I will raise you not only by not registering the insult but also by insulting you back while pretending not to and then we can laugh at you together" stance. I thought this is how you play.

"I date artists," I said. I'd meant for it to be ironic, just not so cutting that he'd fire me before I'd had a chance to square away my sandwich debt. But it came out sounding dumb.

"Really?" he said. He seemed genuinely concerned. "I could introduce you to rich guys."

It was a joke, of course. We all laughed. He laughed the hardest. I was given a nominal cost-of-living raise that was several months overdue.

There was no bonus that year, after all, but we did get Christmas gifts — we each received a remaindered copy of *The Hot Zone*, the Ebola-virus book; and a book about Anita Hill. I quit a few months later. I somehow managed to pay off all the ham.

It felt at once both enormously significant and like no big deal. It was nothing. It was funny. It was just a little piece of absurdity to be saved and turned into art later, when I wasn't working all the time. I'd always had a Goth streak, was attracted to rot, ruin, and decadence for the interplay between truth and its corrosive effect on beauty. It was future-art, as-yet-not-contextualized art. At some later point, when I finally became myself, I would fashion my true self from these stories. I would tell these stories and find a way to make myself the hero.

But it was harder than I'd expected, because there's so much fear that arises. You fear looking bitter, vindictive, overly sensitive. You fear looking like you're blaming others for your shortcomings or settling scores. You worry that somebody will feel bad or attempt to discredit you. "Did you leave the room when your parents fought?" a screenwriting professor once asked me. (Then he said, "We should get a drink. I'd probably get arrested. How old are you, anyway?") He was right about my aversion to conflict. It immediately made me feel guilty. That's how your experience becomes unspeakable and the things that are done to you become your fault, your terrible, guilty secret. The rules of the game as I understood them were just to play along with the game — just do the best you could with the flamingo mallets and hedgehog balls, like Alice did in the Queen's walled garden. You know you'll never *win*, but at least you wouldn't lose *everything*.

So, all of this is to say that this story is not a composite, but it easily could have been. It's not exceptional, just funnier than most. I wasn't traumatized by the experience, I don't think. I think of it as formative. It's not like I was traumatized. I think of it as one of the many experiences that hones my sense of the absurd. It's not like I was traumatized. It's how I ended up making a living, paying attention to moments, locating the cognitive dissonance, saving it for later. It's not like I was traumatized — but it's not like I bear no responsibility for my intermittent hopelessness, either, for the urge to just cosmically give up.

Not long after the Anita Hill hearings ended, my boyfriend and I were invited to another party — Thanksgiving dinner at the home of a friend of a friend, a woman about a decade older than me. After dinner, someone suggested we watch *Pretty Woman*. The women squealed and professed their love while the men engaged in distancing behaviors. I was old enough to know better than to get into an argument, but not old enough to play along. Instead, I sulked. I found a corner of pastel carpet and sat through the movie in aggrieved silence. I knew the movie had fans, of course, I'd just never met them in person. That afternoon, the women enacted for me my greatest fears about womanhood. I resented them for it. I was trying to locate a narrative in real life, in fiction or in nonfiction, that I could relate to and aspire to at once, and I couldn't find one anywhere. And they were happy not to care, or to act like they didn't.

That afternoon, I became aware of something I hadn't been aware of before. Our hostess and her friends could take *Pretty*

Woman at face value in a way I wasn't capable of doing, but apparently I required some kind of a fairy-tale ending, too. It bothered me that women's lives seemed unfinished to me, and that I couldn't resist the longing to see everyone put in her place, either. But even if I'd wanted to, I couldn't unsee the message of *Pretty Woman*. I couldn't unknow what I knew. The role of romantic fiction since the eighteenth century, but especially starting in the nineteenth, was to obscure the transactional underpinnings of marriage, to blur them over with love and romance. Nothing was more high-stakes than marriage for a middle-class girl in Jane Austen's time, yet it was necessary, for obvious reasons, to minimize the appearance of a transaction. The heroine never married for money, of course. But her kind, wise, noble prince just always happened to have it. (To marry for love without money was never not a tragic mistake.) *Pretty Woman* gave us the shameless American capitalist version, predicated on the self as something to be sold. Revisiting *Thelma and Louise* decades later, I was struck by how dated it seemed. At the time, I would never have guessed that *Pretty Woman* would prefigure every romantic comedy for the next two decades, but it did. *Pretty Woman* turned out not to be a throwback at all. It turned out to be the future.

7

Thoroughly Modern Lily

SHORTLY BEFORE THE TURN OF THE MILLENNIUM, ADAM Gopnik wrote a piece for *The New Yorker* about the redesign of the U.S. currency. People found the new money disturbing, he said, because it seemed to mock the old money through use of "traditional satiric devices of exaggeration, displacement, and oversimplification." Whereas the old money recalled the excesses of the Gilded Age, he thought the new money looked like parody money. Like "metamoney," it seemed "to be getting at us in some obscure way."[1]

Money did seem very conspicuous all of a sudden. This hadn't been true before. I'd moved to San Francisco after college, when it was so cheap people used to call it the city "where the young come to retire." Then I moved away, to Los Angeles, and then moved back up right before the turn of the millennium. I barely recognized the place. It seemed like money was mocking us, or some of us, anyway. One day, I stepped outside my ruinously expensive studio apartment, on Divisadero Street, and I saw that someone had stenciled something on the sidewalk outside my building in red spray paint. It was an egregious statement that then mayor Willie Brown had made in the press, to the effect that nobody should try to live in San Francisco on less than $50,000 a year. I tried. My efforts were heroic but doomed. My rent was insane. When my car died, I didn't repair it. My boyfriend bought my groceries for me, because he worked in finance and I worked in journalism, and that was just the way things were always/again. I had just turned thirty and was suddenly acutely aware of both the apparent availability and personal unattainability of money in ways I hadn't been before. I was newly/once again steeped in ideas about how money intersected with sex and relationships. *Sex and the City* had just come on the air.

I don't remember how or when, exactly, I started to come around to *Sex and the City*, but eventually I did. At first, it got on my nerves in the same way *Pretty Woman* had. It struck me as a fantasy for older single women who were oblivious to its regressive message. I associated the show with a coworker in the cubicle opposite mine, who used to spend what felt like hours on the phone with her sister dissecting the show after each episode.

Sure, the situations in which Carrie, Miranda, Charlotte, and Samantha found themselves were often familiar or redolent of my similar experiences, but the characters themselves were too archetypal and one-dimensional to identify with consistently: Samantha was too strange, Miranda was too bitter, Charlotte was too rigid, and Carrie was too infantile. They weren't identifiable characters so much as fantasy projections whose most mundane moments were instantly recognizable, even if their clothing budgets or Park Avenue apartments or sexual rosters were utterly fantastical. Carrie and Charlotte were the romantics, and both were focused on landing rich men. Love, for both, was wish fulfillment. Charlotte wished for traditional high-status domestic-pedestal dwelling, and Carrie for luxury, glamour, and sybaritic pleasures.

The conventional take was that *Sex and the City* was so clever at capturing the modern female archetypes that no woman could fail to identify. To me it seemed that the four friends were not modern archetypes so much as media-created stereotypes, allegorical figures standing in for the divided parts of the feminine mystique. Their conversations weren't conversations so much as referenda on the lady topics of the day, as each character manifested and grappled with an oppressive fantasy of contemporary womanhood, tested against the others. That's what made the show ultimately worthwhile; you could feel the tension between ideology and experience. The war was being waged inside each of the friends' psyches, but at least they were in the foxhole together.

The end of the nineteenth century gave rise to a new American upper class whose wealth seemed unthinkably vast. People lined up outside the Standard Oil offices to catch a glimpse of John D. Rockefeller. Money seeped into the American imagination. Millionaires became folk heroes. How did they do it? Most people didn't have a clue. Most people still don't. But everyone was drunk on champagne wishes and caviar dreams. This time, perhaps, other people's money has ceased to be the object of fascination that it was then, and is regarded with more suspicion and resentment. But at the end of the twentieth century, just as at the end of the nineteenth, money loomed over the culture and colored everything. New fortunes permeated the atmosphere, they got in the groundwater, they demanded attention. During the Gilded Age, wealth worship ran amok.

The popularity of the wedding-as-a-path-to-fortune drama had ebbed during my early life to the point that, save perhaps for Charles and Diana's much-publicized courtship and televised nuptials, my only significant experience with the story had involved Disney princesses. Then, toward the end of the nineties, big, elaborate "dream weddings" as a cultural gesture came roaring back into prominence. Maybe it started with *My Best Friend's Wedding*, the movie that reintroduced the concept of panicking about your "expiration date" to my generation. The website The Knot had been founded a year earlier. It was suddenly rare to open a magazine and not come across an article lamenting the way that money had seeped into romance like damp through plaster, staining and soiling it beyond repair. Men with little money wrote about the unreasonable economic demands made on them by women with little money. Women with little money defended their impossible economic standards while grieving that men with money held them to impossible beauty standards. Women with money (these were rarer) complained that men with no money eventually resented and left them. Magazines from *Forbes* to *Harper's Bazaar* devoted pages to the surplus of available Silicon Valley gazillionaires and provided instructions on how to snag them. *Cosmopolitan* argued that it was just as easy to date a rich man as a poor one. The Forbes 400 list included information on marital status.

Proponents of media consolidation claim that it has given the market freedom to deliver what audiences want. So, what do audiences want? They want what they have been taught to want. Without increasingly consolidated media, there is no "audience" with predictable desires. The rise of social media has allowed for a great proliferation of voices at a time of unprecedented media consolidation, it's true. Yet at the same time it has tended to mask the fact that social media has only consolidated media *even more*. The question also rests on a false premise, anyway: that there is such a thing as a single, collective audience, and that this mass consciousness "wants" something. It's the same false premise that Freud's infamous "woman question" was rooted in. "The great question that has never been answered," he famously said, "and which I have not yet been able to answer, despite my thirty years of research into the feminine soul, is 'What does a woman want?'"[2] Of course, that question is unanswerable, because it is not even a question, it's a trap. The women of Freud's imagination were the symbolic opposite of everything he understood to be *human*, so it's no wonder he was convinced that women by their nature "oppose change, receive passively, and add nothing of their own."[3]

*

In 2000, Terence Davies adapted Edith Wharton's *The House of Mirth*. Davies said he cast Gillian Anderson in the role of Lily Bart because a photograph of her reminded him of a painting by John Singer Sargent. But Wharton's Lily Bart, no matter how beautiful, would never have had her portrait painted by Sargent, nor by his fictional counterpart, the society painter Morpeth; there would have been no one to foot the bill. Sargent's sitters were the wives of very rich men — something that Lily, despite her efforts (or because of them), never managed to become. Lily hates big parties but attends them because it is "part of the business." But she is a lousy businesswoman who chokes every time she comes anywhere near closing a deal. Lily, whose definition of success is "to get all that one can out of life" (by which she means "marry the biggest fortune"), lacks the self-knowledge and the courage to recognize that she may have to sacrifice her romantic ideals in return for wealth and status — or vice versa. As a result, she winds up with nothing. What's poignant about Lily is not that she fails to achieve her goal, nor that she has an unwitting hand in her own failure: it's that, as she finally realizes, "there had never been a time when she had had any real relation to life."

If ever there was a book that disproved the notion that beauty is only skin deep, at least where it comes to self-concept, it is *The House of Mirth*. For Lily, her beauty is the prism through which the world sees her and through which she sees the world. Beauty is her cardinal trait. Her character and her destiny are shaped by it. Without it, she would have been someone else entirely — namely, her poor, plain, and unmarried cousin and only (unappreciated) true friend Gerty Farish. Gerty, a pivotal character in Wharton's story, was omitted from Davies's adaptation. Yet without girls like Gerty, there could be no girls like Lily. Gerty is the standard against which Lily defines herself. "She likes to be good," Lily says of Gerty early on. "I like to be happy."

That Lily equates money with happiness, that she believes it is her birthright to trade her beauty and charm for both, and that goodness, in her mind, is the surest path to poverty are just some of the themes that made Wharton's *House of Mirth* feel so contemporary. Lily doesn't just "enjoy the finer things in life." She is a single-minded junkie. "I am horribly poor," she tells Lawrence Selden near the beginning of the story, "and very expensive. I must have a great deal of money." For some reason, the movie failed to dwell on this aspect of Lily's character. Her greed and her desire for constant adulation were never addressed in the film. I remember feeling like Davies had glossed over the sense of entitlement that her beauty has inculcated in her and her own complicity in her financial ruin. Anderson played her as a tense and lachrymose innocent who is brought down by her own scruples and sense of fair play in a world that has none.

The writer Candace Bushnell, who wrote the novel that *Sex and the City* was based on, expressed an affinity with Wharton, and she struck one mass-market nerve after another not only by not shying away from the same territory but also by making it current. What Bushnell hinted at that nobody else seemed to acknowledge as pointedly was that, where money and beauty are involved, not a lot has changed between men and women in the past hundred years. There have always been women who participate in their own commodification, but suddenly it was a popular dream, the kind of thing people flaunted. Whereas Davies delivered Lily as the victim of a cruel and bygone era, Bushnell and series creator Michael Patrick King saw Lily working it everywhere they looked.

A friend of mine who grew up in New York described it like this: "You walk down Madison Avenue and you see things. Eventually you start to like them, then want them. Then you realize how much they cost." Luxury items have always been marketed predominantly to women, and the women who can afford them invariably become luxury items themselves. In his 1899 critique of upper-class values, *The Theory of the Leisure Class,* economist and philosopher Thorstein Veblen wrote, "The dress of women goes even farther than that of men in the way of demonstrating the wearer's abstinence from productive employment. It needs no argument to enforce the generalization that the more elegant styles of feminine bonnets go even farther towards making work impossible than does the man's high hat. The woman's shoe adds the so-called French heel to the evidence of enforced leisure afforded by its polish; because this high heel obviously makes any, even the simplest and most necessary manual work extremely difficult." Women may no longer wear bonnets, and high-heeled shoes may no longer be seen as hindrances to employment, but the fact remains that "the more elegant styles" are outside the reach of most working women. They require more money, more attention, and more leisure than the average working woman can afford. This is their point.

I remember an episode of *Sex and the City* in which Carrie has her credit card cut in half while she tries to purchase a pair of Dolce and Gabbana shoes: powder-blue mules with a feathery pom-pom on top. The shoes are absurdly expensive, impractical fetish objects. To Carrie's rescue comes Amalita, a woman who lives off her rich, jet-setting boyfriends. Amalita charges the shoes to her boyfriend-of-the-moment's card and sends Carrie off with a kiss. Later, when Carrie runs into the woman and her friends at a bar, she gets herself an invitation to Venice. The financially strapped Carrie wonders, "Is there a line between 'girlfriend' and 'prostitute'?" Ultimately, because she is our heroine, Carrie decides that for her the line does exist, and she declines the invitation and resolves to avoid Amalita in the future. Carrie is a modern version of Wharton's Lily, whose failure to get what she wants (she blows at least three chances to marry a fortune) could be the result of either her moral upbringing or her naïveté. Marriage-obsessed Charlotte doesn't grapple with these questions; the only difference between her and the "professional girlfriend" is that she is not willing to sacrifice anything in return for her never-ending reward.

Despite her notoriously low-paying creative profession, Carrie craves and feels just as entitled to luxury as Lily does. Like Lily, she denies herself nothing, even if it means racking up debt. When it comes down to it, she doesn't have the stomach to face the intrinsic hypocrisy of her life. The things she wants cannot be acquired virtuously — no one who is unwilling to cross a few moral lines can afford $500 shoes. For Carrie, as for Lily, the conflict between their longing for romance and their longing for luxury is unresolvable. In the new Gilded Age, the tragedy of Lily Bart would have been reframed. In the new Gilded Age, her tragedy wouldn't be living in a world that valued her only for her ornamental qualities, or being complicit in her own commodification, or being reduced to a parasite and then discarded, but having everything she needed to succeed and just being unable to go through with it. She knew what she wanted, and it lay within her grasp, but she just wasn't pragmatic enough to pay the price.

8

Bad Girlfriend

ONCE, IN THE LATE NINETIES, I SPENT THREE STRANGE days hanging around the Sheraton Hotel in Universal City — which is not a city so much as a mostly unincorporated area in Los Angeles County that houses Universal Studios and its attendant theme park — reporting on an event that billed itself as an academic conference on the First Amendment and pornography. I was there on assignment for *Salon*'s then new (now dead) education section. The hook was that the conference was being cosponsored by the Center for Sex and Gender Research at California State, Northridge, and something called the Free Speech Coalition, which turned out to be the lobbying arm of the adult-entertainment industry.

Having never attended an academic conference, I didn't know what to expect, but the mix yielded some highly amusing juxtapositions, some bordering on parody. Panels on Victorian pornography and erotic vases from Ancient Greece were presented alongside chats with porn stars. My job, as I remember, was to soak in the ambience, filter it through my disbelief, and report back in arch tones. The article would write itself.

No doubt my experience of the conference was filtered through a trifecta of inexperience, selective focus, and confirmation bias, but I was quickly struck by how hostile to inquiry (for an event cosponsored by a research center) the conference seemed to be. To be honest, I don't recall attending any panels on Victorian pornography or Ancient Greek vases, and maybe if I had, my one-sided experience would have been mitigated somehow. What I do recall, however, is that over the next few days, I found myself absorbing one unrelenting, expertly media-trained "celebratory" paean to commodified sex-positivity after another, and feeling more and more depressed by the hour. The conference's best-known, most vocal attendants seemed to respond to all but the most ingratiating questions by invalidating them and then swiftly shaming the interlocutor. The porn stars stuck to their talking points and stayed on message. "Liking sex" was the preferred euphemism for making or consuming porn. Conversely, harboring even the slightest ambivalence about porn meant that you categorically "hated sex" and were out to ruin it for everyone else.

A dominant narrative soon emerged in which pornography—and not the Victorian kind with the bloomers and the spankings, but the kind with the record-breaking gang bangs — was presented as a bastion of orgiastic disinhibition; a filthy fun-time Arcadia from which sprang nothing but joy and empowerment and marriage and children and unicorns. Like all good stories, this one had a villain: the sex-hating, man-foiling "girlfriend" whose cruel, withholding ways sent armies of disconsolate men into the tender embrace of their "favorite" porn stars daily. I was the girlfriend! Was I *that* girlfriend? I didn't feel like that person, but in this alternate universe I undoubtedly was. I'd had an upsetting encounter with a boyfriend's porn stash recently, and I felt both upset and upset about being upset. In the late nineties, it was not cool to be upset about porn or sex work of any kind. In the shame hierarchy of the day, just as now, it felt much more shameful to feel bad about it in any way than to produce, distribute, or consume it. The more this version of reality was reiterated and reaffirmed throughout the event, the sadder, more isolated, and more diminished I felt. The worst thing about it was how totalizing the experience was, and how deviant it made me feel.

About a decade and a half later, I was reminded of those strange few days while watching the Showtime series *Masters of Sex*. Ironically, what reminded me was the dogmatic and intolerant sexual milieu. Created by Michelle Ashford and based on the book by Thomas Maier, *Masters of Sex* followed the sex researchers William Masters and Virginia Johnson, whose landmark 1966 book, *Human Sexual Response,* would eventually tear down barriers and help pave the way for the sexual revolution, through the early stages of their research and their relationship. The show "begins" in 1956, when Bill Masters (Michael Sheen), a hormone-replacement-therapy specialist, hires Gini Johnson (Lizzy Caplan), a thrice-divorced former nightclub singer and mother of two, as his secretary, and together they lead the charge to bring sex out of the Middle Ages. The characters go through seismic changes brought on by their own repressed, unexamined, and eventually uncontrollable urges.

Whereas *Mad Men* took a fictional character, loosely based on a real person, and threw him against the cataclysmic events of his time, *Masters of Sex* cast historical figures, fictionally enhanced for dramatic effect, as agents of change working with clockwork precision on the most intimate level. Don Draper was a mind reader, a diviner of feelings, a mystic capable of imbuing simple products with magical, emotional qualities. Bill Masters and Gini Johnson, as imagined here, were clinicians intent on shining the hard light of science on a mysterious, transcendent thing. Still, both shows looked back from a distant future, trying to pinpoint the moment that everything changed. *Masters of Sex* was a contemporary show about a bygone time known for its retrograde attitudes, groping around blindly for the moment when the "old-fashioned" way of thinking about sex gave way to the "modern" way. Both shows exhibited signs of posttraumatic stress. Most interestingly, though, *Mad Men* was about a man whose job it was to replace reality with prejudicial stories — stories that take away agency, that dominate and control — whereas *Masters of Sex* was about what the stories do to people and their humanity, which they are forced to sublimate to the big lie.

• • •

Advertising pervades our inner lives and dreams in ways that Don Draper (had he existed) could never have imagined. Still, the backward glances — did it all go right or wrong? — have the air of trying to work something out. In that metamagical way that zeitgeisty things sometimes have, the worlds of *Mad Men* and *Masters of Sex* merge and overlap in the present, where they've mutated into something big, strange, and intractable — a mutant octopus carcass galvanized by commerce lurching toward Tokyo.

Masters of Sex was about how women's sexuality and sexual identity were once constructed, more or less exclusively, by men, out of conjecture, projection, fear, and very little actual information, all of which is then irradiated and mutated into something monstrous by media and corporatism. Not only was research of the kind carried out by Masters and Johnson virtually unheard of, but also there were hardly any female scientists in the field. The character of Gini — however closely she hews to her real-life counterpart — is a galvanizing force herself, not to mention a lightning rod, who goes around upending people's schemata and otherwise not fitting in. A mildly harried single working mother with limited resources — that is, a perennial poster girl for bad life choices — Gini is nonetheless portrayed as by far the happiest, most satisfied, least frustrated character on the show. She comes across as ambitious, curious, fulfilled, and free. There's some guilt involved, but she's not racked by it and she doesn't punish herself. And the show's writers aren't in the least bit equivocal in this: she derives her happiness and satisfaction from asking nothing more and nothing less from sex than pleasure (unlinking it from money), and from being creatively engaged in her work. As often as she says she needs the job to support her kids, it's obvious she needs it for herself, too.

Gini's charm and allure upset the absurdly brittle and buttoned-up Dr. DePaul (Julianne Nicholson), the hospital's sole female doctor, who resents the way Gini is allowed to flaunt her beauty and allure and still be mistaken for a doctor, whereas she herself feels obligated to hide such aspects of herself if she wants to be taken seriously as a professional. Bill Masters's wife, Libby, is a mother-in-waiting who spends her days making a home for nobody; Betty, the prostitute, is prepared to do anything for the chance to live the "normal" life of a wife. One of the things *Masters of Sex* keeps returning to is how out of control of their sexual identities women were in those days; how blithely sorted into slots; how casually they were idealized or debased, dehumanized, reduced to a single function within this system of total control. Of course, the in-joke is that every character on the show "deviates" in some way, or longs to, or feels stifled by the phantom expectations that hang over him or her like a toxic cloud. As Bill tells Gini at one point, 80 percent of the women who come into his office think they're frigid, because Freud had issues in bed. Only Gini manages to be free of this, which is why there's something about her that feels somehow modern, even anachronistic.

Masters of Sex dwells in the moment just before control over women's sexuality and reproduction shifted from men to women. Sex may be completely out in the open now, but it's still defined and controlled by a powerful subset of elite men. In the past thirty years, ideas about what makes women sexy have become narrower, more rigid, and more pornographic in their focus on display and performance. Nancy Jo Sales wrote an article in *Vanity Fair* about the "porn star" aesthetic and young girls' behavior on social media, observing that pornography is not about liberation but about control. The more pornography, the more control. "Girls talk about feeling like they have to be like what they see on TV," the director of a youth-counseling service for teens told Sales. "They talk about body-image issues and not having any role models. They all want to be like the Kardashians." The pervasiveness of the porn aesthetic, combined with the underrepresentation of more multidimensional female characters, affects the attitudes, behavior, and ideas about gender roles in both girls and boys, but it's especially insidious for girls' self-concept, as they constantly absorb the message that the choice comes down to either duck-faced selfies across a portfolio of social-media accounts, or abject invisibility. I'm not sure where the idea comes from that frank presentations of sexuality are somehow "daring" or "iconoclastic" or otherwise exist outside of a repressive norm. If anything, it's the other way around.

Would Gini have been out of the place in the fifties? I don't know. All I know about it I learned from movies and TV shows. It's easy to look back and cluck at the innocence of a time when sex was hidden behind closed doors, especially now that we take for granted that all the doors have been flung wide open. But the majority of female characters are still reduced to a single, salient trait (the mean one, the dumb one, the romantic, the slut), which makes Gini's character seem all the more modern, and as out of place as ever. She's complex and contradictory, a sympathetic homewrecker, a sexual woman who's smart. She stands out even now.

High-gloss cable shows are the house that frank depictions of sex built. You can't sell a cable show today that doesn't also function as a delivery system for hot, writhing, naked people. Part of what's interesting about *Masters of Sex* is that it is a show about a reactionary, prudish time nestled like a pearl in a relentlessly, almost compulsorily lubricious media landscape. It's interesting to look at this from the other side, from a time when "prude-shaming" is as common as "slut-shaming." The idea that frank presentations of sex are somehow daring or iconoclastic is an enduring notion whose time has, perhaps, finally come and gone. As a symbol of a repressive norm, we may have simply replaced "fifties housewife" with "porn star." Given the current environment, it's clear that the biggest imaginative hurdle that viewers of *Masters of Sex* have to overcome is to imagine a time when sex, in any form, was even remotely taboo. *Masters of Sex* is the first such show to be expressly about sex itself — about how people respond to stimulation, what constitutes attraction, and how sex is used for purposes other than procreation or pleasure. Observing strangers having sex has become so pervasive and commonplace, not to mention such big, influential business, that the *New York Times* yawned at a new crop of celebrity-sex-tape "scandals," calling them no more scandalous than a press release, and only marginally more effective. How do you make a show about sex in an era when it's hard to find anything that isn't, at least where women are involved, about sex? *Masters of Sex* demonstrated how. Just because we were always watching people have sex didn't mean we couldn't also be learning something.

9

The Kick-Ass

JUST AFTER THE 2000 FLORIDA ELECTION RECOUNT, MY boyfriend and I flew to Vero Beach, Florida, to spend Christmas with his parents. They were elderly and Republican and, unlike many Floridians, had voted for George W. Bush on purpose. This could have made for some chad-related awkwardness at the dinner table, but we stuck to safe topics during our nightly excursions to Chili's and Outback Steakhouse. By the end of the holiday, I was exhausted, depressed, and very bloated. All I wanted was to get back to California, where I could resume trashing Katherine Harris from a safe distance while eating at restaurants that didn't require waiters to memorize lines. On our last day, on the way to the airport, we stopped in Orlando to visit my boyfriend's brother and his tiny manicurist girlfriend. They suggested we eat lunch in the then newish fake town of Celebration. I perked up. I had just seen *The Truman Show*. I was dying to go.

Celebration was a master-planned community built by the Walt Disney Company. I don't know what the master plan was, exactly, but it looked truly diabolical. The town was built according to Walt Disney's original vision for what he called an experimental prototype community of tomorrow, or EPCOT, which turned out to be more of an experimental prototype community of yesteryear — a themed, sanitized version of a small American town from a time before never. The strangest thing about it was that it felt scrubbed free of all branding and advertising, with the exception, of course, of constant allusions to Disney — the brand residents were literally inhabiting. Celebration wasn't a place so much as an idea made manifest: the idea of transferring your entire existence into a controlled, frictionless fantasy where time could be denied and the world remade to conform to the brand's values. Celebration was a celebration of fear sublimated into nostalgia, of longing for a time that never existed, when nothing was confusing. It was all super-scary totalizing-ideology speculative fiction, except it was non-fiction. After lunch at a bright, colorful Cuban restaurant, where in short order I consumed a mojito the size of a watering can, we stepped outside into the dazzling Florida sunshine, and we were suddenly caught in a regularly scheduled fake snowfall, accompanied by piped-in Christmas music. Oh, sure, nobody blinks an eye now. Sure, now I'll meet my friends for dinner and fake snowfalls at the Grove, an outdoor mall in Los Angeles, around Christmas because the kids like it. But at the time, probably because I was buzzed and really excited to get on that plane, something shifted, and I felt myself yield like butter to the frictionless, engineered, pathologically dishonest pleasure of the experience.

*

Maybe I expected too much from life. Maybe a fake approximation of winter, of snow, of a town, of a Cuban restaurant, of an election, of a democracy, and of a president should have been enough. Maybe I should have counted my blessings and shoved down the bad feelings, but things took a very dark turn for me after we went back to my boyfriend's brother's house to pick up some guns, and I sat slumped in the backseat of the SUV like a sullen teenager, listening to Rush Limbaugh fulminate at top volume as the euphoric effects of the cocktail wore off. Suddenly, I had no idea who I was or how I'd arrived in this curious place — not just Florida, all of it. What was I doing here? Could I be here and still be myself? Who was I? By the time we reached the shooting range, I was in the grip of a full-blown identity crisis, and within seconds of stepping inside

I burst into tears, bolted for the door, and spent the rest of the afternoon alone in the backseat of the car, reading Jane Austen.

Later, on the plane ride home, I found myself wondering: If this story had been a scene in a movie and I had been the heroine, would I have qualified as a "strong female character"? And if not, then what was I? What would an ass-kicking heroine do in a situation such as this? Toss off an epigram while shooting up the satellite radio in the Escalade? Reveal a hidden talent for martial arts by jumping over the rifle-range counter and beating the gun guy to a pulp? What would she be wearing, flats or stilettos? How about flip-flops?

I did not feel strong. I was in my early thirties, and I had no idea where my life was headed. Everything felt fake, somehow, arbitrary, like the life next to the life I wanted to be living but had not managed to have. I was writing a lot of reality-show recaps at work—early chronicles of *Big Brother*, *Temptation Island*, *Chains of Love*, stuff like that. I recapped a one-time reality FOX special called *Who Wants to Marry a Multi-Millionaire*, a pageant in which a group of women competed for a rich husband they'd never met, and the winner, in this case an emergency-room nurse, married him on the air. The rich husband turned out to be not so rich and not so nice, or insufficiently vetted by the producers, and the marriage was swiftly annulled. I assume the nurse went back to work—rescued again, only this time from an actual villain, not from her perfectly good life.

Charlie's Angels: The Movie came out later that year. It was a fun, fun, fun pastiche of one of my favorite childhood shows. It was also a corrective to the "strong female characters" of the eighties and nineties. Throughout my tweens, teens, and twenties, female action heroes (with the notable, and notably glorious exception of Goldie Hawn in *Private Benjamin*) had been portrayed as damaged women in the mold of Demi Moore's *G.I. Jane*—all sublimated rage channeled into upper-arm strength. It felt like they all had no kid, a dead kid, or something terrible happened to their kid — they were sad. Their strength had to be explained in this way: robbed of their maternal fulfillment, they became lady-dudes. Because you couldn't just have them running around fighting crime or exploring space or whatever without explaining where the hell their kids were. You couldn't show them having *fun*. You couldn't show them running around in bathing suits with no muscle definition, like *Wonder Woman* or *Charlie's Angels* in the seventies — at least not with a straight face — and get away with it. So, *Charlie's Angels: The Movie* did it as a joke. It gave us the postfeminist kick-ass, the pastiche heroine.

Like Celebration, *Charlie's Angels: The Movie* made it safe to be nostalgic about problematic old times by stripping them of their context. Reframed as pastiche in a social and political vacuum, Cameron Diaz, Drew Barrymore, and Lucy Liu allowed us to enjoy the problematic action heroines of their/our childhood ironically and therefore unproblematically. It was commentary and commentary on commentary, a dizzying hall-of-mirrors representation of the cultural cloning that was peaking around that time. Remakes have a lot more in common with cloning than just copying. Like cloning, a remake involves tricking an idea into thinking it has been fertilized. But the idea is not fresh, the idea is old. It has been reproduced many times. Its telomeres have degraded over the years. The new movie is not the identical twin of the original, which sprang from a temporal context that is now gone forever. It is a product of the present moment, with all the experience that entails. It is genetically grown-up. It can't unknow what it knows. That it pretends not to know makes it suspect.

Unlike the characters on the original TV show, or the heroines of a Jane Austen novel, the sexy, self-reliant, unruffled ass kickers of *Charlie's Angels: The Movie* were at once highly destructive and apparently indestructible. They were girls removed from history, from time and space. In this ahistorical vacuum, consequences don't exist. There is no cause and effect, nor does anyone care about cause and effect (we infer), because caring about consequences, and even acknowledging that there is any such thing as a fact or reality, is for suckers. (The president would soon confirm this.) On the bright side, at least the heroines of *Charlie's Angels: The Movie* had fun together, as friends. At least they had adventures, even if they were utterly fantastical. The following year, the girl most removed from history was *Lara Croft: Tomb Raider,* one of the first movies based on a video game. The kick-ass kicked ass in a vacuum — she kicked theoretical ass. She was the exceptional girl, the one to whom the rules did not reply, the one who wasn't a person but an idea.

The phrase "reality-based community" was still three years away from being coined when, in the aftermath of 9/11, President Bush suggested we all go shopping and book our Disneyland vacations. But it's clear we were already living in a world where discernible reality was already hard to locate, especially on-screen. If *Flashdance* introduced the aesthetic of the music video (all style) to the movies, then *Charlie's Angels: The Movie* turned the movies into a commercial (all reference, all association, all echo). It was a new reality created out of the weakened chromosomes of past realities, taken out of context, scrubbed free of problems, idealized, and dehistoricized. We were so sophisticated. We were so postmodern. We were so above it all. As Karl Rove would tell the *New York Times,* "We're an empire now, and when we act, we create our own reality. And while you're studying that reality — judiciously, as you will — we'll act again, creating other new realities." *Judiciously, as you idiots will.*

In a 2013 interview in *New York* magazine, screenwriter Damon Lindelof talked about the entropy that afflicts Hollywood movies now that their budgets have become so gigantic they require gigantic special effects and "larger-than-life characters wielding those effects" to match. It's a proportionality issue. Anything that isn't puffed up to monster size and steeled against the whims of the marketplace by a force field of sheer humongousness looks weak, puny, and doomed by comparison. Lindelof called this "story gravity" and credited it with distorting everything from plots to characters. "It's almost impossible to, for example, not have a final set piece where the fate of the free world is at stake," he said.

This Dr. Seussian "biggering" of stakes (*"The Avengers* aren't going to save Guam, they've got to save the world," Lindelof said by way of example), coupled with the usual sense of moral and historical unassailability, has a deadening effect on contemporary blockbusters. Characters are reduced to performative types (the hero, the villain, the girl) and planted against one interchangeable backdrop or another to enact the same story over and over again. Watching these movies is like being hit repeatedly over the head with a monolithic ideology obsessed with rehearsing its goodness and rightness. It also rewires your brain. This is the story we're told again and again: no matter how bad things get ecologically, financially, corporately, health care–wise, or inequality-wise, our exceptionalism, embodied by a "regular guy" pumped up and morally enraged to mythic proportions, will save us. And it takes a viewer who thinks of himself as a "regular guy," the unobjectionable center of the universe, to tell the story of this story without impugning its agenda, with a straight face.

The difference, according to Slavoj Žižek, between the way ideology used to work and the way it works now is that we used to accept it at face value. Now our naïveté has been replaced by a cynical awareness — what he calls the "paradox of an enlightened false consciousness."[1] We see the gap between reality and the distorted representation of reality, and we understand it's lying to us. We don't renounce it, we just note that we are noting it. We mock it. Susan J. Douglas talks about a similar shift in feminism in her book *The Rise of Enlightened Sexism*. If you grew up in the seventies and eighties, then you thought of yourself as living in a postfeminist world. You solved the problem of living in a sexist world that pretended not to be sexist anymore by noticing it in quotation marks and not caring, by detaching and shrugging it off as though it were all a joke, or unreal. But it wasn't.

The Lindelof interview is a perfect example of this complex mental adjustment in action. No fewer than five times, he alluded to his awareness of the problems inherent in this mode of storytelling and his fundamental inability to do anything about it. "But ultimately I do feel — even as a purveyor of it — slightly turned off by this destruction porn that has emerged and become very bold-faced this past summer," Lindelof said. "And again, guilty as charged. It's hard not to do it, especially because a movie, if properly executed, feels like it's escalating." He said this "destruction porn" was almost inescapable: "Once you spend more than $100 million on a movie, you have to save the world. And when you start there, you are very limited in terms of how you execute that. And in many ways, you can become a slave to it."

I was reminded of the Lindelof interview recently while watching Alfonso Cuarón's technically marvelous but emotionally weightless *Gravity*, which despite its surface soulfulness eventually gives way to the relentless, if-it's-not-one-damn-thing-it's-another thrill ride we've come to expect. On a routine space mission with veteran astronaut Matt Kowalsky (George Clooney), the ship suffers damage and Dr. Ryan Stone (Sandra Bullock) winds up all alone, in space. In the first few minutes of the movie, during a deep-space getting-to-know-you scene with Kowalsky, it's revealed that Ryan had a very young daughter who died in a freak playground accident and untethered her from the world.

I'd expected *Gravity* to be a meditation on existence. I thought that Clooney would remain in Bullock's ear throughout, prompting some existential exploration, leading her to some liberating insight. Why I'd expected this, I have no idea. I should have expected the obstacle-course plot with its tedious oscillation of progress and setback, like a football game. In *The Martian*, Matt Damon's character, Mark Watney, is also struck by debris and stranded in space, and it is presumed that we will care about him and like him even though he has no family and no backstory, because he requires no justification. He's a person, and we care about people unconditionally. But the dead-baby detail seemed to say that we couldn't care about this character, a woman in her forties, unless she was both impressively toned and a tragically bereaved mother. There had to be a kid, and the kid had to be dead. How else could we be OK with this woman drifting so far, far away from home?

Watching Ryan (the boy's name implies you can trust her) struggle to overcome impossible odds all by herself didn't really make me feel good. It didn't make me feel empowered. I didn't identify, except maybe with her loneliness and insignificance, and with the coldness and cruelty of the world around her. (Was it a world, even? She has no context.) It didn't make me feel anything, except slightly anxious and clenched, because what in the world is this lady if not a long-suffering Job in space? I mean, it's one thing after another. The calamities that befall her are biblical. A plague of boils would not have come as a surprise. By the time she swims her way to the surface of the water at the end of the movie, I was half expecting her to encounter and single-handedly fend off a ravenous shark, possibly even an entire "sharknado." I wasn't moved by this ritual performance of steely individualism and emotional compartmentalization against the world. I'm tired of the same binary battles between good and evil. I'm tired of fascist allegories; they exhaust me. I reject being told over and over again that even our basic survival in a vast, cold, indifferent universe is 100 percent dependent on us and our biceps. That even George Clooney is deadweight, and Sandra Bullock must pull herself up by her own parachute cords, all alone in the universe, and crawl back into her womb capsule and shoot back to Earth.

I did not expect to have all these thoughts and feelings validated while watching *Doll and Em*, a tiny show about two Englishwomen in America, but that's exactly what happened. Written by real-life best friends Emily Mortimer and Dolly Wells, the show is in many ways about the alienating effects of story gravity on real women — even movie stars. It is the aesthetic and ethical opposite of *Gravity*. Everything about the show is small: the moments, the stakes, the teeny-tiny slights and misunderstandings that trigger emotional cataclysms — which are, of course, mostly repressed. In the first season of the show, waitress and late bloomer Doll breaks up with her boyfriend in London, so movie star Em invites her to come to L.A. and be her personal assistant on a movie she is doing. It is, of course, a terrible idea; not just because Doll and Em grew up together under uncannily similar circumstances (they are almost mirror images of each other) but also because the power imbalance is too great. Em has "everything": a husband, two kids, a home, a successful acting career; and Doll has "nothing": no marriage, no children, no success, no home.

And yet something weird happens when Doll joins Em in L.A. on the set of a dumb movie she is making for an awful young director who treats Em, who is forty, like shit: the imbalance of power is unsustainable, and it starts to spill over into resentment, envy, passive aggression, and outright sabotage. In *Doll and Em*, Emily is struggling with her role as a "strong woman" whom her director describes as "the female *Godfather* — the strongest woman ever!" She's supposed to cry in one scene but can't, even though, as she tells Dolly, in real life she cries every day. She can't relate to the part at all and feels completely alienated from it. Dolly responds by demonstrating her amazing ability to trick herself to cry on cue by thinking of something else; and Em is required to praise her. Em's inability to connect emotionally with the idiotic role, coupled with the blatant contempt of her self-important director, erodes her confidence until it's completely gone. The problem is that "she keeps on being told how wonderful it is that she gets to play this strong woman and how there aren't nearly enough parts for strong women," Mortimer said in an interview. "It's such a cliché conversation in our business. 'God, it's such a wonderful opportunity to play this strong woman!' It was just amusing to us that the more Em gets told how lucky she is, the more freaked out she feels about how she's not nearly strong enough to play this strong woman." This fictional strength only makes the real woman playing her feel silly and weak.

Here was a story I could relate to. I'd been so tired of "strong female characters" for so long by then. I was so tired of the way female strength was made to look cold and humorless; the way it was characterized as deviant and "unnatural" and always lonely and exceptional. I was tired of the grim undertone of tragedy that lurked under its surface. "Strong female characters" were never funny, and they never had any fun, either. More often than not, they were celibate, friendless, and clinically depressed. Their monomaniacal devotion to crime fighting made them lean, cranky, and impatient. Naturally, they had axes to grind: they were avenging brides, poker-faced assassins, gloomy ninjas with commitment issues. Who were these characters? What were they trying to tell us? Why didn't they ever say goodbye before hanging up the phone? And why were they always being reborn or remade as killing machines after losing everything they held dear?

Maybe it's because I've given birth that I'm not necessarily keen on reliving the experience, nor prone to burden it with metaphors. I'm indifferent to images of rebirth, unless what's being reborn is the whole system. I don't want to see another symbolic woman start all over again. I want to see the symbolic world change to acknowledge her existence. I don't want to see the young girl get a makeover or go shopping with her boyfriend's credit card. I want to watch her blow up the Death Star — metaphorically, of course.

PART THREE

You Wouldn't Have Come Here

"In *that* direction," the Cat said, waving its right paw round, "lives a Hatter: and in *that* direction," waving the other paw, "lives a March Hare. Visit either you like: they're both mad."

"But I don't want to go among mad people," Alice remarked.

"Oh, you can't help that," said the Cat: "we're all mad here. I'm mad. You're mad."

"How do you know I'm mad?" said Alice.

"You must be," said the Cat, "or you wouldn't have come here."

— LEWIS CARROLL, *ALICE'S ADVENTURES IN WONDERLAND*

10

Surreal Housewives

IN 2000, THE FEMINIST FILM-AND-TELEVISION SCHOLAR Charlotte Brunsdon published a book called *The Feminist, the Housewife, and the Soap Opera,* which chronicled the story of second-wave feminist theorists' obsession with soaps. In interviews with prominent scholars, she asked why feminist critics of the 1970s were so interested in the genre. The consensus came back that because soaps "were perceived to be both for and about women," feminists studied them as part of "a commitment to knowing thine enemy." The personal was suddenly political in those days, and soap operas helped feminists define themselves in opposition to "an imagined other, the soap opera–watching housewife."[1] More than thirty years later, these venerable tropes — the angry feminist and the happy housewife — remain locked in the same musty semiotic cage, at least they do in the public imagination.

Every new generation of women, it seems, feminist and housewife alike, is encouraged by popular culture to disavow its forebears and rebrand itself as an all-new, never-before-seen generational phenomenon, completely different in every way from what came before. The "housewives" of the 1970s gave way to the Martha Stewart "homemakers" of the 1980s, then the "soccer moms" of the 1990s, then the stay-at-home moms of the 2000s. Next may come the homeschooling homesteaders of the impending postapocalypse — who knows? What's significant is that the cycle of idealization, devaluation, and revision gives an appearance of progress, of superficial change, that distracts us from the big picture. The word *housewife* itself went from connoting drudgery to evoking the privilege to indulge in self- and home care 24/7. We loathe the housewife now, but we love her modern rebranding — now with complicated new signifiers! If the Stepford Wife was the Victorian "true woman" of the mid- to late twentieth century, the movie *The Stepford Wives* gave us permission to reframe and vilify her as the "angel in the house" of the "me decade" and to hold her entirely responsible for choosing to devote herself to domestic perfection. By the time the label "Stepford Wife" entered the lexicon, it had completely turned in on itself. She was no longer a murdered wife replaced by a robot but a shallow, conformist woman who chooses to turn herself into an automaton and who deserves what she gets. Three decades after the movie came out, *The Stepford Wives* was remade as a corrective to the original. In the remake, the problem is not that marriage snuffs out women's humanity and turns them into robots, but that their jobs do. The villainous patriarch Diz, the head of the Men's Association, is recast as a woman: a former neurosurgeon and engineer played, of all people, by Hollywood's favorite loneliness-crazed, career-lady menace, Claire (Glenn Close), whose husband has left her for her assistant and who therefore vows to turn back the clock to a time, as Claire says, "before overtime, quality time, a time before women were turning themselves into robots."

It can be easy to forget that the ubiquitous *Real Housewives* franchise was born of a housewifely renaissance kicked off by the long-gone *Desperate Housewives,* which in turn evolved from 2004, when Frank Oz remade *The Stepford Wives.* Given the archconservatism of that moment, it's not surprising that the show — or, perhaps more accurately, the cultural meme it rode in on — struck such a cultural nerve that then First Lady Laura Bush made a joke about it at the 2005 White House Correspondents' Dinner: "Nine o'clock, Mr. Excitement here is sound asleep and I'm watching *Desperate Housewives.* With Lynne Cheney. Ladies and gentlemen, I am a desperate housewife."

At the time, the phrase "desperate housewives" had only recently been reappropriated, and it still carried with it the easy shock of the original pejorative. Or maybe the *Real Housewives* are the legacy of eighties nighttime soaps like *Dynasty* and *Dallas*. Producer Scott Dunlop had been wanting to make a film about Coto de Caza, the exclusive gated community in Orange County where he lived, when it occurred to him that the housewife subculture of Coto de Caza would make for the ideal reality show. As much as the realism of the original Orange County version was self-consciously constructed by its stars, the germ of something organic was there — basically, Bravo lifted a rock and found *Real Housewives,* a hit show.

The housewives are so far removed from housewifery that they're not even all married. Whether they are single, married, or divorced, whether they work or have children, and whether they came by their money through marriage or made it themselves, what they pride themselves in is their ability to pass for ladies of means, leisure, and indulgent patronage. The "real housewives" fill their days with shopping, grooming, lunching, feuding, and self-promoting. What they don't do, actually, is housework — although some of them take offense at the suggestion that they employ others to manage their households and do the drudge work. Even assuming that the intended audience is made up primarily of married women, the feminist intellectual and the soap-watching housewife are not so diametrically opposed anymore. If anything, the contemporary reality-show consumer is conscious of the fact that what she is watching is a performance based on the theme of housewife, which is being performed in service to a personal brand. The "real housewives" have as much in common with June Cleaver as she had in common with Cleopatra.

The spin-offs, however, didn't have quite the same "found" quality. They are much more self-consciously constructed. These shows were predicated on the ability of their members to have married "well," and some of the later spin-offs have a more artificial, less anthropological feel.

Across the various iterations, the "real housewives" flaunted their refusal to conform to the happy modern housewife ideal as though they were breaking the law by spending their days drinking, sparring, and shopping. They proudly showed off their incompetence in the kitchen (as when Adrienne of Beverly Hills washed a chicken with hand soap), or their disinterest in sex (as when Lisa Vanderpump joked about treating sex as a twice-annual gift to her husband), or their limited patience for parenthood (like Camille, who gave birth to her kids via a surrogate and employed one nanny per kid). Some, like Camille, made a point of treating their employees like beloved friends and their beloved friends like employees, whereas others, like Larsa Pippen, bragged to friends about their deep-seated nanny hatred and their compulsive need to fire them. Their lives were constantly being exposed as shams in the tabloids as they continued to deconstruct the feminine mystique on-screen and reconstruct it for the New New Gilded Age (Gilded Age III: More for Me). They hawked their lifestyle brands. When wronged, they became pure vessels for sorrow. They fell apart in public and wasted away in plain sight. They suffered exquisitely.

Back in the seventies, when the women Brunsdon wrote about were busy creating a new idea of themselves, a housewife was something a middle-class woman had to resist becoming by default. Today, far from having to actively resist falling into the role of housewife in a traditional marriage, a young feminist (or even a not-so-young, not-so-feminist) woman is more likely to find herself outside of that role as a matter of course. There are twice as many women in their early forties who have not given birth now than there were in the mid-seventies. The "real housewives," in many cases, seem to have become, to paraphrase Gloria Steinem, the women the men they wanted to marry would have married had not the whole enterprise gone bust.

For women of this peer group, it's the retro designation "housewife" — with its shades of housework and mothering stripped away, and its connotations of laziness and sluttiness dialed way up —

that confers a perverse status and allows them entry into the televised Have-It-All Olympics. These are the Veblen housewives, the women whose job it is to make a performance of excess in the service of the status of their husbands, even when their husbands are less rich, or less famous, or simply not in the picture. Skills are not necessary, but shame is not allowed. Here's how it works. A group of highly competitive, thoroughly confused women are pitted against each other in five events: wealth, youth, beauty/body, husband, and glamour career. In order to participate, a housewife must qualify in at least three of these categories. She does not need to have all of them in order to win, but it helps. Some categories trump others. For instance, wealth trumps beauty, and husband trumps glamour job. Kids plus husband trump job, too — unless the process of acquiring them leads to a show of one's own. Every show features at least one aggressive instigator whose job it is to ratchet up the jealousy and paranoia and to keep the interpersonal conflicts coming. All you really have to do to be a "real housewife" is take pride in your privilege, your leisure, your profligacy, and your willingness to ratchet up the melodrama at every possible opportunity. You can't win unless somebody else loses.

As a product, this is not so terribly different from what previous "real housewives," the descendants of Julia Child and, more directly, Martha Stewart on cable, were selling. The big difference is that it isn't designed to make you feel bad about your incompetence, or lack of ease, or shortage of creativity, or crushing scarcity of time to do anything but get by with the bare minimum in the domestic sphere. A few channels over from Bravo, on the Food Network and the hipper, cuter Cooking Channel, a new generation of Nigellas is focused on the sensual and communal pleasures of home cooking — just as across the cable landscape, a new generation of crafters and gardeners and decorators and DIYers offers visions of what it would be like to spend one's days ministering to domestic surroundings. These shows cater to a whole different set of fantasies: the fantasy that there is a gracious, lovingly created domestic sphere that needs tending to in the first place, for instance; the fantasy that there is time and energy left over after work, commute, and unglamorous chores to swan around one's beautiful kitchen dipping one's manicured fingers in bowls of chocolate or whipping up mini crème brûlées for unexpected guests; the fantasy that such a thing as unexpected guests who show up demanding crème brûlée even exists.

The "real housewives" are nothing like these people. They are not gracious nor accomplished nor poised. They do not handle themselves with aplomb or display grace under pressure. They do not have housewifely tips to hand down, tips on getting the kids to eat their vegetables or saving on the grocery bill. They will never make you feel bad about your own lack of domestic perfection. What they're selling is the idea that they have it better, or at least easier, than you do — even though they really don't deserve it. This appropriation of the term *housewife* may be somewhat ironic, but it's not at all apologetic. Whether or not they are in on the self-parody, their purpose is not to be emulated or admired but to be envied and despised.

It's interesting how pop culture has recast housewifery as leisurely and lucrative, especially given that the issue of unpaid gendered labor (a.k.a. "the second shift") has not been resolved. On the contrary, it has been found, conclusively, to be the number one thing holding women back in their careers. A survey of Harvard Business School graduates in the *Harvard Business Review* discovered that women disproportionately failed to meet the goals they set for themselves in their twenties not because they'd "opted out" but because their husbands' careers were prioritized over their own. Researchers found that "Harvard MBAs value fulfilling professional and personal lives — yet their ability to realize them has played out very differently according to gender."[2]

Upon graduation, more than 70 percent of male HBS grads who were Gen-Xers or baby boomers said they expected their careers to take precedence over their partners' careers — and only 7 percent of Gen-X women and 3 percent of baby-boomer women said they expected their careers to come first. Women, overwhelmingly, expected egalitarian marriages in which both careers would be treated with equal seriousness. Their expectations were unmet. In the end, about 40 percent of the Gen-X and boomer women surveyed said their husbands' careers ended up taking priority, even though only about half of them had planned on putting their own careers on the back burner. Child-care statistics painted an even more unequal picture: 86 percent of Gen-X and boomer men said their wives were responsible for most of the child care. Women Harvard Business School graduates with jobs said this was true to the tune of 65 percent of Gen-X women and 72 percent of boomer women.

The entire *Real Housewives* franchise is predicated on the assumption that we bring a healthy dose of contempt for such people to the table. We aren't just conditioned to not have any empathy for the housewife character, we're constantly reminded not to. The *Real Housewives* are never deserving of our empathy because they aren't real people, even as, somehow, tales of their desperation keep getting produced and dismissed. Or maybe the "real" modifier refers to their true, essential nature, and is intended to smear its own heroines as ornamental, parasitic, venal. Either way, they are built for hatred. And yet, ironically, as Laura Miller writes in a 2016 *Slate* essay called "The Resurgence of the Housewife Novel," "to be so materially lucky that you're not allowed to experience any discontent at all turns out to be just another way of being swallowed up by your social role."

The *Real Housewives* spin-offs (which I love! and recapped for years!) are arenas where ideas about how women should live — what they should do, how they should self-identify, how they should be judged — duke it out in the dirtiest, most extreme, most performative way possible. And the "real housewives" themselves are the embodiment of all that is impossible to reconcile in women. Maybe the women's willingness to turn everything we've been simultaneously conditioned to expect and to reject about the feminine ideal into a stylized performance for their own profit is progress of a kind — for them, anyway. For the rest of us, symbolically, it doesn't help much. The people who make these shows aren't stupid. They might even be evil geniuses, subverting the housewife mystique once and for all, crawling into its navel Matrix-style and exploding the myth from the inside. Or maybe they are unconsciously perpetuating the categories they've been made into prototypes of. Either way, they remind us that we're a little screwed.

What the *Real Housewives* creators — clever devils — did was professionalize the role of wife entirely outside the parameters of marriage: they turned wifeliness into a scalable, husbandless brand. More than the Martha Stewart–style domestic lifestyle gurus that preceded them — with all their tiresome skills and fussy creative endeavors — the Bravo housewives have turned the role of housewife into a job whose main purpose is to sell a ruinously expensive and hard-to-support lifestyle to a generation that is at once ideologically opposed to and functionally barred from such a lifestyle. They reinforce the already widely accepted idea that what you represent is much more important than what you do — and representing housewifely leisure has turned out to be a surprisingly lucrative line of work.

11

Real Girls

OVID'S PYGMALION IS A SCULPTOR WHO CARVES A GIRL out of ivory, falls in love with her, and prays to Venus to make her real. The reason he goes through the trouble, instead of just popping out to the agora and meeting someone nice, is that all the women he knows in real life are whores. And it's true: Venus has turned them into prostitutes as punishment for refusing to worship her. There's a lesson in there somewhere: like so many love stories, Pygmalion stories aren't about love at all — they're about compliance.

You can learn a lot about the longings and generalized gender anxieties of an era by the kinds of fake women it dreams up. In *The Iliad*, Hephaestus, the god of metalsmithing and technology, created, among other human-looking machines, two female automatons made of gold. In Fritz Lang's *Metropolis* (1927), a mad scientist constructs the evil-robot doppelganger of a beautiful labor organizer to destroy her reputation. In the sixties sitcom *My Living Doll*, a psychiatrist is entrusted with a sexy, artificially intelligent gynoid and programs her to be the perfect woman (hint: she is silent and completely subservient). In *The Stepford Wives* the same thing happens on a bigger scale. In *Weird Science*, nerdy teen outcasts program a 1980s power glamazon on their computer, who starts out scary and destructive but eventually helps them self-actualize. In the 2004 remake of *The Stepford Wives*, the husbands turn their wives into robots so they can play video games without being nagged. Scarlett Johansson's voice in *Her* (2013) is a disembodied, artificially intelligent operating system that exists only as an iterative idea between Joaquin Phoenix's head and the cloud, and it/she becomes so perfect that she surpasses him and escapes his control. In *Ex Machina* (2015), a young programmer named Caleb wins a contest to spend a week with his multibillionaire search-engine-creator boss, Nathan, at his isolated bunkerlike compound, where Nathan introduces him to Ava, a sentient AI in a female body. Eventually, Caleb finds out that Ava is a composite of his porn preferences and other online behavior, and that he wasn't selected at random but was recruited to test Ava not for sentience but for the capacity to love. Ultimately, she surpasses her creator. She kills him, locks up Caleb, and lets herself loose upon a world full of men conditioned to feel something like a love response for their algorithmic porn preferences. She's the fear, personified, automated, weaponized.

So what else is new. Almost all movies about artificial women are *Frankenstein* stories, if they have any self-awareness at all. Some are cautionary tales, warning that perfection is inhuman, that it's monstrous to play God. Some pity the monster — the girl. In *Ex Machina*, the AI robot is a princess locked in a tower, isolated and alone. She understands she's not real, but she feels real — not just to the people who made her; to herself. She seems real to us, especially in contrast with Nathan's inhumanity. In *Westworld,* a whole alternate world full of fake women created to cater to fantasies forged by violence and porn is created. All of the fake girls are perfect. The question they raise, though, is: perfect for what?

Around the time I attended the academic porn conference, in the late nineties, a friend sent me a link as a joke. It was the website of a then new company called RealDoll that made hyperrealistic sex dolls that started at about $5,500. The dolls were fully customizable, like MINI Coopers. Customers designed their own dolls from a menu of options, including face and body type, breast size, hair (head and pubic) color and style, nipple circumference and hue, and number of functioning orifices. The dolls' weight and height approximated human proportions (small, except in the breast area, where they tended to range from large to enormous), and they could be warmed up to body temperature by being placed in a hot tub. You could play around with the options and preview your doll online. So I did. I did it again. I couldn't stop doing it. I completely freaked myself out. I felt like Joanna in *The Stepford Wives* when she walks into the room at the Men's Association and confronts the dead-eyed, silicone version of herself staring back at her vacantly.

Until the moment I went on the RealDolls website, my image of sex dolls had been more or less fixed on what it was when I first saw the movie *Airplane!*, when I was nine. In my mind, a sex doll was a joke, a novelty item or gag gift. I imagined an inflatable pool toy. I was shocked and unnerved by the dolls' verisimilitude. They looked so uncannily real yet unreal, only silent and completely inert. And yet creepy as the dolls were, nothing scared me more than the customer testimonials on the company website; these rapturous, highly emotional testimonials from satisfied customers thanking the company for finally solving their problems with women by providing them with an alternative to women. They loved their dolls so much. The dolls were everything the customers wished real women were, but weren't.

Last I heard, the company was diligently working on artificially intelligent models, like Stepford Wives. Maybe they will be official sponsors of the real-life *Westworld*, whenever that comes. A new world made just for them.

Stories about men making artificial women have always been around, but they've started to migrate from fiction to nonfiction, and they're not morality tales anymore, they're wish fulfillment. The stories were fantastical and the debate was hypothetical. You could only speculate on the ramifications of choosing artificial women over real ones. Now you don't have to. Afterward, I discovered a BBC documentary called *Guys and Dolls*. The film interviewed RealDoll owners who thought of the dolls as girlfriends. One of the subjects was "Davecat," a Goth in his thirties who lived with his parents and his doll outside Detroit. Davecat explained that he had saved for a year to buy the doll. He called her Sidore, or Shi-Chan, for short. At first, his interest in her had been merely sexual, but he'd come to see her as a companion. He said his father had a hard time accepting their relationship, but Davecat tried not to let it get to him. To him, the doll was not a substitute for a real woman, she was better. He said that not only was she more beautiful than any real woman he could ever "get," but she was exactly whatever he wanted her to be — nothing more and nothing less. "Shi-Chan is an anchor to me because I know what to expect," he said. "With women, you don't really get that."

In 2012, Davecat resurfaced in an episode of the TLC show *My Strange Addiction*. By now, he'd gotten his own apartment, bought matching rings with the inscription "Synthetik love lasts forever" for himself and Sidore, and started referring to her as his wife (which he said many of his friends, in particular his female friends, were very accepting of). He had also ordered a second doll to join them in a polyamorous relationship. Asked if he ever dated real women, Davecat replied that he had had flings with "organic" women in the past but that he never felt secure in them. He took his doll out to dinner with a female friend. His friend was very accepting, and the waitress was curious and cool. Davecat said the relationship with his doll Sidore made him happy, and "if that's what makes me happy, well, that's what makes me happy. And I really see no reason to change."

In 2013, Davecat was featured in an *Atlantic* article sounding less weird and abject, and more empowered, like an advocate. He called himself a "technosexual" and described himself as "an activist for synthetic love and the rights of synthetic humans." Throughout the segment, he referred to "organic" women as "organiks." He chose his words carefully to reflect what appeared to be a slight shift in his position. He no longer distinguished between dolls and women but rather separated women into "organic" and "synthetic" ones. Not only did he not think of his "synthetic" girlfriend as a substitute, he preferred her silicone skin and slightly stilted movements. He wrote an e-mail to the interviewer:

> Now the important thing to remember is that gynoids and androids are like organic humans, but they would lack the qualities that make organics difficult to deal with. They would be pleasant, agreeable, non-judgmental, aesthetically and mentally pleasing, and more. In day-to-day existence, most people have to deal with at least one person whom they'd rather avoid at all costs. The way I see things, your spouse should be easygoing and a joy to come home to, to counteract having to deal with all manner of undesirables when you're out and about. I think the best way to reach that goal is through humanoid robots. It's like having your cake, and eating it too.[1]

In 2014, Davecat was interviewed in *Vice*. He told the reporter that he preferred his relationship with his doll wife to "messy" human relationships, because "when you love an organic, you're really loving two people: there's the idea of the person that you fall with love with and then there's the actual person—and at some point, the idea is going to disappear and you are going to bump straight into the actual person. You have to come to terms with the discrepancy between those two people. And for that matter, they're doing the same thing with you too."

"So, with a synthetic," the reporter said, summing it up, "the fantasy and the reality are identical."

"Exactly," Davecat said.

Of course, Pygmalion himself was an artificial creation. As a character in a story, he existed entirely as a symbol in a larger system of meaning. Davecat, by contrast, is a character in this chapter, and in an episode of a TLC show, and in several documentaries and magazine articles, but he's a real guy who has invented a fictional universe around a doll that he expects the world to validate and normalize, and in doing so he raises a lot of interesting questions. For example, this one: Does appropriating the language of inclusivity to talk about a plastic fuck doll help promote tolerance, or does the existence of the dolls degrade the actual people they've been designed to replace? Because the more I read new interviews or caught his appearances in new videos, and the more ensconced he was in this worldview of the dolls as real women who just happened to be made of silicone, the weirder about it I felt. Was it OK to be creeped out? Or was I a horrible, judgmental organicist? To be honest, I was relieved when I came across the person in a website comments section who expressed the feelings I was scared to express, or even to feel. "He is trying to insist to the world that dolls are women. He doesn't refer to them as dolls, and actually bristles at the fact that other people do," the person wrote. "He comes up with dehumanizing language for women and bristles at imagined slights towards his toys."

About two years later, Davecat reappeared in a *Reason* article called "Sex, Love, and Robots." By then, he'd added a third doll to his collection. Asked about how he felt regarding a sex robot currently on the market, he replied, "All told, I'd rather have a Gynoid than a Doll," he wrote to the author of the piece. "Dolls are fantastic, but realistically speaking, they can only do so much, and with a completely Synthetik lover, I'd have all the opportunities that are afforded in relationships with Organiks, but without all the drama." The article entertains all the possible repercussions of a robot-surrogate sexual future, both optimistic and pessimistic. One technologist quoted wondered if it would lead to more unrealistic expectations of women. Regarding this, the author of the piece wrote that "some men are already predicting this day with glee, crowing on blogs and Reddit boards that human women will have to lower their expectations, step up their beauty rituals, or face the fact that many men will find sex robots a 'better option.'"

By then, I didn't feel so bad about being creeped out.

In 1970, a Japanese roboticist named Masahiro Mori conducted an experiment in which he graphed people's emotional reactions to humanoid things that weren't human. He plotted people's feelings along the y-axis, as they reacted to things like toy robots, stuffed animals, androids, Bunraku puppets, prosthetic hands, and zombies, which were plotted along the x-axis. What he found was that people loved things that looked vaguely human, but only up to a point. Past a certain threshold, too much verisimilitude was freaky. Most people agree that toy robots are cute, for instance, but that highly realistic sex dolls are repulsive. There are differing theories on why this is. It may be because, when looking at something that looks almost but not quite human, we sense that some ineffable thing is missing. The cognitive dissonance that arises from meeting something that's at once incredibly lifelike and clearly lifeless fills us with dread. Mori called the effect the "uncanny valley." The "valley" was the steep dip on the graph where hyperrealism yielded revulsion. The "uncanny" (which doesn't exactly correspond to the Japanese word Mori used) comes from Freud, who used the word to describe the nightmarish feeling you get from things that are familiar yet deeply strange: seemingly human bodies with dead eyes, corpses that walk, bodies reanimated by sorcery or science. For Freud, a monster was just that: an uncanny mirror of humanity.

The theory of the uncanny valley doesn't technically apply to images of women in pop culture, but it's still a useful metaphor. Girls in pop culture are also often represented in ways that feel almost, but not quite, human. They are lifelike rather than alive, and more than anything they resemble the "idea of woman" in late capitalist culture; the twenty-first-century "true woman." There isn't a girl in the world who has not, at some point, come across an image or portrayal that made her feel a sense of recognition and alienation at the same time, a me/not-me, real/not-real, true/not-true feeling that, once experienced, never quite goes away. Sure, these images and portrayals do not share the same qualities as the objects Mori first mapped — they are not, at least to start with, artificial beings. They aren't cyborgs or replicants or reanimated corpses. But we don't recognize them as human, either, at least not like any humans we know. Some ineffable thing is missing.

12

- - - - - - - - - - -

Celebrity Gothic

Accursed creator! Why did you form a monster so hideous
that even you turned from me in disgust?

— MARY SHELLEY, *FRANKENSTEIN*

IN THE BLUSTERY WILDS OF SUFFOLK COUNTY, IN A SEA-
side hamlet that was once a prominent whaling village, a young girl
is born to a prominent local family in the most decadent decade
of the last century. Soon, her father — an impulsive, reckless, and
moody figure given to fits of sudden rage — is beset by legal trou-
bles and sent to prison for three years. During this time, the girl is
pressed into service — in part, perhaps, to help with the cost of raising her younger siblings — and becomes famous around the world.
When the patriarch emerges from prison, he is enraged to find
that his wife's parasitic family is controlling his daughter's affairs
and that the girl has fled to the far end of the continent and taken
up residence in a gloomy (though recently remodeled) chateau
perched high atop a hill above town. There, she experiences a series
of mysterious afflictions and ailments, and she is repeatedly institutionalized by her family members and business associates struggling to gain control over her estate. The excesses of her ancestors
— cocaine abuse, alcoholism, insider trading, DUIs — come back to
haunt her, and, having escaped from the castle, the girl finds herself
imprisoned once again, electronically shackled in her home, after
a valuable necklace mysteriously appears in her possession. Tragically, her mother is declared mad in a Mother's Day poll on Holly-

scoop.com of the "ten craziest Hollywood moms," which basically seals it: Lindsay Lohan is a textbook persecuted gothic heroine.

In the space of about two months just after Christmas 2006, Lindsay Lohan entered rehab; Anna Nicole Smith was found dead in her suite at the Seminole Hard Rock Hotel and Casino, surrounded by prescription-pill bottles, nicotine gum, and empty cans of SlimFast; and Britney Spears, trailed by paparazzi, walked into a Sherman Oaks tattoo parlor and shaved her head. Each time women like these made headlines, the headlines shot to the top of the most-read lists. The hunger for Britney's pantyless crotch shots dominated even as troop surges, systematic layoffs, and a rise in global warming and global terrorism took place, and as global credit and asset bubbles headed for a pop. It was as though the tabloids were not just distracting us from the scary stuff but enacting our fears and honing our outrage to bite-size pieces. (What were suspect sites and credit-default swaps, anyway?) More virgins were sacrificed to the god of war. Because that's who got it the worst by far: the former child stars and erstwhile Mouseketeers who had the temerity to grow up.

Tabloid stories about celebrity scandals are nothing new, but in that period there was something about their accelerated pace and their recurring themes of excess, addiction, transgression, decadence, madness, alienation, and confinement (jail! rehab! house arrest!) that seemed both new and familiar. Like the pursued heroines of eighteenth-century novels, the young celebrity heroines of the tabloid stories were doomed to wander the wilderness, being poked at by villagers wielding sticks and telephoto lenses, or to remain trapped, sealed off in the glass dungeon of their fame. Gothic tropes and motifs spilled over from fiction and permeated reality. In the tabloids, on the Internet, and on reality TV, familiar monsters and villains were created daily: menacing foreigners, corrupt plutocrats, and, most of all, grotesque, abject celebrity train wrecks.

Gothic is the genre of fear. Our fascination with it is almost always revived during times of instability and panic. In the wake of the French Revolution, the Marquis de Sade described the rise of the genre as "the inevitable product of the revolutionary shock with which the whole of Europe resounded," and literary critics in the late eighteenth century mocked the work of early gothic writers Anne Radcliffe and Matthew Lewis by referring to it as "the terrorist school" of writing. As Fred Botting writes in *Gothic*, his lucid introduction to the genre, it expresses our unresolved feelings about "the nature of power, law, society, family and sexuality" and yet is extremely concerned with issues of social disintegration and collapse. It's preoccupied with all that is immoral, fantastic, suspenseful, and sensational and yet prone to promoting middle-class values. It's interested in transgression, but it's ultimately more interested in restitution; it alludes to the past yet is carefully attuned to the present; it's designed to evoke excessive emotion, yet it's thoroughly ambivalent; it's the product of revolution and upheaval, yet it endeavors to contain their forces; it's terrifying, but pretty funny. And, importantly, the gothic always reflects the anxieties of its age in an appropriate package, so that by the nineteenth century, familiar tropes representing external threats like crumbling castles, aristocratic villains, and pesky ghosts had been swallowed and interiorized. In the nineteenth century, gothic horrors were more concerned with madness, disease, moral depravity, and decay than with evil aristocrats and depraved monks. Darwin's theories, the changing roles of women in society, and ethical issues raised by advances in science and technology haunted the Victorian gothic, and the repression of these fears returned again and again in the form of guilt, anxiety, and despair. "Doubles, alter egos, mirrors and animated representations of the disturbing parts of human identity became the stock devices," Botting writes, "signifying the alienation of the human subject from the culture and language in which s/he is located." In the transition from modernity to postmodernity, the very idea of culture as something stable and real is challenged, and so postmodern gothic freaks itself out by dismantling modernist grand narratives and playing games. In the twentieth century,

"Gothic [was] everywhere and nowhere," and "narrative forms and devices spill[ed] over from worlds of fantasy and fiction into real and social spheres."[1]

Our fascination with the gothic peaks in times of anxiety, panic, and upheaval. The Victorian gothic revival of the 1890s was stoked by scientific, technological, and social change. Industrialization and urbanization sparked feelings of alienation, Darwin's theories of evolution and the changing roles of women fanned racist, misogynistic, homophobic, and colonialist fears of "primitivism," moral decay, and sexual depravity. In the nineteenth century, terror-inducing imagery had shifted away from crumbling castles to crime-infested cities, and fear of villains and ghosts was supplanted by a fear of madness and degeneration. In the twentieth century, we celebrated/mourned the death of authorship, of the grand narrative, of the self, "going-one-better in eschatological eloquence," as Jacques Derrida put it, "the end of history . . . the end of the subject, the end of man, the end of the West, the end of Oedipus, the end of the earth, *Apocalypse Now.*" A few years into the new millennium, we were zombie hordes, stalking social media for brains. The gothic is the fucked-either-way-and-freaking-the-fuck-out school of artistic interpretation, the hysterical framework of doom. And this tension between horror as morality tale and horror as decadent spectacle is, I believe, what fueled the pandemic of tabloid stories about wayward starlets that raged throughout 2006 and 2007. Celebrity train wreck stories begin, conservatively, as cautionary tales. A young woman, unprotected or legally emancipated, has moved alone from the relatively sheltered and secluded condition of parent-managed child stardom (because who, nowadays, is more cut off from the world than a child star?) into a corrupt and dangerous world, where her beauty, fame, youth, fortune, and sexual allure are regard with a charged, ambivalent awe. She is instantly besieged with dangers, and preyed upon by unscrupulous adults. Until they can be contained again, by marriage or paternal protection, she exists in a constant state of uncertainty and peril. The peril is created, of course, by the "author" — the media outlets that shape the train wreck's life, again and again, into thrilling, chilling tales of suspense.

Britney Spears, Lindsay Lohan, Paris Hilton, Nicole Ritchie, Anna Nicole Smith, and Michael Jackson (so fascinating for playing Frankenstein to his own monstrous self and so terrifying for his refusal to stay within clear race and gender binaries) also soon found themselves inescapably trapped in the same story of the vulnerable young girl brought down by hubris, ambition, or uncontrolled appetites (by the same libidinous freedom that attracted us in the first place) and transformed into a disorderly, histrionic grotesque.

In telling chilling tales of tabloid train wrecks, we resort again and again to all the gothic themes, motifs, and stock characters.

For instance: Themes of excess, decadence, madness, addiction, depravity, alienation, dispossession, transgression, and confinement. (Fat! Slut! Drunk! Psycho! Drug addict! Bad wife! Bad daughter! Bad mother! Jail! Rehab! House arrest!) Motifs of lost or dispossessed fortunes, haunted castles, fakes and counterfeits, long-buried secrets and hidden pasts, repressed alter egos, and, of course, the constant, looming threat of financial ruin. (Bad-vibe hotels, bad plastic surgery, stripper past, secret bigotry revealed!) Stock characters like controlling patriarchs, exploitative Svengalis, ineffectual or absent mothers, and callous or abusive boyfriends, husbands, and other cads. (Sued dad! Sued momager! Married business manager! Husband took money and kids!)

Between 9/11 and the financial panic of 2008, these lugubrious tales of lost innocence piled up, one after another, not only distracting us from the real horrors of the modern world but also somehow enacting them. Celebrity train wrecks *captured the American imagination*, giving us a reason to be outraged that we could wrap our heads around (as opposed of, say, "suspect sites" and credit-default swaps), and a clear, easily identified object for our rage.

The celebrity train wreck was disgusting. She was fat. She was a bad mother. She was a whore. One by one, the increasingly erratic heroines transgressed the boundaries of taste and decorum, tarnished their vaunted innocence (or their highly-publicized virginity), and were cast out of the protected sphere of acceptable femininity and into lurid tales of abjection. They stumbled around in the streets of Hollywood, drunk, drugged, terrified, distraught, catapulted into madness, and/or temporarily blinded by the exploding flash bulbs of the jeering predators that pursued them everywhere they went ("Britney! Britney! What's wrong? Are you sad?"), then mocked and reviled by the "'baying mob' intimidating its subjects" online. The train wrecks became the stars in a grand Foucauldian "theater of punishment."

If 2007 seemed like the year celebrity gossip turned gothic, it's probably because that's the year celebrity worship was eclipsed by the more lucrative business of celebrity denigration. Even at work, there seemed to be a TV tuned to *TMZ* all day. Everybody seemed to be up on the comings and goings of the fallen starlets. A *New York Times* article about the invention of the twenty-four-hour celebrity-news cycle described a business model that set out to create "online addicts" by providing a continuous flow of fresh gossip, sometimes provided by family members. Michael Lohan, Lindsay's dad, a former commodities trader who had gone to jail for contempt of court while being investigated for insider trading, had a sideline in trading insider information on his daughter.[2] The article alluded to the scandal sheets of the 1950s, of which *Confidential* magazine was the best known and most notorious. *Confidential* was known for paying for information on stars, and for demanding ever more celebrity sacrifices. The deal Dexter made with *Spy* magazine's publisher in *The Philadelphia Story*, then, was not unheard of. In exchange for getting *Confidential* not to out Rock Hudson, his manager threw his other clients Rory Calhoun and Tab Hunter to the wolves.[3] Finally, the movie studios asked the California state attorney general to intervene. An investigation was launched, and the magazine was taken to court in 1957 and eventually shut down. Another *Times* story, on the Rupert Murdoch phone-hacking scandal, noted that the media conglomerate Time Warner, which during peak train-wreck time still owned both the Warner Bros. movie studio and *People* magazine, also owned *TMZ*. When *Confidential* was put on trial in 1957, it was largely because the celebrity scandals it trafficked in cost the studios a lot of money. In these days of vertical integration, however, when the studio and the tabloid likely have the same parent company, it's less crucial to protect a celebrity's untarnished image. Now, whether a celebrity is making a movie or making a scene at a nightclub, the money ends up in the same place. In 2011, advertising analysts estimated that the twenty-four-hour gossip sites, magazines, and TV shows generated more than $3 billion in revenue per year. That's Frankensynergy at work.[4]

Like the genre itself, twenty-first-century gothic heroines had not only transgressed their original limits but possibly also vacated them. People were interested in the saga of their lives writ large. They were corrupted innocence and squandered potential, with all the bad behavior, screwups, meltdowns, and crack-ups that implies. This was much more emotionally compelling and cathartic than any role they'd be likely to play in a mainstream Hollywood movie. Which story was more lucrative for Time Warner, in the end — some *Herbie* remake, or the ongoing saga of Lindsay Lohan's tragic flameout? Whether Britney is making a movie, making an album, making a drunken scene outside a nightclub, or making hundreds and hundreds of clickbait headlines, she is making a lot of money. The former child stars did not make it on the perilous journey to marriage. They transgressed all the boundaries and became grotesques. Some of them found their way back, some didn't, some died. But the year 2007 was the year they become our id monsters, our cautionary tales of terror and abjection. We didn't just consume their suffering as entertainment, we also produced their suffering as entertainment. And we were entitled to it, too, because they were rich and wore short skirts and drank too much and asked for it. We turned them into the ghostly embodiment of our collective anxieties about privacy, identity, consumption, social decay, financial collapse, and the increasingly blurred line between reality and fantasy. And for a while there, they came back to haunt us relentlessly, sometimes more than thirty times a day.

13

Big Mouth Strikes Again

"OH, DO SHUT UP, DEAR!" IS THE NAME OF A TALK BY MARY Beard, a professor of classics at the University of Cambridge. It's a rollicking tour through Western culture's foundational tradition of silencing women who speak out in public, which Beard gave at the British Museum in 2014 after being harassed on Twitter for her vocal support of putting Jane Austen on the one-pound note. In the speech, she talked about how such harassment was nothing new, how it's totally been a thing since antiquity. She explained that the deliberate, boastful, and even performative exclusion of women from public speech was considered, in ancient Greece, "an integral part of growing up as a man." It was how a man took power. She traced the first recorded example of it to a passage in Homer's *Odyssey* in which a bard is singing a song about the Greeks' suffering on their return from Troy. The song upsets Penelope, so she tells the bard to stop, which triggers Telemachus, her young son, to berate her in front of his friends. "Speech will be the business of men," he tells her. "For mine is the power in this household." Then he sends her to her room, and she goes. After all, Penelope is Telemachus's (temporarily single) mother. It's her job to raise him not only as a man but as the king.

Not everyone is granted the power of authoritative speech. Even when it's not expressly denied, the freedom to exercise it isn't evenly distributed, or appreciated, or forgiven. It has always taken courage for women to speak up for themselves and to speak out against the way things are, especially against female oppression. Alice's predicament in Wonderland is a familiar one to modern women: She's a post-Enlightenment girl in a persistently feudal world. She perceives herself as a subject with inalienable rights, but she's perceived, variously, as an interloper, a servant, a threat, an object, a bother, a girl. Alice believes this can be remedied with information. She believes that if she explains and asserts herself, if she reasonably points out the facts, then she will shift the perception. At the very least, she thinks, she can learn the rules and fit in. So, she tries. She takes others' good faith for granted. She makes her case again and again. She tries to learn their rules. But she is eternally frustrated, because Wonderland is governed not by reason or rules but by ideology, faith, superstition, and fear. Something is real if you believe it's real, if you continually affirm its existence. It disappears if you don't, subsumed into a parallel universe.

I was in my teens the first time I jumped into a heated argument about a book or movie or band with a boy I liked, only to watch his face fall in dismay or harden instantly into anger. It baffled me. I liked boys who were attractive but also smart and funny and original. I assumed this was mutual, but it usually wasn't. A tarot-card reader once told me that I was a ninja who looked like a geisha, so some boys might feel ambushed. I once had an argument with a boyfriend in college about Pearl Jam, and we both walked away crushed — I at the fact that he liked Pearl Jam, he at the fact that I hadn't thought to hide my contempt. Another boyfriend told me that he didn't want to know what I thought about Paul Auster — if I didn't like the books he liked, then I didn't like him. One boyfriend invited me to watch him play squash as we were leaving a museum where we'd argued about a painting. I went but ended up sitting out the whole game at the bar, furiously writing an essay about the painting on a napkin. The essay was a gift to him in the same way a dead mouse is a gift from a cat to its owner. He reacted accordingly. So many aesthetic impasses, so many relationships dashed against the rocks of critical variance. I come from a line of refractory women adept at dismantling male authority through underhanded mockery and satire, which is how my grandmother survived my grandfather. I believed that the days of telling girls to keep their opinions to themselves were over, because I'd been encouraged to speak up in class my whole life. When I started the movie-critic job, in 2004, I was warned by my predecessor, also a woman, to brace myself for nasty e-mails that would inevitably come — but they never did, at least not with the fury I'd expected. Maybe it was because when I had something not-nice to say, I made sure to be as funny about it as possible. I made sure to tuck it in the very best dead mouse I could find.

In December 2007, not long after Isla Fisher's quote about playing the girl was repurposed as clickbait all over the Internet, Katherine Heigl, who had starred in *Knocked Up* earlier that year, was profiled in *Vanity Fair*. Leslie Bennetts, author of *The Feminine Mistake*, which argued against women staying home to take care of kids full-time, wrote the profile. In it, Bennetts remarked that although many critics had liked *Knocked Up*, "quite a few discerned an underlying misogyny that made female characters into unappealing caricatures while romanticizing immature and irresponsible male behavior." Heigl agreed that the movie felt "a little sexist" and that it painted "the women as shrews, as humorless and uptight," and the men "as lovable, goofy, fun-loving guys." She admitted that the disparity bothered her. "I had a hard time with it, on some days," she said. "I'm playing such a bitch; why is she being such a killjoy? Why is this how you're portraying women? Ninety-eight percent of the time it was an amazing experience, but it was hard for me to love the movie."

It wasn't the first time that Heigl was criticized for criticizing her employers in the media, but for some reason, this time she was sent to the corner for it. Nobody was scandalized when George Clooney called *Batman and Robin* "a difficult film to be good in," but the backlash against Heigl was swift and merciless. Her comments were considered bitchy and traitorous. Even though in her next two movies, *27 Dresses* and *The Ugly Truth*, she also played sad, lonely, uptight, insecure, workaholic, relationship-obsessed single girls, and even though she recanted her statements in *People* magazine almost immediately, calling *Knocked Up* "the best filming experience of my career," it was too late. She'd become a cautionary tale, the abject poster child for what happens to ungrateful women who not only question their roles but also dare to point out that the story doesn't match the reality.

After *The Ugly Truth* came out, Judd Apatow, the director and writer of *Knocked Up,* and Seth Rogen, another of the movie's stars, discussed the incident on Howard Stern's radio show. "That looks like it really puts women on a pedestal in a beautiful way," Rogen said. Apatow said he'd heard there was a scene in *The Ugly Truth* in which Heigl wore underwear with a vibrator inside, so he'd "have to see if that was uplifting for women." The idea that Heigl had been calling for women to be "uplifted" or "put on a pedestal" was so bizarrely Victorian and off the mark that it made me doubt my perceptions. Even stranger was how Apatow and Rogen took Heigl's comments personally, when she'd been careful to say the experience had been "98 percent" positive. In the Hollywood liege mentality, her criticism of the movie was construed as personal betrayal, punishable by exile.

"We never had a 'fight,'" Apatow said. "Seth always says, it doesn't make any sense . . . She improvised half her shit . . . She could not have been cooler."

He wondered if maybe Heigl had just gotten tired after six straight hours of interviews and "slipped." To which Rogen retorted, "I didn't slip, and I was doing fucking interviews all day too! I didn't say shit!"

Apatow said that he'd waited for the call to come saying, "Sorry, I was tired," but it never came. Rogen was skeptical. "I gotta say, it's not like we're the only people she said some batshit crazy things about. That's kind of her bag now."

It was peak train-wreck coverage time in the media. Jeff Robinov, who was then the president of production at Warner Bros., had recently announced that his studio would no longer be making movies with female protagonists (I guess they aren't called Bros. for nothing). Hillary Clinton was losing her lead in the polls against Barack Obama after having been subjected to a merciless double standard for months. The question of whether women are funny was being debated in earnest. For these and other reasons that all seemed to fit together in some way, the backlash against Heigl really got under my skin. I'd hated *Knocked Up* with a passion, but I'd been afraid to say so, and I'd been afraid to say why. In fact, I'd gone back to see it a second time to make sure I hated it. And here, six months later, was the star of the movie proving that I'd been right to be afraid. The context in which this opinion could be expressed did not exist.

Nearly a decade later, Rogen regretted that Heigl was hurt by criticizing the film, while still objecting to the criticism. He told the *Hollywood Reporter* that he sympathized with Heigl and that he did not think that her comments should have affected her career; but all those years later, he still didn't see the bigger picture. "I respect the fact that perhaps she realizes that it has hurt her career, and I don't want that to have happened to her at all because I've said a thousand stupid things and I really like her," he said. "The only people who in this situation should in any way take anything from it is me and Judd because we're the ones she was talking about. For other people to not work with her because she didn't like her experience with us is — I think is crazy."

In his book *Fearless Speech,* Michel Foucault traced the Western tradition of criticism to the Greek idea of *parrhesia. Parrhesia* can be translated as "free speech," "frank speech," or "truth" that is both grounded in personal experience and expressed with conviction.

The word *parrhesia* is derived from a word that means "to say everything," so it implies risk, because there's always risk involved in spilling your guts. The *parrhesiastes*, or "one who speaks the truth," is, according to Foucault, "always less powerful than the one with whom he speaks." The word is also "linked to courage in the face of danger," and it "demands the courage to speak the truth in spite of some danger." *Parrhesia* is fundamentally antiauthoritarian, so it's always a bit of a risky stance. It's heroic, because it's dangerous. It can cost you your head. "In its extreme form, telling the truth takes place in the 'game' of life or death," Foucault writes. People take it on in the cause of justice.

Foucault writes, "In *parrhesia*, telling the truth is regarded as a duty." Who is responsible for telling the truth in the cause of justice? If the civilized world is built on injustice, who is allowed to call it out? Who has a duty to call it out? What does that person risk? Greek philosophy, he went on, "problematized" truth telling as an activity. It asked,

> Who is able to tell the truth? What are the moral, the ethical, and the spiritual conditions which entitle someone to present himself as, and to be considered as, a truth-teller? About what topics is it important to tell the truth? (About the world? About nature? About the city? About behavior? About man?) What are the consequences of telling the truth? What are its anticipated positive effects for the city, for the city's rulers, for the individual, etc.? And finally: What is the relation between the activity of truth-telling and the exercise of power? Should truth-telling be brought into coincidence with the exercise of power, or should these activities be completely independent and kept separate? Are they separable, or do they require one another?[1]

In other words, who gets to say who should be believed? When and why, in a civilized society, does truth telling become a target for social regulation that eventually becomes so cultural? The backlash against Heigl looks like nothing compared to the backlash against women who speak out online now. "It doesn't much matter what line of argument you take as a woman," Beard told *The New Yorker*. "If you venture into traditional male territory, the abuse comes anyway. It's not what you say that prompts it — it's the fact that you are saying it." The British journalist Laurie Penny compared a woman's opinion to "the short skirt of the Internet" for the same reason. Women who express their views, especially their critical views, are construed as "somehow asking an amorphous mass of almost-entirely male keyboard-bashers to tell you how they'd like to rape, kill and urinate on you." Telemachus would have loved Twitter.

Like Telemachus, sexist online trolls "become men" by actively excluding women from public speech. When women speak out against social constructs that are easily mistaken for reality, their words are construed as revolt. Whenever I wrote a critical review of a mainstream movie and someone took the time to write me an e-mail telling me to "relax" and reminding me it's "just a movie," that person was not only invalidating my interpretation but also questioning my sanity. Male reviewers were subjected to abuse as well, but "relax" was gendered advice, advice that felt intimately familiar. Sometimes, I'd get an e-mail like this and I'd wish I could just take the advice; that I could write "It's just a movie," file it, and go to the beach. But alas. I'd have to find a way to be opinionated without being too opinionated, authoritative without being a bitch about it, smart without being elitist, fair without being a pushover. If the boyfriends of my youth found me too authoritative when I should have been cheering on the sidelines as they kicked and tossed and smacked balls toward the vanguard, the male colleagues of my adulthood kept reminding me of my lack of authority as they unconsciously displayed theirs. I was always failing someone's standards of legitimacy, as a girlfriend, as a producer of opinions. It was an eternal no-win. I was always too big or too small, like Alice, and forever being told, in one way or another, "Eat me."

• • •

It just so happens that at the time that *Knocked Up* came out, I was trying to get knocked up myself. I was spending a lot of time worrying about how I would manage my job after having a baby, even though I wasn't pregnant yet. I was also simultaneously thinking about and trying not to think about how I would be able to afford to raise a baby. My job paid well, but Los Angeles was getting more expensive by the day. I worked very long hours; Craig had only recently started working in TV production, and his hours were long and irregular. On the days he worked, he left at the crack of dawn and came home late at night. I wrote and edited and did administrative stuff from home, and sometimes went to meetings or screenings during the day. I drove to screenings across town at rush hour two or three evenings a week and got home at ten. My once-a-week cleaning lady wanted to become a full-time nanny, and she used to joke that I should have a baby for her. I'd laugh, then I'd crunch the numbers and panic. There was no way I could afford her full-time.

Meanwhile, the "mommy wars" raged — mostly in the pages of the *New York Times,* the *Atlantic,* books, and other magazines — the ad-supported bards sang of an epic battle between mommies who cleaved to the private sphere (angels in their walled gardens) and mommies who struck out into the public sphere, "paying other people to raise their kids," as it was often tendentiously put. In this narrative, the choice was made out to be moral: between selfishness and selflessness. Dig deeper and the choice was actually between what kind of woman you chose to be: Were you a "true woman," born to nurture and give yourself over to others (the kind of person for whom, as Virginia Woolf once put it, "if there was chicken, she took the leg"), or a woman who remained a person first? The mommy wars were presented as a debate about practical modes of living, but they weren't that at all. They were entirely ideological, and as divorced from practical reality as it was possible to be. The argument wasn't what is best for women and children so much as what and whom are women for. It's an argument that is ongoing today. A "mommy" was understood to be financially dependent on a husband of decent means. The word did not refer to women who had had children while single or poor. Money and husbands were never mentioned as factors in the decision, which was always framed as a choice between selfless motherhood and selfish careerism. The argument also assumed that the responsibility of caring for children naturally fell to mothers, and that business could not be expected to accommodate parents' schedules. Finally, because working women, especially working mothers, tended to make less than men, especially fathers, it "made sense" for mothers to eventually drop out of the workforce and stay home. Rarely did the debate take a macro view of the system. Instead, it pitted the self-sacrificing mommies, who were "giving it all up" to get up at 5:00 a.m. to pack bento-box lunches, put them on Tumblr, drive the kids to school, and still make it to Pilates by 9:00, against the bitchy, aggressive ones in heels, who felt guilty about missing recitals to fly to Singapore. These were the mommies people made movies about and wrote novels about.

As a kid, I'd worried about what would happen when I grew up and had children of my own. I imagined it would be like a *Twilight Zone* episode in which I studied and studied and prepared and prepared and then, just as I was entering adulthood (my mom had me at twenty-three, and her mom had her at twenty-three), I'd have a daughter, and I'd have to shut down operations as myself and divert all my energy to making sure she studied and prepared until the day she became a mother, and so on. It reminded me of a recurring nightmare I had in which a cop pulled me over and whipped off his mirrored aviator glasses to reveal another identical pair of mirrored aviator glasses, then another, then another. Needless to say, I didn't dream of this day when I would give myself over to my uncanny double, I lived in fear of it. I didn't quite understand how it would work without my making a conscious choice to marry for lifelong support. My goals for myself had varied over time, but I'd always known I never wanted that. There was something mercenary about wanting to become "a mother" that nobody ever talked about; an economic aspect that was unspeakable. I feared that a strategic middle-class marriage would be the very thing that would make a creative life impossible. If I didn't have to write to survive, my writing would lack urgency. If it wasn't urgent, it wouldn't be relevant. If it wasn't relevant, it wouldn't be necessary. If it wasn't necessary, it wouldn't be worth the money it would cost to pay for child care. I'd always wanted to marry an artist. I'd always wanted a daughter. I'd always wanted to write. I'd always been terrified of disappearing.

Given all the confusing and anxiety-provoking mixed messages about motherhood and work that the culture was bombarding me with, I was glad when I was assigned the review of *Knocked Up*. It would be a light, life-affirming comedy about love and babies and how everything would be OK and nobody would end up living in the car. I was even more than receptive to this goofy tale of role reversal and nontraditional family values because I was the one with the secure, much higher-paying, stressful, high-profile job in my relationship, too. I was ready to relate, to have my perspective validated and my anxieties soothed. Besides, I'd loved *The 40-Year-Old Virgin*, especially for the relationship between Catherine Keener and Steve Carrell, which was sweeter and more offbeat and more real than anything I'd seen for a long time. I knew it would be a hit, of course, and that people would like it no matter what, but I fully expected to like it, too. I took a friend. We got popcorn. We settled into our seats excitedly. The dread that came over me when I realized just how much I hated it came as a complete surprise.

Knocked Up is about two strangers who go home together after a drunken night at a club, have sex, accidentally get pregnant, and decide to try to make a go of staying together for the baby. The joke of the premise is that Ben and Alison are a role-reversed odd couple: Alison is a beautiful and successful on-camera entertainment reporter, and Ben is an overweight, unemployed, eternal adolescent with limited social skills who is working on a stupid idea for a website with his many roommates. It's not the premise that's the problem, however. The problem is that the movie would sooner chew off its own arm than explore its premise in any honest way. It is so intent on avoiding reality that it becomes, with every further complication, a Jenga tower of lies. Alison is given all the attributes that signal power, agency, autonomy, status, popularity, and happiness, yet she is portrayed as a miserable, lonely, and friendless wretch. Ben has none of Alison's advantages, but he's happy. He doesn't need to be attractive, hardworking, smart, prepared, or dedicated. It doesn't matter how much time he's wasted or how many brain cells he's killed. When the baby comes, all he has to do is decide to get his act together, and the doors fling open. The system is ready and waiting. All he has to do is walk through the door.

What bothered me was not that the movie didn't hew to some strict standard of realism. What bothered me was that its many moments of through-the-looking-glass misrecognition worked in unison to form an alternate reality. There was a montage of bizarre visits to the ob-gyn as imagined by someone freaked out by the idea of an ob-gyn; a shopping scene in which Alison, Debbie, and Ben choose a crib that costs nearly $1,000, and nobody bats an eye; a scene moments later when they run into Alison's catty frenemies, the only friends she's shown to have; a couple of scenes at work where her female boss tries to sabotage her because she's jealous, but Alison gets promoted anyway because audiences love that she's pregnant. In the upside-down Wonderland of *Knocked Up*, the woman has no friends, but getting pregnant boosts her career. It seemed like more evidence that, as the George W. Bush administration had made clear, the "reality-based community" had lost. We were strictly faith-based now. By the mid-2000s, you had to look to the fantasy genre if you wanted to see your social or political reality reflected in any recognizable way. You had to read *The Hunger*

Games. Realism had jumped the shark into ideology. The more fantastical the story, the more "naturalistic" the look.

The problem with *Knocked Up* wasn't that it was full of moments that made it more than a little bit sexist, even though it was.
The problem was that it presented an adolescent boy's perspective
of what it means to be an adult woman in a world that has not yet
come to terms with the idea of women as autonomous subjects.
The problem was that it reveled in its hero's unearned advantage
in this world while at the same time refusing to acknowledge what
it's like on the other side. The movie refused to so much as utter the
word *abortion*. (It makes somebody say "smashmorshun" instead.)
Knocked Up wasn't interested in Alison's life or in her experience
or in her options; it saw the life stages of a woman as they are seen
in fairy tales: child, maiden (hot chick), mother, and crone. Alison
was an incubator, not only for her baby but also for Ben's maturity, just as Debbie was, long past the point when her own chicks
had hatched. Alison and Debbie grew old and angry waiting for
their men to grow up, even though they knew — said the movie —
they would never grow old. The women braced for their terrifying
decline, whereas the men retained their childlike wonder forever.
Their growing old was without cultural meaning; it didn't count.
The problem with *Knocked Up* was that it was self-satisfied, tri-
umphalist swagger barely concealed under layers of sentimental-
ity. It was its bad-faith premise. The trouble wasn't only *Knocked
Up*, of course. This take on gender relations circa 2007 was the
only perspective anyone got. It was the most suffocating dude-bro
imperialism; patriarchy rebranded as "fratriarchy." Watching it, I
felt the way I imagine Khrushchev must have felt as Nixon tried
to undermine his self-esteem with a tour of a modern American
kitchen. Khrushchev was, like, we have kitchens in Russia, too, you
know . . . But nobody listened.

The low point of the movie for me came when Debbie, who is
forty, and Alison, who is pregnant, go to a club one night when Pete
and Ben are in Las Vegas. The bouncer at the club, played by Craig

Robinson, allows a parade of younger girls in and sends Debbie and Alison to the back of the line. Debbie explodes with rage at the bouncer.

"I'm not going to go to the end of the fucking line!" she yells at him. "Who the fuck are you? I have just as much of a right to be here as any of these little skanky girls! What, am I not skanky enough for you? You want me to hike up my fucking skirt? What the fuck is your problem? I'm not going anywhere! You're just some 'roided-out freak with a fucking clipboard. And your stupid little fucking rope! You may have power now, but you're not God. You're a doorman! OK? You're a doorman! So . . . fuck you, you fucking fag with your fucking little faggy gloves!"

The bouncer just listens to her homophobic tirade, and then he does something unexpected. He empathizes. He recognizes her vicious, homophobic tirade for the impotent howl of pain that it is. He grabs Debbie, pulls her aside, and whispers to her. "I know. You're right. I'm so sorry," he says. "I fucking hate this job. I don't want to be the one to pass judgment and decide who gets in. This shit makes me sick to my stomach. I get the runs from the stress. It's not because you're not hot. I would love to tap that ass. I would tear that ass up. I can't let you in because you're old as fuck . . . for this club, not, you know, for the earth."

What *Knocked Up* said to me was that when it came down to it, it really didn't make a difference if, on earth, the hero was a slob with dreams of getting rich by creating an Internet database of female nudity in mainstream movies and the woman who agrees to marry him is beautiful and successful. It didn't matter that, as he told Alison over an expensive sushi dinner at Geisha House, he had been living off an insurance settlement for years and had only eleven dollars left in the bank. In fact, it didn't matter so much that the scene ended before the check came. It didn't matter that he wasn't smart, or good-looking, or sexy, or funny, or capable of empathy. It didn't matter in the same way that Alison's career, salary, accomplishments, looks, or other advantages didn't matter. Without a husband and a baby, she was just Emily Dickinson in a back-yard, without the poetry. He still got to be the hero. He still got to decide. What *Knocked Up* said to me as I tried to get pregnant at the last possible moment of thirty-nine while fretting about how I'd manage to do my job after the baby came (if a baby ever came) was "Fuck you."

*

In the fall of 2007, a few months after seeing *Knocked Up*, I went to a screening of a movie called *Lars and the Real Girl*, which turned out to be the weirdest Pygmalion story ever told. The movie poster featured Ryan Gosling in a bad sweater and worse mustache, clutching a bunch of flowers and smiling shyly next to a silicone sex doll. At the beginning of the movie, Lars is living alone in the con-verted garage behind his brother's house. Because he's lonely but terrified of human contact, he orders a life-size sex doll online for companionship and invents a chaste and utterly dependent person-ality for her — an unbeatable Madonna/whore combination. When the doll arrives, Lars introduces the doll to his brother, Gus, and sister-in-law, Karin, as "Bianca," an orphaned, disabled, celibate, child-loving Brazilian missionary. Bianca might look like a rubber replica of a sex worker, but her mystique is all "true woman." Sure, believing it requires contorting your subjectivity into a pretzel, but if Lars — that beloved, temporarily insane, universal everyman — insists she is a virginal and demure girlfriend, selflessly devoted to him and to "children," then so it is. Gus and Karin are horrified, as is everyone else in town. But at the request of Lars's therapist, they all agree to play along with the delusion that Bianca is real until Lars is good and ready to snap out of it. For this particular course of treatment (and for the movie) to succeed, however, certain things must be accepted as true: that underneath the temporary psycho-sis, Lars is a nice, decent guy going through a rough psychologi-cal patch who deserves the town's support and the audience's emo-tional investment until he's ready to come around and find a real girl to love — Margo, the cute coworker whose crush on Lars never flags, not when he turns heel and bolts each time she tries to talk to him. Not when he ignores her when she asks him a question. Not when he fails to stand up for her when his cubicle-mate is rude to her. Not when he brings his sex doll to church with him and it becomes patently obvious that he's not in his right mind. Not when he brings it to another coworker's Christmas party, talks to it, dances with it, and tells everybody that she doesn't like it when he drinks. Every time she appears on-screen, it's to gaze longingly at Lars. Nothing Lars does can dampen Margo's affection and commitment to Lars, because she is a "real girl," too. Margo is almost as passive and inert as Bianca. She is entirely devoid of needs, for example, the need for a boyfriend who is not crazy. No social or conversational skills? No grip on reality? No problem! No matter how many times he rebuffs her in favor of his sex doll, she's there for him. She's even there for the sex doll. She considers her a friend.

Somewhere between the arrival of the doll and the shrink's insistence that everyone in town collude with Lars's delusion, the townspeople get over their discomfort at being asked to pretend a sex doll is a person, and they begin to treat her like a person even when Lars isn't around. They take her shopping and to the hair salon. They elect her to the school board. They embrace her as a valued member of the community.

As I watched the movie, a feeling kept nagging me. Lars and Bianca reminded me of someone. They looked so familiar. He was dowdy, she was hot. He was active, she was passive. He was maladjusted, she was placid. He was unreliable and immature, she was patient and forgiving. He was funny and charming, she was conventional and dull. He was the subject, she was the object. He was human, she was a piece of plastic with a fantasy projected onto it. They were Man-Boy and Dream Girl, and the audience was the community who had stopped noticing that something wasn't right with the girl.

This would have come as a shock regardless, but it was especially strange given that I'd been fully expecting a metaphor about a psychotic man-child with a Manchurian Barbie doll, whose psychiatrist insists that the everyone else disregard their own senses and go with the story, for his sake. It takes the story of a guy who has purchased a fuck doll, gives her Mother Teresa's biography, insists that the world accept her as real, and then tries to bury this story under a feel-good, completely bonkers message of inclusion and acceptance: sex dolls are women, too. It says, sure, he ordered the thing and forced his family and his community to deny their own reality and take his messed-up fantasy at face value, but, hey, he loves and respects his fake woman. He makes it sleep in his brother's guest room!

In order for *Lars and the Real Girl* to function as the kind of edgy yet wholesome entertainment it is trying to be, it has to sell you on its absolute sincerity. It has to remain resolutely oblivious to its own symbolism and categorically refuse to engage with its own premise in any meaningful way. It has to ignore the glaring fact that Bianca is the literal objectification of "the unbeatable Madonna-whore combination" of Robin Morgan's worst nightmares. The movie is so hell-bent on forcing our identification with Lars that it tries to pass off its own perfect metaphor for the symbolic annihilation of women in pop culture (where they are systematically replaced with fantasies, robots, or sex dolls) as a supercute tale of redemption. This is why we never see Lars ordering Bianca from the website, cobbling together his womanly ideal from a diverse selection of faces, bodies, heights, cup sizes, hair color, pubic styles, and number of working orifices. To face the reality of what Lars is doing — to even so much as acknowledge it — would make it impossible to identify with or root for him. Instead, the movie decides to mirror its delusional main character and insist that the audience go along with its delusions as well. As the movie critic Dana Stevens wrote in *Slate*, "*Lars and the Real Girl* suffers from an even stranger delusion than Lars does. The movie is convinced that its man-loves-mannequin premise is uplifting, when actually it's just kinda gross." Confronted with its own ontological horror, the movie squeamishly averts its eyes.

I wasn't assigned to review the movie. Instead, I wrote a long essay about how the sex doll represented what had happened to female characters in the movies over the past decade. I wrote, "The idea that a girl might play anything other than 'the girl' in a studio comedy is so far out of the mainstream that it's considered an experimental idea, not to mention a major financial risk. It seems that not a week goes by without a dust-up about the alleged misogyny of studio executives or a lament about the state of women's careers in Hollywood, or an explosion of frustration on feminist blogs." I got more than a hundred e-mails from all kinds of people: from teenagers saying they'd never understood why so much of what they saw made them feel bad; from men who were irritated by the presumption that this was what they wanted; from frustrated writers, directors, and producers, most of them women. I felt like Miss Lonelyhearts. Nine days after the piece ran, Kira was conceived. It's true. I looked it up.

Sometimes, it really helps to talk about your feelings.

"The best directors of romantic comedy in the nineteen thirties and forties," wrote David Denby in *The New Yorker* that summer, "knew that the story would be not only funnier but much more romantic if the fight was waged between equals. The man and woman may not enjoy parity of social standing or money, but they are equals in spirit, will, and body."[2] It was commonplace for the heroine to play the clown to the hero's straight man, because he, after all, was the hero. He had a patriarchy to uphold. So, it fell to the frivolous, irrational ladies to play the fools. In coming together the couples locked in a struggle to preserve their identity and individuality. You rooted for them to get together, because it was clear from their dynamic that once they got past whatever hump they were trying to get past — no money, an interloper in the form of Ralph Bellamy, whatever — their lives would from then on be a glorious expanse of witty banter, fun times, and incredible sex. You understood that one would not extinguish the other but would reflect the other, and we would recognize this as love.

The women in *Knocked Up* were based not on people but on an idea of woman that hadn't changed very much since the Victorian era. Following a decade of rom-coms about girls with low self-esteem, the script had flipped. In the new comedy of the sexes, as Denby observed, the main purpose of the female lead was to make the hero grow up. Once again it was incumbent on women to uphold the patriarchy while men enjoyed the fun perks of disenfranchisement — things like flouting convention, mocking authority, and shirking responsibility, Lucy Ricardo–style. Still, this didn't entirely explain what appeared to be a strict prohibition against female characters' being funny, even when played by funny women. It was as if a law had been passed barring female characters from making jokes, or having fun, or letting anyone else have any fun. They were backlash personified. In the "new comedy of the sexes,"[3] there were sad girls in the public sphere, like Alison, or demons in the house, like Debbie. The women were trapped in their tiny psychic spheres. They were petty, jealous, shallow, and self-loathing. They spent their split-second youth lamenting the passing of that youth. The boys' world, meanwhile, was as expansive as ever; mediocre looks and penury notwithstanding, their lives felt full of possibility. The message was clear: women might be smarter, more responsible, and more together than men now, but men were still happier — because this was still a man's world. You don't get to make jokes if the joke is on you. This was the new sexism; "enlightened sexism," as Susan J. Douglas called it. It was the sexism of people raised on *Free to Be . . . You and Me,* of people brought up to believe that sexism was a thing of the past, so they didn't have to worry about perpetuating it anymore.

My time as a TV and movie critic overlapped with the second Bush administration, when power aligned itself with populism in such a way that criticism of its power and hegemony was dismissed as "elitist." If intellectualism and even intelligence had been ridiculed as smug and effete since the 1980s, in the 2000s it began to be cast as evil and somehow exploitive. The image of the critic as a sneering, smug, supercilious, and quite possibly monocled bully — an unholy cross between Addison DeWitt and Mr. Peanut — was invoked every time a terrible movie was universally panned but made zillions of dollars. The zillions of dollars were paraded as proof that "normal people" loved and cherished stupid movies, the dumber the better. To engage critically with popular culture was to out yourself as one more out-of-touch elite, a natural enemy of popular culture and, by extension, the people. Criticism became more fan-based, as politics became branded and faith-based. There was no arguing with popularity. To argue with popularity was to be "elitist," and "elitist" was the "Communist" of 2007 — one insinuation and you were toast. The paper even changed our bylines, from "film critic," to "movie critic," for a while.

"Don't you want to know why?" my new editor asked.

I knew why.

"Why?" I asked.

"Because it sounds less elitist."

In the end, it wasn't my elitism that did it, though. It was the lack of authority in my authorial voice that was the problem. I was instructed to be more authoritative and to state more clearly whether I liked or didn't like things, but I thought, well, if I'm going to write about consumer products as consumer products, I should just go into advertising. I agreed to try harder. I was hugely pregnant, and I cried during the meeting. The paper was laying people off like crazy. Exactly a month after returning from maternity leave, I was laid off, too, over the phone. I blamed myself for having cried in the meeting, for having failed to be authoritative enough with my adjectives. But then I remembered that I'd been hired for my mouthy antiauthoritarian style, or so I'd been led to believe. I have problems with authority. Craig said losing the job was the best thing that had ever happened to me, and eventually he was right, but for a long time he wasn't. When I think back on the months that followed, all I can remember are tears falling on the baby.

As it happened, four or five months later I did get a job at an ad agency. I worked there for about eleven months. While there, I acquired a whole new vocabulary, composed of many darkly hilarious terms of art; things like "emotionally competent stimulus" and "touchpoints" and "reasons to believe." "Reasons to believe," often abbreviated to "RTBs," was my favorite. It refers to a kind of proof or persuasive fact from real life that supports the "brand promise" — such as "because it's 30 percent faster and creamier" or "because it's trusted by lepidopterists and moms." It occurred to me that some of these terms would have come in handy for describing some moviegoing experiences for which I'd previously had no words.

At the agency, I worked briefly, with an otherwise all-male team, on a light-yogurt campaign aimed at women. Research had provided us with some findings linking light-yogurt consumption to reduced waist measurements, as well as the "insight" (another good one; "What's the insight?" someone was always asking; I always had an insight, insights were my thing, except they were always the wrong kind, the non-reassuring kind) that a "smaller waist" is something women specifically desire. I was the person suggesting that basing the campaign on women's collective yearning for reduced waist measurements was stupid, but maybe I was wrong. It made no difference anyway, because nobody was listening. I didn't really care. I was just biding my time, riding out the crisis, keeping the baby in blueberries and baby-gym-class passes. Advertising is extremely authoritative, though. It broadcasts the master's voice. It is the last word.

14

The Redemptive Journey

THE LOVE STORIES OF THE SEVENTIES WERE DIVORCE STO-
ries. Or maybe the divorce stories of the seventies were love stories.
Either way, they were about learning to love yourself. This love had
to be extracted from underneath the rubble of a ruined marriage,
like a sparrow from an avalanche, and nurtured back to health. I remember it as an archetypal story, one I saw again and again. A wife
is abandoned and cast out into a cruel and unfamiliar world she is
unprepared to navigate. After a slew of bad dates and other humiliating experiences, she slowly starts to regain her confidence and
find her way. She acquires new interests. She meets new people.
She learns to stand on her own. She locates herself. Her ex chooses
this moment to come back, but she is over him. Her style has become flowy and bohemian, and she gently rebuffs him in favor of
freedom and batik. It is incredibly romantic.

I feel like I saw this story told in a million movies, but it is entirely possible that I'm thinking exclusively of Paul Mazursky's *An
Unmarried Woman* (1978). It loomed that large. What impressed
me the most was how, when Erica's (Jill Clayburgh's) husband tells
her after lunch one day that he's leaving her for a Bloomingdale's
salesgirl that he met while buying a shirt. Erica doesn't cry or yell.
Instead, she asks if the girl is a good lay, then walks half a block and
throws up on a mailbox. The vomiting really impressed me as being very authentic and visceral, not to mention a pretty good special effect. After making it through the requisite rough patch, Erica
has a personal renaissance that includes a job at an art gallery and
a relationship with a hot painter who asks her to quit her job and

spend the summer with him in Vermont. She declines and he gives her a painting, which she drags out into the street by herself. Turning down the hot painter was a very big deal: a happy ending without a prince was not a thing a heroine snubbed her nose at. It was even stranger and more impressive than watching the heroine lose her lunch.

For a few years before and after Kira was born, I resisted buying a copy of Elizabeth Gilbert's *Eat, Pray, Love*. This wasn't always easy. I'd have a long layover at an airport and find myself staring at a solid wall of copies at the bookstore, and before I knew it I'd be flipping anxiously through a copy, half skimming, half looking, trying not to look. I didn't want to buy it. I didn't want to read it, exactly. What I wanted was for it to comfort me, to lie to me, to reveal its secret powers to me. I wanted its spiritual uplift to work on me, or its success to rub off on me. I wanted to believe in it, truly. As a little kid in the 1970s, I'd loved watching *The Phil Donahue Show* and then when I was in high school, my friend Susan turned me on to Oprah Winfrey. Oprah was magical. Where Phil had explored feelings, Oprah had a gift for turning setbacks into fairy tales of transformation. On the status of the fairy-tale genre as socialization for children in the nineteenth century, Jack Zipes wrote that as "notions of elitism and Christian meritocracy were introduced into the stories" by authors such as the immensely popular Hans Christian Andersen, the emphasis shifted to "extraordinarily gifted individuals who owed their rise in fortunes to God's benevolence or miracles of destiny represented metaphorically through the intervention of a fairy or powerful magical people and objects. Another aspect that appealed to children and adults was the Horatio Alger attitude that encouraged taking advantage of opportunities and pulling oneself up by one's bootstraps."[1]

Oprah was like the talk show version of a story by Hans Christian Andersen.

Eat, Pray, Love should have been exactly the story I was looking for — the one I should have wanted to read, and write. It was everything I identified with, but wasn't. Liz, the heroine, leaves her husband, has an affair with an actor that ends badly, spirals into depression, and embarks on a quest for identity and enlightenment that takes her to various international vacation spots funded by a book advance, a trip that yields a new boyfriend and a best-selling book that transforms her life. As Steve Almond wrote in a profile of Gilbert in the *New York Times Magazine*, *Eat, Pray, Love* was Gilbert's chronicle of "an effort to balance her pursuit of pleasure with a spiritual life."[2] Like philosophy, it examined the problems of the body and the material world and the soul and the spiritual world. Like religion, it saved. Like a romance novel, it offered a fantasy of hedonic escape in exotic lands. Like a self-help book, it made the dream seem accessible and somehow about you, the reader. No wonder it has sold nine million copies.

I wish I could say I was immune to the promise of the redemptive narrative, but I found it hard to resist its mass-market allure. I also wanted very badly for it to save me. It wormed its way into the space where I had no faith and called out to me. In about six months, I had given birth to a baby, lost my job, and moved to a new city to work in a new industry, neither of which I liked much. I was lucky, considering. My disaster was part of a much bigger, global disaster. There were so many redemptive narratives bubbling up everywhere, so many stories of catastrophe leading to the best thing that ever happened, the thing that was fated to happen all along. I remember standing in line at Starbucks staring at a wall of books — the same book — about some terrible thing that happened to someone, spun into a gilded Oprah pick. All around me, people like me were turning their catastrophes into lessons of uplift, writing about the unexpected redemption of jam making, or gardening. I couldn't spin wisdom from catastrophe, because I was still too terrified. I needed someone to tell me it was all going to be OK. Or rather, I needed to be able to tell that to myself. I didn't buy this kind of stuff enough to be able to sell it.

This only made me feel worse. I could have chosen a year of

off-the-grid baby bonding and creative production, maybe an un-sponsored freelance sabbatical in Slovenia or Slovakia, could have started a parenting blog or a YouTube channel about how raw food changed my life. Everyone seemed to be casually launching em-pires. What kind of a failure was I that I had failed even to make lemonade from the lemons I'd been handed? I'd taken a job I didn't want, for half the money I used to make. I'd marvel at the blossom-ing Facebook pages of all these out-of-work journalists and screen-writers. Where did they find the emotional resources? the where-withal? the inexorable story arcs that would translate into salable book proposals? I was not capable of writing whimsical Facebook updates. I was not graceful under pressure. I was a train wreck. My anger was not purifying, it was contaminating, boring, paralyzing. I had nowhere to put it. My marriage was falling apart. I couldn't write. I thought I was going to die.

What was the name of this problem, though? I couldn't quite name it.

In her *New York Times* review of *Eat, Pray, Love,* Jennifer Egan wrote, "[Gilbert's] crisis remains a shadowy thing, a mere platform for the actions she takes to alleviate it . . . [She] acknowledges the 'almost ludicrously fairy-tale ending to this story,' but reminds us, 'I was not rescued by a prince; I was the administrator of my own res-cue.' Rescue from what? The reader has never been sure. Lacking a ballast of gravitas or grit, the book lists into the realm of magical thinking. Nothing Gilbert touches seems to turn out wrong; not a single wish goes unfulfilled."

It's true. At the start of the book, Gilbert paints herself as a des-perate suburban wife in the throes of a nervous breakdown. But she was already a prize-winning journalist. She was rich. She'd had sto-ries made into movies. She talked about having shopped for appli-ances on credit for the big house with enough rooms for children, despite not wanting children. Something about the way she pre-sents herself as "Liz," a regular girl blindsided by love and doubt, a girl in desperate need of comfort in the form of pasta, gelato, scenic vistas, fun friends, and exotic spiritual uplift, feels not entirely honest, or not fully explored. Maybe she felt she had no choice but to get married and buy a house and buy appliances and discuss children. Or maybe she had to pretend that she had once almost wanted it, because we were being relentlessly hammered with this message all the time. Gilbert and I are almost the same age, and I can attest to the vast gulf between her early-eighties young girl's yearning for adventure and her turn-of-the-century, Edith Whartonesque angst about houses and things and what you were supposed to want.

Say *Eat, Pray, Love* was a "journey of transformation" — what kind was it? Can a "journey of transformation" really be preplanned and undertaken under contract? What if you start out mildly dissatisfied and end up wildly depressed? Or if, instead of realizing what's truly important in life, you end up hopelessly dwelling on what's wrong? Zipes writes that fairy tales "reinforced the patriarchal symbolical order based on rigid notions of sexuality and gender. The stereotypes, not archetypes, depicted in printed and staged versions of fairy tales tended to follow schematic notions of how young men and women should behave."[3] I believe the feelings behind the idea were sincere, once it was sold it could turn out a certain way. The redemptive narrative was the new heroine's text for the late twentieth and early twenty-first centuries. It was the Eileen Fisher phase of the fairy tale — the fairy-godmother phase. It was tasteful, flowing, and calming, it had one foot in the beckoning foamy wavelets.

My fortieth year had very little calm and wisdom in it. Mine was not a story of courage, hope, and chai tea. It was a story of stress-eating Cheetos and Googling things like "voodoo" and "how to put a hex on someone's balls." It was neither a redemptive narrative nor a revenge fantasy. I did not travel the world or transform into a kick-ass. Mine was a Douglas Sirk melodrama about the tragedy of privileging romanticism over pragmatism, or some other inexcusable thing. You follow your heart at your peril. I was a dreamer, so I was an idiot doomed to wander the hinterlands in a fallen state. Unlike Liz Gilbert (or "Liz Gilbert"), I'd failed to use my adversity to locate my inner strength and courage and big paycheck, so the universe, too, had responded with indifference. I'd failed to believe in the unified theory of female redemption. This was unforgivable.

Eat, Pray, Love felt about as authentic to me as the heroine's "journey" on *The Bachelor.* Either she triumphed against all odds, or she quietly disappeared. It had to be a certain kind of redemptive narrative for a certain kind of lady at a certain stage in life when perhaps she has taken to wistfully wearing caftans on the beach at dusk while holding a mug of herbal tea. I am not making fun of this lady. I don't believe this lady really exists. She was invented by Celestial Seasonings and *Real Simple.* Her greatest desire in life is "balance." She wants balance so badly. This lady wishes that she, too, could escape her suburban life and her annoying husband. Imagine going off to Italy, India, and Bali and eating all you want, flirting with hot Italian guys, falling in love with a Brazilian, and then getting to call it a mystical journey because of a layover in an ashram! Gilbert's mantra in the book is "Tell the truth, tell the truth, tell the truth." But she doesn't really. She tells around it. Nobody is expecting the truth here. What's being sold is a fantasy of reassurance. The movie of Gilbert's book only amplifies this, both because it's unable to exteriorize Liz's inner life and because the person taking the journey is Julia Roberts. Julia Roberts is the vehicle. The reassurance that everything is going to be OK is the product.

*

The women on *The Bachelor* fight each other for a prince, a stranger to whom they have been presented like a portfolio of options. The bachelor on *The Bachelor* then begins to exercise his preferences, slowly winnowing the ranks of options as he zeroes in on the girl who best embodies his ideal. The girls, meanwhile, are trapped in a nightmare palace where the booze is more accessible than the food.

All that's left to do is drink, wait, and hope to meet the prince's requirements. (He seems to really like them. He really liked them five
minutes ago. He is making out with twenty other girls right now.)

The Bachelor is a game of attrition. The point is to stick it out
at whatever cost to your dignity. There are two proven strategies
for survival. The safe one, of course, is to hew as closely to the pre-
vailing ideal as possible. Conformity works. The ideal girl is pretty,
sexy, submissive (the whispered thank-yous as they survive one
more rose ceremony!), demure (adjusted for the twenty-first century), and domestic (in the theoretical future). The younger, thin-
ner, prettier, more submissive, more agreeable, and more insecure,
the higher her value. Her ladylike demureness should exist in inverse proportion to her sexual adventurousness — although virgins
who look like porn stars are also highly valued. It is always a risky
strategy to try to stand out from the crowd, especially in an environment as fiercely competitive as this one. Women who express
their needs or let their personalities or emotions show are immediately written off as weird or crazy; and the ones who let their personalities show except when the prince is there to see are labeled
troublemakers. It's inappropriate to be anything but sunny and accepting and sweet and to make statements beginning with "I." The
crazy and weird ones are often kept on the show for entertainment
value, as examples of how not to be, but they never win. They know
that confrontation is a fatal strategy and that the prince doesn't like
being made to feel guilty about kissing all the girls. This is not how
it is put to them, of course.

The girls and the bachelor talk constantly about their "journey."

It's not an accident that *journey* is one of the most overused words
in reality TV. On *The Bachelor*, which has been on the air since
2002, and its spin-offs *The Bachelorette* and *Bachelor in Paradise*,
host Chris Harrison kicks off every season in the same way. "Let
the journey begin," he says. Then the limo pulls up. Although efforts are made on the show to avoid too much word repetition in

general, an exception is made for *journey*, which participants—
who are not allowed to acknowledge that they are participating in a
constructed, televised experience—are encouraged to use as a syn-
onym for the bubble they are living in. They're not allowed to use
words like *process*, or *situation*, or *human experiment*. It is only,
always, a "journey."

The journey has been a central framework for storytelling
since the earliest works of Western literature. Homeric epics recount journeys as foundational myths that either reinforce or question cultural values, and the way heroism gets constructed around
them. Reality shows borrow a documentary style to tell very deterministic stories that reinforce cultural values and make heroes out
of the people who participate. *The Bachelor* naturalizes its beauty-
pageant-as-courtship contest as an open-ended journey or "quest"
for love. "Life" and "experience" may be random and chaotic, but a
journey, in theory, has a purpose. It suggests destiny. It elevates the
speaker from clueless bumbler to epic hero; it confers a mythic fate
onto whoever uses it, turning ill-advised entanglements and poorly
handled interpersonal conflicts into scenes from the foundational
myths of a brave new culture.

But there is almost nothing open-ended about the doomed
journeys on *The Bachelor*. There is travel involved, and an emotional trajectory, but the "journey" is as controlled and shaped by
the show's producers and editors as is the inclusion of a typecast
group of women. There is the weepy one, the slutty one, the down-
to-earth one (She is so nice and funny! Why do looks have to matter as much as they do?), the batshit crazy one, the tragic one, the
backstabber—it goes on. It's less about reality than about the re-
moval of reality from the process of finding a mate; a kind of systematic decontextualization of love distilled to a luxury shopping
experience. Audiences are trained to expect the "journey" to unfold
along a well-worn path, and on a strict timeline, and they get upset
when it doesn't unfold exactly as it should. Then, in real life, non-

reality-show people are allowed to use the "journey" to reframe dumb moves, selfish decisions, and other personal mistakes as externally imposed trials on the path to triumph.

The Bachelor presents itself as a show about beautiful young single people finding love, but the show is less a matchmaking service than a sporting event. The sport is femininity. Part human experiment, part longitudinal study of the effects of enculturation on the self-concept of the hot-girl cohort, *The Bachelor* games marriage — it is a game (where the prize, presumably, is all the housework) that is won by the woman who is best able to mold herself into the current ideal of "true womanhood." The constructed ideal looms larger than ever. If you don't believe me, watch all the seasons. Watch the red-carpet coverage of every awards show ever broadcast over the past fifteen years. Sometimes, it seems like popular media exists primarily to set impossible standards and then to shame people who don't try their hardest to meet them. It is, after all, the greatest myth-making machine the world has ever known. And the purpose of myth, as Roland Barthes pointed out, is to turn culture into nature. You can't argue with nature. Everybody submits.

In one season I followed, the bachelor on *The Bachelor* is an Iowa farm boy plucked from his Walmart-vanquished town and transported to a fantasy world of mansions, helicopters, Grand Canyon picnics, mink eyelashes, and bikini parades in downtown L.A. Temporarily recast as a savior prince, as the guy to take you away from it all, this guy, it turns out, really is the guy to take you away from it all. His town boasts a population of about four hundred people. It no longer has a restaurant or a grocery store. Why these women are torturing themselves to win him is unclear. One of the finalists is a fertility nurse in Chicago. She wants to give it all up for love. All of it: fertility nursing, income, independence, Chicago, purpose, life. I am not *not* romantic. I am, if anything, exceedingly romantic. I believe completely in the primacy of feeling. I lived my whole life in hot pursuit of the "unappeasable yearning for unattainable goals," as Isaiah Berlin put it. But this is bullshit. The women on *The Bachelor* shows aren't interested in marriage except as a certificate of completion; proof that they've become what a girl is still expected to become. What they're looking for is the chance to embark on the singular adventure they've read about and seen acted in movie after movie their whole lives: the chance to be the heroine in a marriage plot on the grand, transcendently validating, superstar scale that is so tantalizingly within reach. Of course, the "journey" undertaken on *The Bachelor* is nothing like an actual journey. It's an instructional guide for girls at home about what matters, what should be displayed, and what should remain hidden. The farm boy is their best shot at the fairy tale, a fairy tale that will conclude on the suggestion that a marriage is imminent. It's not. Marriage is immanent. Judging by the show's outcomes so far, the bachelor and his chosen bride will not marry each other. Maybe they will date for a while, then break up. Maybe they will eventually meet their spouses on Tinder, or stay single. Marriage is not the actual goal. The actual goal is to be shown to have the winning strategy, to be seen winning, to balance what should be displayed with what should be hidden — to understand how a girl can be a winner.

Once, when Kira was two and I was in a bad place — depression, but also Texas — I took her with me on a visit to New York — a work journey. And one evening, we were walking back to my friend's place in Brooklyn at dusk, and it was a beautiful night, and then suddenly in my memory, we were running — then, flying. I was carrying Kira like a koala pup, her arms and legs wrapped around me, and an impenetrable force field grew around us, a glowing energy shield of love and power. I felt invincible then, like nothing could ever hurt me again. It was the first time I'd felt not-afraid since she was four months old. Maybe it was the change of scenery, or feeling reconnected to the world again, or the depression lifting. Maybe it was a brief, psychotic break after months of cratering sadness and loss of hope. Whatever it was, it was transporting.

There's a show I like called *UnREAL*, a scripted drama about a fictional reality show called *Everlasting*, modeled on *The Bachelor*. The main characters are two female producers: Rachel, who has a complicated emotional history; and her borderline sociopathic boss and mentor, Quinn. Rachel's job is to produce the show's dramatic story lines by "producing" the girls on the show. The producers typecast the contestants (wifey, villain, slut) and tell their stories accordingly. They probe their psychological pasts, exploit their insecurities, and feed them all sorts of fantasies and lies. Rachel has a gift for psychological manipulation, having been "produced" her whole life by her controlling psychiatrist mom. Reality is produced through storytelling is produced through framing; what's in and what's out.

UnREAL is about authorship and authority, speech and reality, fairy-tale romance and social control. Rachel is gifted at her job but lacks authority, because people think she's crazy. Quinn has authority, but everyone hates and fears her, and she does all the work while getting none of the credit. Chet, her married boyfriend and the do-nothing, drug-addicted creator of the show, originally stole the idea from her and never gave her a controlling partnership. Moreover, the network executives feel comfortable dealing with Chet, not Quinn. If they can avoid dealing with Quinn, they do. In the second season, Quinn takes over the show and promotes Rachel to her former job. Then Chet returns, having completed a men's paleosurvival course, and tries to take the job back. In a power play, Rachel goes over Quinn's head and tries to gain control of the show, telling the head of the network that Quinn and Chet are making two different versions of the story: Quinn is producing the usual treacly fairy tale, and Chet is making a pornified "man version." The head of the network listens but doesn't put Rachel in charge. Instead, he brings in an award-winning, Ivy League–educated documentarian, Coleman, with an overall deal at the network. Coleman has no idea how the show is made, so Rachel shows him. She and Quinn convince a claustrophobic contestant with an abusive past to hurt another girl, then they lock her up in a basement cell as punishment, knowing she was locked up as a child. They tell her that her only shot of staying is by telling the "suitor," Darius, all about her tragic childhood in foster care. She does, and then they bring in an actress to play her mother, to say she is lying. Darius cuts her from the show for being dishonest, and she goes crazy. Coleman worries that she'll sue the show, but Rachel reassures him. They have the network, the lawyers. Who's going to believe the girl?

Besides, doesn't he get it? That's how you make the story.

15

A Modest Proposal for More
Backstabbing in Preschool

A FEW YEARS AGO, I WAS DRIVING KIRA TO HER PLAY-based, shoe-optional, sugar-free Arcadia of a preschool — a magical place where chickens roam free and grow fat off the spilled Pirate's Booty of the land, and where the major areas of academic focus seem to revolve around turn-taking, problem solving, and Rosa Parks — when suddenly I experienced a moment of self-doubt so paralyzing I almost had to pull over. The radio was tuned to an NPR show where callers were debating the decision by Yahoo!'s then new CEO Marissa Mayer to ban employees from working from home. I'd been thinking about Mayer since early that morning, having accidentally fallen into an Internet rabbit hole and spent half an hour scurrying frantically around her contemporary art collection, her standing Saturday-morning salon appointments, her Oscar de la Renta addiction, her $5 million penthouse atop the Four Seasons in San Francisco, her Craftsman in Palo Alto, her $117 million annual compensation package, and her estimated $300 million net worth before managing to claw myself out. I was thinking about the way she'd rather high-handedly dismissed her need for maternity leave as if unaware that having built a nursery next to her office elided her need for it. The boast suggested a lack of self-awareness and insulation from reality so egregious they would make Marie Antoinette roll her eyes. The suggestion that people who didn't like it go elsewhere added insult to injury. In the only industrialized country without family leave, where else was there to go?

I was in a bleak and self-censorious mood by the time I got in the car and was visited suddenly by an apocalyptic vision of the future. I saw my daughter, once a bright sunbeam of pure potential, as a frustrated former liberal-arts major stuck in bonded servitude to a midlevel job at a company where employees were required to "live from work" and occasionally to beam themselves home for some cursory family face time, despite the easy availability of 3-D holographic telepresence software that allows people all over the galaxy to interface with each other in real time, surround sound, and smell-o-vision from the comfort of their own brain implants. I saw with blinding clarity that I was to blame for this dismal state of affairs, that it was all my fault, all mine, because I'd accidentally gone and raised a hothouse serf.

Oops.

It's hard to find your bearings in the middle of a cataclysm. That's what I tell myself when I get confused, anyway. Do you fight or surrender? Beat 'em or join 'em? How can you be sure which way is up? During Kira's last year at preschool, I was consumed by the question of where she would go to school. In the process, I toured at least half a dozen schools of every possible description. I visited public, private, progressive, academic, bilingual, charter, and magnet schools. I inventoried my values and checked my privilege and confronted my low self-esteem and insufficient feelings of entitlement. After touring one particular bastion of privilege (I don't even know why anymore; I was obsessed) with a parking structure so gleaming and immaculate I thought I was at Barneys for a second, I had fever dreams all night of having consigned my child to being a nameless cog on a *Matrix* power grid through my own selfishness and stubbornness. How could I have been so stupid as to not have joined the corporate world or at least married into it? How profligate did I have to be to have blithely chucked my shot (the good college! the brass ring!) out the window? Who did I think I was to get away with anything? What did I even think I was doing?

I had fevered dreams about that parking structure, too, about how it would never be ours to park in. I felt so bereft, and so relieved not to belong there.

A friend told me about a mother at her daughter's school who, when asked about her work, looked at her sadly and said, "I'm lucky. I don't have to work." We thought a good product would be a punching bag with a chip in it that says that every time you smack it.

For a word as dominant as *choice* in the contemporary woman's life narrative, I am struck by how rarely I have heard people in my acquaintance actually use it to describe what happens after they have children. Most of my friends are journalists, writers, and other creative people with unconventional careers, but the narrative of "choice" — the idea that women reach a fork in the road and freely choose between two distinct but equally valid and available paths, each with its own moral implications — has always bothered me. It isn't just that the idea of choice assumes a privilege most people don't have (though it does) but also that there is a choice to be made, that motherhood is a job one chooses over a host of other jobs, like firefighter or ballerina. But it wasn't until I made my Goldilocks tour of schools that I was struck by how pernicious and illusory the notion of choice really is. Stress over choosing a child's school — even when you don't have much of a choice — comes down to anxiety over the child's future. What will give the child the best chance in life? And when the child is a girl, the question becomes more fraught. We don't live in an equitable society, we just pretend we do and are punished when we suggest otherwise. We force women into a false choice that isn't a choice, really. Then we make them feel bad no matter which option they "choose."

I was in my mid-twenties when I first started hearing about how women fell behind men in the workplace because they "chose" to take time off to have kids, and then had a hard time reentering the workforce. And I was in my early thirties when the "mommy wars" really took off. I remember feeling very suspicious of this narrative. After Harvard Business School published a survey that showed how motherhood impacted its graduates' careers, *New York* magazine's Lisa Miller mused,

> Perhaps it is a uniquely American desire to uphold the myth of the meritocracy, the ideal of the level playing field. If we can pin a woman's stalled trajectory on the fact that she took too much maternity leave, or she was devoted to the point of obsession to her progeny and took her eye off the ball at work, or she conceived and bore too many children, or she can't or won't do the hours or the face time needed to succeed, or she didn't find the right mentor, or she couldn't figure out the rules of the game, or she didn't try hard enough — then at least we preserve the possibility that some women, if they play their cards exactly right, can succeed.

That's what it was: the feeling that it was your fault, that you had nobody to blame but yourself.

Once, I was having a drink in San Francisco with a friend who'd gotten pregnant as a teenager and kept the baby, even took her with her to college. At the bar, we ran into a guy she knew. He asked about her daughter and then asked me if I had kids. I said I didn't. He smiled at me sadly and said, "Didn't you want any?" *Didn't I?* I was barely thirty.

The culture pushes women to "become moms," but it's not until you have a child that you understand what the culture thinks becoming a mom is. It comes as a shock, after a lifetime of Hallmark commercials and the constant idealization of motherhood, to realize just how socially devalued mothers really are. Becoming a mother is bad for your career. It's also bad for your image. The functional role of "mom" as portrayed in media is all-consuming. It eradicates personhood. No more fun, sex, fashion, music, tech, or autonomous existence for you! Everything you do, own, think, and wear will be devalued by its association with you, becoming the most degraded version of itself. Your jeans will become "mom jeans." Your dinner out with a friend will become a "moms' night out." Your technology will be deemed simple enough for you to use it. If somebody wants to fuck you, it will be as a "mom" — which is to say, in defiance of all known rules governing human behavior, kinkily, and with a sense of humor (but it will beat what people think of you if you are "childless," of course). A friend of mine, a mother of two who has a big media job, told me that her younger, single boss kept using the expression "cool mom" whenever he wanted to describe something that he thought was cool, but wasn't. Like, my friend would ask his opinion on a video, and he'd say, "I don't know, that's so cool mom."

She waited for him to realize that he was saying this to her, and that it was denigrating. He never did.

Even today, a "mom" is a person for whom the need for an income — forget about the need for meaningful, productive work — is strangely obviated, as though babies filled their diapers with hundred-dollar bills. Echoing Charlotte Perkins Gilman a century later, Alison Gopnik wrote in the *Wall Street Journal* about the problem of thinking of parenting as a job rather than as a function of being human. A job is either a project undertaken with a specific goal in mind or paid labor — the place where you go to exchange your time for wages. It's weird that we even use the lowly word *job* to refer to the exalted task of child rearing; if we're going to go with employment-related metaphors, doesn't *career* seem more appropriate? "Job" implies we have a specific outcome in mind, we expect something from the product of our labor. But a child is not a book you are writing or a cake you are baking or a PowerPoint deck you are assembling. "Working to achieve a particular outcome is a good model for many crucial human enterprises. It's the right model for carpenters or writers or businessmen. You can judge whether you are a good carpenter or writer or CEO by the quality of your chairs, your books or your bottom line. In the 'parenting' picture, a parent is a kind of carpenter; the goal, however, is not to produce a particular kind of product, like a chair, but a particular kind of person." Gopnik reminded us that there are a few years when combining motherhood and work is difficult but that it gets easier as children grow up, and that having children and work should not be mutually exclusive for anyone.

> Let's recall that "parent" is not actually a verb, nor is it a form of work. What we need to talk about instead is "being a parent" — that is, caring for a child. To be a parent is to be part of a profound and unique human relationship, to engage in a particular kind of love, not to make a certain sort of thing. After all, to be a wife is not to engage in "wifing," to be a friend is not to "friend," even on Facebook, and we don't "child" our mothers and fathers. Yet these relationships are central to who we are. Any human being living a fully satisfied life is immersed in such social connections.[1]

Here's something I didn't know until quite recently: During World War II, the United States had federally funded, government-administered child care.[2] An amendment to the Lanham Act in 1942 authorized the funding of a massive system of federally and locally funded high-quality day-care centers, which were established in every state except New Mexico. Over the course of the war, the government provided care for some six hundred thousand children — approximately one in ten of those who needed it. For fifty cents a day, a mother could drop off her child for enriching care that was found to have lasting positive benefits on the children's well-being.[3] After the war, the centers were closed despite appeals from working mothers, civic groups, and educators. As Eleanor Roosevelt wrote in a newspaper column, "The closing of child care centers throughout the country certainly is bringing to light the fact that these centers were a real need. Many thought they were purely a war emergency measure. A few of us had an inkling that perhaps they were a need which was constantly with us, but one that we had neglected to face in the past." She quoted from a letter she received from a woman that she believed expressed "the kind of thing a great many people are feeling," including the fact that, to her surprise, women were "organizing to express their feelings on this subject." The woman wrote to say that not all husbands returned from the war, and some came back unable to work, and their children had benefited greatly from attending centers that they couldn't have afforded otherwise.

As the closing of the centers helped move women out of jobs that could then be given to returning soldiers, and the feminine mystique kicked in full force, the need for child care didn't go away. More women worked outside the home in 1955 than at any point in American history.[4] That number increased to 40 percent by 1960. Forty percent of married mothers worked in 1970, and only about 24 percent of them had kids under a year old. In 1971, on a bipartisan vote, Congress passed the Comprehensive Child Development Act, a bill cosponsored by Senator Walter Mondale and Representative John Brademas to establish a very similar system of government-funded centers, which they hoped would eventually lead to universal child care. Mondale's intent was to make the centers high-quality and available on a sliding scale, so as "to avoid typing it as a poor person's program." On the advice of political commentator Pat Buchanan, however, President Nixon vetoed the bill, saying that it would "commit the vast moral authority of the National Government to the side of communal approaches to child rearing over against the family-centered approach." Opponents attacked it with Red-scare rhetoric. According to New York Republican senator James Buckley, the law would create pressure "to encourage women to put their families into institutions of communal living."[5] By the mid-seventies, the economy was tanking, interest rates were sky high, and married mothers entered the labor force in huge numbers. By 1984, 59 percent of married mothers worked. The government was aware of these statistics but did nothing to address the problem of child care or equal pay. Instead, psychologists continued to dispense helpful advice about how working mothers were scarring their children for life — but, hey, go "find yourself" — and the media latched onto hysteria about an epidemic of satanic abuse in day-care centers.

Now, decades later, the mothers of more than 64 percent of pre-kindergarten-aged children are in the labor force, yet our country's work-family policies are worse than they were in the mid-forties, when that number was only 10 percent (and the supply still didn't meet the demand).[6] As Rhaina Cohen wrote in the *Atlantic*, "Now, in 31 states and the District of Columbia, the average annual cost to send an infant to daycare can exceed a year's tuition and fees at a public university. High childcare costs do not merely strain parents' budgets; they often pressure women to drop out of the workforce, because in many cases the price of childcare would surpass earnings from a job. A lack of affordable childcare has contributed to the yawning long-term earnings gap between women and men."

My friend Darby told me a story about when her daughter (and Kira's good friend), Sydney, heard the expression "throws like a girl" for the first time. She took it for a meaningless tautology. "Of course she throws like a girl," Sydney said, like it was the most obvious thing in the world. "She's a girl." Darby had to explain that "like a girl" was intended as criticism, that it expressed a belief "some people have" that girls are less good at doing things than boys, just in general. Sydney listened patiently for the punch line or the corrective. She waited. It didn't come.

Finally, she said, "Whatever. I throw better than Daddy." Then she walked away.

Around the same time, Kira brought home a library book about a brother and sister who time-travel to Ancient Greece. Upon arriving in Athens, they are greeted by Plato (because all time travelers get the celebrity VIP treatment), who informs them that girls are not allowed to watch the Olympic Games. Girls aren't allowed to go to school, either, or learn to read and write. Then he introduces them to a great poet who can't put her name on her work or she'll get in big trouble. "What?!" Kira yelled, indignant. "That makes no sense!"

It bothered me that the book framed this as a thing of the past, that it didn't go beyond simply noting the unfairness. It's easy to deplore past injustice. It makes you look good. It's much harder, especially in a children's book, to confront why injustice arises, how injustice is consciously and unconsciously perpetuated, and why it is allowed to continue while we are fed fairy tales about the way things are now. Kira's shocked disbelief was made possible only by her innocence. Eventually, she'll shed it and no longer be shocked. The stories still won't make sense, but she'll stop expecting them to.

In the meantime, what should we tell our daughters about fairness? How should we raise them? Maybe we should consider types of pedagogical approaches better suited to the current environment — wilderness survival camp, maybe? gladiator school? Should I start organizing Lean In Circle playdates? Driving to preschool that morning, Kira got (understandably) annoyed with NPR and asked, "Is there anything about Rosa Parks on that thing?" And, you know, there wasn't. But now, several years later, all through the third grade, she has gotten to know a lot about Donald Trump. At what point, and how, do I prepare her for the existence of that?

PART FOUR

A Mad Tea Party

"No room! No room!" they cried out when they saw Alice coming.
"There's *plenty* of room!" said Alice indignantly.

— Lewis Carroll, *Alice's Adventures in Wonderland*

16

Let It Go

FORMER UKRAINIAN PRIME MINISTER YULIA TYMOSHENKO was released from prison, and every time I opened my browser to the *New York Times* home page, I saw Elsa, queen of Arendelle. Like Elsa, Tymoshenko has the folkloric fairy-tale look of a Disney princess combined with the forbidding *froideur* of one of its villains. And it's not every day that a blond, peasant-braided head of state unseated by a murderous rival dominates the news. Naturally, you lump them together. Or maybe I'd started to see Elsa everywhere, in everything, all the time.

Kira saw *Frozen* something like thirty times. I took her to the theater the first time, after her dad and I had a fight and he jumped out of the car at a stoplight and walked home. She got scared during the scene where Prince Hans's soldiers storm the ice palace and arrest Elsa, and ran out of the theater screaming, "I have to get away from this movie!" Then someone gave us the soundtrack, and we played it on loop in the car for two months. A few days after Craig and I decided to separate, I took her to the sing-along screening at the El Capitan in Hollywood on my birthday, where we joined Darby, Sydney, and roughly another thousand tiny Elsa impersonators in heartfelt, tuneless song. It was as if we'd discovered in Elsa some kind of mystical instrument magically attuned to our emotions. After that, we got an Oscar screener and the movie took over our lives. We couldn't stop watching it, and we especially couldn't stop singing "Let It Go." For a while, I was swept away by the histrionic fun of it all, and then the pitch of our fixation started to give me pause. I couldn't decide if "Let It Go" was about submitting or rebelling. What was Elsa saying? What did I think she was saying? What did Kira? One night, as I tucked her into bed, I asked her what she thought Elsa's anthem was about, and she looked at me like she didn't know who I was anymore. "It's about her powers," she said.

I pressed her. "But what about her powers?"

She squinted at me. "It's about her *powers*!"

"OK," I said, no clearer. Then she launched into one last rousing bedtime rendition of "Let It Go," and I tried to join in, and she punched me in the eye.

Frozen is loosely based on Hans Christian Andersen's fairy tale "The Snow Queen" — so loosely, in fact, as to be nothing like it. "The Snow Queen" had been kicking around Disney for seventy years, since Walt Disney's day, defying attempts to adapt it for the screen. "The Snow Queen" is divided into seven parts. The first part consists of an explanatory myth about an evil mirror made by the devil (or, in some versions, an evil troll) that has the power to distort everything it reflects. The mirror causes "all that was good and beautiful when it was reflected therein, to look poor and mean; but that which was good-for-nothing and looked ugly was shown magnified and increased in ugliness." Excited by the possibilities, some demons (or trolls) decided to take the mirror up to heaven, but dropped it on the way up so that it shattered on earth and sent specks and shards flying. The specks and shards lodged in people's eyes and hearts, distorting their vision and making them cruel.

In part 2, we're introduced to Kai and Gerda, two little neighbor children who love each other like siblings. Kai and Gerda love to listen to Gerda's grandmother's stories about the beautiful but frightening Snow Queen, who peeps into people's windows at night and covers their panes with flowers made of frost. Kai threatens to melt her on the stove if she comes near their houses, and the Snow Queen appears in his window that night. The next summer, he feels a pain in his heart and his eye, and soon he's mocking Gerda and rejecting her in favor of the big boys in the square. ("His games now were quite different to what they had formerly been; they were so very knowing.") The Snow Queen comes for him soon afterward, freezes his heart with kisses, and spirits him away to her ice palace, where she tasks him with working out pointless logic problems until he's literally blue in the face.

Meanwhile, an inconsolable Gerda sets out to find him. On her journey, she meets some magical talking flowers, a witch who wants to keep her, a prince and a princess who tempt her to stay with them, a band of robbers who capture and threaten to kill and eat her, a fierce little robber girl who frees her from the robbers, and a Finn woman and a Lapp woman who help her reach her destination. Eventually, Gerda reaches the Snow Queen's castle and finds Kai alone, "quite blue, yes, nearly black, with cold," trying to solve math problems in a near catatonic state. Gerda throws herself at him and weeps hot tears upon his breast. In real life, we know, this tactic usually backfires, but in this instance her weeping "melted the lump of ice and consumed the splinter of glass that was in his heart" and broke the spell.

"The Snow Queen" is sometimes considered a feminist fairy tale, because it's the girl who undertakes the brave quest to save the boy, but this interpretation relies on a fundamental misreading of the story. Andersen was not remotely interested in subverting the patriarchy — on the contrary. The working-class son of a cobbler and a washerwoman, he was brought up and educated by a wealthy bourgeois Copenhagen family. His life with them inculcated a worshipful attitude toward elites, an enthusiasm for essentialist ideologies, and a deep sense of inferiority. Andersen continued what Jack Zipes describes as "the Brothers Grimm mission of remolding oral folktales explicitly for a bourgeois socialization process."[1]

"The classical fairy tale for children and adults reinforced the patriarchal symbolical order based on rigid notions of sexuality and gender," he writes.

Stereotypes, not archetypes—depicted in printed and staged versions of fairy tales tended to follow schematic notions of how young men and women behave and should behave. Though it is somewhat of a simplification, most of the heroes are cunning, fortunate, adventurous, handsome, and daring; the heroines are beautiful, passive, obedient, industrious, and self-sacrificial. Though some are from the lower classes and though the theme of "rags to riches" plays an important role, the peasants and lower-class figures learn a . . . set of manners, customs, normative behavior, and thinking that enables them to fulfill a social role, to rise in social status, and to distinguish themselves according to conventional social class and gender expectations.[2]

If anything, the fact that adorable little Gerda prevails over the terrifying specter of the frosty and aloof but lethally enchanting Snow Queen can more accurately be read as a moral about the benefits of girls remaining pure and childlike forever. Gerda, in the story, represents innocence, whereas the Snow Queen, as Naomi Lewis writes in her introduction to Andersen's *The Fairy Tale of My Life: An Autobiography,* is "neither good nor evil: She is Experience." Kai is corrupted by the latter and redeemed by the former. Gerda becomes a "true woman," and a "true woman" never grows up, never wakes up, never learns. She's there to help, and to save the boy from himself.

That's a weird story. Then what happened?

The Disney project was revived in 2010, then shelved again after the disappointing box-office results of *The Princess and the Frog.* *Tangled,* with its prominent male lead, was put ahead of it on the production slate, and it did well enough to convince Disney to try again. Jennifer Lee was brought on to write the screenplay, and later to codirect.

What is Frozen *even about?*

In *Frozen,* Jennifer Lee's adaptation of the story, Elsa and Anna are sisters. Elsa has magical powers that allow her to create things made of snow and ice. Originally, Elsa was modeled after the Snow Queen and conceived as the villain of the piece. At some point, however, the songwriters asked themselves what it would feel like to be cursed with an awesome power that you are taught to be ashamed of. The song made Lee rethink the Snow Queen entirely. The queen was renamed Elsa and made queen of Arendelle. Gerda became Anna, her little sister. One day, while playing as children, Elsa accidentally zaps Anna in the head with an ice beam and nearly kills her. Their parents spirit her away to the land of the trolls, where Anna's consciousness is restored and her memory is erased. From then on, the girls are kept locked up in the castle. Elsa is made to wear gloves and told not to touch things and to keep a lid on her feelings. This makes her fearful and anxious. Nobody tells Anna anything. All she knows is that Elsa used to love her and now she doesn't. This makes her needy and desperate. The isolation warps them both. Trapped in a story they had no hand in creating, the sisters spend their time enacting their respective pathologies: Elsa struggles to contain her feelings while Anna projects herself in fantasies into the paintings on the walls and dreams of imaginary loves.

On the day of her sister's coronation, Anna falls instantly in love with a visiting prince she's just met, named Hans. "Can I say something crazy?" she asks during their falling-in-love number. "I love crazy!" he says. And at the end of it he says, "Can I say something crazy? Will you marry me?" he asks. "Can I say something crazier?" she replies. "Yes!" When Anna tells Elsa about her engagement, Elsa says that she can't marry a man she just met, and they fight. The stress unleashes Elsa's powers, and she is outed as a freak — a princess with powers! The Duke of Weselton, a visiting potentate, brands her a monster, and the mob runs her out of town on a rail. Elsa flees to the North Mountain, where she builds herself a glittering ice palace, transforms into the Snow Queen, and declares her intention to be "alone and free" forever. Perhaps her anthem can be interpreted as Elsa's intention to break with bourgeois convention and step into a radical void. And yet Elsa's flight from repression and her big creative awakening coincide with her transformation into a showgirl sex kitten.

"Let it go, let it go," she belts out, "that perfect girl is gone!" as she transforms into an even icier and more perfect girl than before, a sexy version of her uptight self in a skintight dress slit up to here and high heels made of jagged shards of ice.

Meanwhile, Anna sets out to find Elsa and bring her back to Arendelle, leaving Hans in charge. On her journey, she meets a scrappy ice salesman, Kristoff, and an enthusiastic snowman, Olaf, whom Elsa created as a kid and who represents her long-suppressed youthful exuberance and creativity. The three of them eventually reach Elsa's castle, and Anna tries to persuade her to return to defrost Arendelle. The realization that she has frozen Arendelle sends Elsa into a spiral of self-loathing, and she zaps her sister again — this time in the heart. Kristoff brings Anna back to Arendelle so Hans can bestow upon her "true love's kiss" and prevent her from turning into an ice sculpture. But Hans is only too happy to get Anna out of the way so he can assume the throne. He doesn't love her: he only just met her. Who does love her, of course, is Elsa, and vice versa. Just before she turns to ice, Anna prevents Elsa's execution; and Elsa, in turn, weeps hot tears upon her frozen sister and brings her back to life. Hans is arrested, peace is restored, and Elsa — presumably back on the throne again — becomes a kind of magical, mystical, celibate hostess, using her magic to turn Arendelle into a playground; her creativity has been tamed, her fundamental aloneness confirmed. Nobody gets married at the end.

What actually is a princess, anyway (part 1)?

When I ask Kira what she thinks a princess is, she replies without hesitation: "It's a very fancy woman who gets her own way." But a few weeks later, we're at the part in *A Little Princess* where Sara Crewe learns that her father has died penniless and that she is now at the mercy of the horrible Miss Minchin. Kira protests indignantly that being a princess has nothing to do with having nice things but with being a kind and good person.

Modern princesses, both real and fictional, are symbols at war with their own symbolism. The commonplace that every girl is a princess has morphed into the expectation that every princess be an everygirl: from Rapunzel to Anna to the Duchess of Cambridge. Her delight in life's simple pleasures contains an equal measure of contempt for its more sophisticated ones. The platonic everyprincess as imagined by Disney is a girl of simple tastes: She loves hot dogs but hates aspic, loves ball games but hates opera. She is baffled by silverware placement. She talks, acts, and comports herself like a middle-class American teen, or a reality-show contestant. She contains all the princess tropes as well as their inverse opposites. She's not just an idea made flesh, she's the *history* of an idea made flesh: the personified record of our relationship to the archetypal princess. A princess, real or fictional, must project a persona that is active, independent, spunky, free-thinking, unpretentious, approachable, accomplished, inherently democratic, and intrinsically cool. That is, she has to be these things, if she wants to go on being loved by the taxpaying, ticket- and tabloid-buying public. For a princess to maintain her sovereignty and/or her market dominance in a society that can tolerate pretty much any degree of unfairness (as long as it's not made to confront how insurmountable the unfairness is), she must reject the role of the princess and act instead like a celebrity: lucky, grateful, and humble, the beneficiary not of privilege but of random, unbiased, equitable chance.

The clearest indication that Anna is *Frozen's* protagonist, for instance, is that she is presented as the "normal" sister: ordinariness, in the popular culture, is the most exalted condition to which a girl can aspire. If Elsa is locked away from view and told to conceal her powers and repress her ice-triggering emotions, Anna not only seems to have been the victim of an unconscionable level of neglect, she also appears to have received no education whatsoever. It's not Anna's lack of magical ice powers that distinguishes her from Elsa but rather her inexplicable discomfort with her position. Anna's every endearing quirk underscores a neurotic uneasiness with authority. Despite having been born in a castle and remaining there her whole life, Anna talks, acts, and generally behaves like a tween in a Disney Junior show. This makes more sense when a princess is a commoner who marries a prince and gets to experience the life of a princess without inhabiting the role. But the qualities that make Anna "common," "likable," and "relatable" (her vulnerability, low self-esteem, eagerness to please, and insecurity) are actually maladaptive and ultimately counterfeit, because they are born from her being systematically deprived of the truth of her situation. No one tells her about Elsa's powers or about why she and her sister have been locked away from the world. Her parents are trying to protect her, but by not cluing her in to the truth, they've set her up to make herself vulnerable to anyone who shows her an ounce of affection, like the nefarious Prince Hans, who tries to use Anna to usurp Elsa's throne.

Pop culture now operates on an infinite, self-referential, constantly accelerating feedback loop. Meaning is contested almost as quickly as it's produced, and the amalgam becomes the new meaning, which is contested almost as quickly as it's produced. Eventually, there comes a point when an archetype is subverted so many times that it ceases to mean anything. As Peggy Orenstein relates in *Cinderella Ate My Daughter: Dispatches from the Front Lines of the New Girlie-Girl Culture*, Disney executives were deliberate in making sure that the concept of princess was defined broadly enough so that it could mean anything or that "it actually has no meaning." Or if the meaning is that a princess is no longer to be defined by her marriage or her lineage or her manners or her duties, then how is she to be defined? By her beauty, her sexiness, her finery, her jewelry, her isolation, her sadness, her lack of power.

What actually is a princess (part 2)?

Once, Kira and I waited in line for more than an hour at Disneyland to go through a princess receiving line, after which she darted back to Cinderella to ask, "Are you princesses real?" The girl playing Cinderella held out her arm for Kira to touch, which struck me as a brilliantly evasive move. How else to answer the question? Kira dutifully stroked the proffered limb, but I could tell she was disappointed. It's not what she was asking. She wanted to know if the mystique was real. She was trying to reconcile the story with reality.

The highly processed femininity is fascinating, because it's so obviously fake and put-on. Yet it's precisely this unabashedly artificial, performed femininity of Disney princesses that adults don't like and little girls love. It's like candy. The more artificial, fantastical, exaggerated, and abstracted, the better. It's not enough for candy to be candy. It has to symbolize candy, too.

Removed from their social and historical context, fairy tales are transvalued as human nature, but using "Snow White" as an object lesson in gender is kind of like using the Venus of Willendorf for anatomical reference. "When history falls away from a subject," Marina Warner writes in her book *From the Beast to the Blonde: On Fairy Tales and Their Tellers*, "we are left with Otherness, and all its power to compact enmity, recharge it and recirculate it."[3] The story becomes another delivery system for ideology passed off as truth. It becomes a narrative system, a feedback loop, recursive and inescapable.

What was a fairy tale originally?

In her book, Warner writes about the origins of fairy tales as cautionary tales for girls. Until they were collected, recorded, and published by academics and writers like Charles Perrault, the Brothers Grimm, and Hans Christian Andersen, fairy tales (the word *fairy*, in the Romance languages, has etymological roots in *fate*) were the domain of old women — grandmothers, nurses, and servants — charged with caring for children. Stories like "Snow White," "Cinderella," and "Sleeping Beauty" — with their often nameless or descriptively named archetypal characters, their generic and remote backdrops and vague time periods, and their magical, terrifying, flamboyantly implausible plots — served a pedagogical function: to wise up a girl by dramatizing some of the real-life scenarios she might encounter, like losing her mother, or encountering a hostile mother-in-law in her new husband's house, or losing her father and finding herself in competition for resources with his second wife. Warner describes fairy tales as "successfully involv[ing] their hearers or readers in identifying with the protagonists, their misfortunes, their triumphs" while presenting "pictures of the perils and possibilities that lie ahead" and pointing to "possible destinies, possible happy outcomes."

Fairy tales were old wives' tales for soon-to-be new brides, at once universalizing and disguising certain inescapable realities. They were a way of giving girls the lowdown and a heads-up, as Warner writes, "us[ing] terror to set limits on choice and offer consolation to the wronged, draw[ing] social outlines around boys and girls, fathers and mothers, the rich and the poor, the rulers and the ruled, point[ing] out the evildoers and garland[ing] the virtuous," and "stand[ing] up to adversity with dreams of vengeance, power, and vindication." They reflected the experience of being a young girl in a patriarchal system. They testified to the powerlessness, injustice, and exclusion that were par for the course, and offered strategies for self-protection. Marriage was a way, if it worked out, of transcending these conditions. If it didn't, it would become those conditions themselves.

Literary fairy tales — that is to say, fairy tales that have been collected in books or made into films for wide audiences — since their appearance in sixteenth-century Italy, have always played a significant role in the acculturation of children. With their simple, stock characters, their fantastical plots, and their indeterminate, ahistorical settings, they have relied on the appearance of childish fantasy to mask their ideology. But whether they have been selected and modified to shape and mirror the social and political realities of the times or to subvert, critique, and challenge them, they're almost always prescriptive. Fairy tales set down norms for behavior and make clear the consequences of conforming to or rejecting the established codes of conduct. Such clarity naturally appeals to children and helps them think about what their place and function in the world will be when they grow up.

So, then, what do people mean when they call something a fairy tale now?

Oh, now, what we are usually describing is an unrealistic fantasy that only a very naive or ignorant person really believes in. To call something a fairy tale is to dismiss it as a naive, frivolous dream; lazy magical thinking; a promise of romance and rescue that can't be kept that allows a princess to stay a princess forever and never grow up to be a queen. Fairy tales involving princesses are also among the few popular entertainments made for girls that feature girls as protagonists.

"It is significant," Warner writes, "that when the Russian folklorist Vladimir Propp analyzed the wonder tale, he broke the form down into seven spheres of action, to which correspond different functions of the dramatis personae: the villain, the hero, the donor, the helper, the princess and her father, the dispatcher, and false hero." The indivisibility of the princess and her father, plus the absence of the mother, Warner notes, reveals "unwittingly, the patriarchal character of traditional marriage plots." The princess is leverage used to reinforce her father's power in alliances that pit women against other women. "The effect of these stories is to flatter the male hero; the position of the man as savior and provider in these testimonies of female conflict is assumed, repeated and reinforced."

On a podcast on screenwriter John August's website, the screenwriter Aline Brosh McKenna asks *Frozen* screenwriter Jennifer Lee why Elsa's transformation had to be so sexy. McKenna says, "What I had sort of admired until then was how kind of sporty they were, especially Anna, how sporty she was. And then all of a sudden she [Elsa] was sort of pageanty and she has the slit and everything. Tell me about that." And Lee replies, "Well, I can tell you. What's interesting, that actually we did a lot of push and pull. There were two things we were feeling. One is that freedom moment where you strut and you just go for it. And I was fine with that and that was great. There was a lot of pull, I will say, from the guys, of loving her as the — every man in the studio, and some of the women, were in love with Elsa."

> We used to joke, like, "Just put Anna in a closet. Just push her." There was one shot where someone was, like, "Can you push Anna further back, further back?" And I was, like, "Just take her off, just get her out of the stick. Just go stick her outside." Because Elsa was — everyone was seduced by her. And so there was this tug of war I think, a bit, of letting people have a little — people who wanted to have that a little and not be afraid of it, but not make it a sexual statement. It's more a moment of, for me, it was like you strut and you say nobody is looking, this is what I'm going to — I'm not going to be afraid of my sexuality. I'm not going to be afraid of who I am. I'm not going to be afraid of anything about myself.[4]

"But her sexuality is definitely part of it," McKenna replies. "It's text."

"I think what we have found is [that] the reaction to it" — she was referring to Elsa's transformation into a sexy showgirl on ice — "has been bigger than what we had thought it was," Lee tells McKenna. "But, that's OK. It's a moment that was — so many people worked on it that it was, yeah."

"Well, what's fascinating is it's a sexual outfit," August insists, "but she's not actually a sexual character."

"No," Lee says, "she's not."

"She doesn't even talk to a boy other than Hans for a brief second," August continues. "So, it's not that she's trying to seduce a man. There's no man around for her to seduce."

If, as Marina Warner wrote, fairy tales were meant to help identify their hearers with the protagonists — their misfortunes and their triumphs — while at the same time giving them a sense of the good and bad things that awaited them, "universalizing and disguising certain inescapable realities," and generally validating the experience of being a young girl in a man's world, then what did Elsa have to teach us? What did Elsa have to tell little girls in 2013 about what to expect?

Elsa's parents' response to their daughter's awesome powers is to fear them and lock her up. As a young princess, Elsa is kept in solitary confinement. As a young adult, she goes into self-exile on the remote North Mountain. Later, she is captured by the evil Prince Hans and imprisoned in a tower. And finally, she is returned to Arendelle, where she entertains the populace with glittering ice flurries, like a party magician. This presumed newfound freedom is confusing, too. When Elsa runs away from Arendelle, she replicates the conditions from which she escaped almost exactly (castle, gown, isolation). In fact, her transformation is a rather astonishing and unexpected dramatization of Simone de Beauvoir's observation that "one is not born but becomes a woman." When she finally gets in touch with her "authentic self," the persona that emerges is a sashaying, bedroom-eyed Celine Dion impersonator. And her song — the heartfelt expression of her deepest feelings — is rendered into a performance for an internalized audience.

Whatever. Elsa still makes no sense to me as a character. What does she actually want? What exactly is she "letting go" of, her perfectionism? her desire for approval? her internalized self-loathing? her rightful claim to the throne? her concern for what other people think of her? her superpowers? It really could be anything. Is she submitting or rebelling? "Let it go" isn't what anybody says when they want to encourage you to own your strength. It's not really ever used as an incitement to let loose your creative or destructive powers. It's what people say to other people when they want them to get over themselves, to move on, give up. "Let it go" is silencing. Maybe the makeover scene means nothing and was simply conceived as an attractive backdrop for the show-stopping musical number. It's supposed to signal that the heroine has finally come into herself by running away, giving herself a makeover in isolation, and putting on a show for nobody. What is she doing?

Well, it would seem to indicate that, rather than waking up to reality, Elsa is finally breaking with it. She's not awakened after all but split off into her own inner fantasy world. Maybe Elsa is not only Disney's first neurotic princess, but its first psychotic one, too.

Maybe it was all the mixed messages that did it. For example:

- Girls can be powerful, but their parents won't be happy about it.
- Girls are too emotional to be trusted with power. Look at Elsa. Her powers are linked to her feelings, and her feelings are out of control. She is fear of a female president personified. A monster who could unleash a snow monster on the Senate while on her period.
- Power is perhaps the most unnatural trait for a girl to possess, but other characteristics are problematic, too — creativity, especially. Spending vast quantities of time alone, doing your own, creative thing, will only make you weird and miserable. The sooner you accept this and focus your efforts on making yourself useful and doing nice things for others — for instance, building them a lovely skating rink in the courtyard of your castle — the happier you will be.
- Although it's nice to make yourself useful to others, a girl's greatest mission in life is to make herself as attractive as possible in the most impractical way possible. What is considered most attractive in a girl involves limited range of mobility (the skirt is tight and the shoes look murderous), extreme discomfort (she says the cold never bothered her, but she's far more bundled up in Arendelle before her escape than she is in the frozen North Mountain), self-abnegation (Where is the food in that castle? Where are the beds?), and crazy expense (clearly, the outfit, the hair, and the makeup cost a fortune). Natural prettiness is nice, but highly stylized hotness

(available to anyone who really puts her mind and money to it) sends the message that you really care what everybody thinks of you. It demonstrates how transforming yourself into a trophy is a good outlet for any strength of will or creativity you may have been cursed with at birth, and helps ensure that you will not be excluded from your community or abandoned by your loved ones. It teaches girls that self-objectification is a great strategy for neutralizing the qualities others may find threatening, and deflects attention away from them. It also communicates that you have your priorities straight.

• It says that the exceptional girl may be admired, but it is unlikely that any one person will love her, because she will be too intimidating. Should this happen, your best option is to make yourself useful — again, maybe by building the populace a nice skating rink?

That's it?! That's messed up.

I know. *Frozen* was sometimes talked about as a feminist princess movie because it did not end with a wedding. But, if anything, it was a feminist movie in that its heroine is being gaslit and put into one impossible double bind after another. It was not so feminist in the way independence is conflated with solitude and loneliness, and creativity and power with madness. Despite her rehabilitation, Elsa still bears all the vestiges of the Disney villainess, but she isn't bad. She just does bad things. She can't help it. She can't control her powers, because she can't control her terrifying feelings. It's her feelings that are dangerous.

Ultimately, Elsa does manage to break free, sort of. But the forces that hold her back are diffuse and insidious, and she never really embraces her desire. Apart from her PTSD reactions to her childhood abuse (after all, her parents all but chained the kid to a radiator), the questions remain: Who is Elsa? What does she want? Where do her magical powers come from, and why does nobody else in the family have them? Why do her parents fear and loathe her powers so much? Why, as Arendelle's legitimate and uncontested sovereign but also, as we have established, a person possessed of superpowers, does Elsa abdicate her position so readily, with so little resistance? Why does she turn her back on everything that belongs to her? Why does she give up so easily, and why don't we care that she never fights back?

"The idea of awakening," Warner writes, "sometimes erotically, but not exclusively, goes to the heart of the fairy tale's function. But Sleeping Beauty's angle of vision, when she opens her eyes, is different from the point of view of the prince . . . The uses of enchantment are extremely powerful, what is expressed and what is denied, what is discovered, and what is rejected, form a picture of the possible world to which Sleeping Beauty will be waking up. Who tells the story, who recasts the characters and changes the tone becomes very important: no story stays the same as its source or model, the chemistry of audience and narrator changes it."

Did you know that Jennifer Lee was the first woman to write and direct a Disney movie, not counting Brenda Chapman, who was fired from Brave *even though it was based on her experiences as a mother?*

Of course. *Brave* was basically Atalanta from *Free to Be . . . You and Me.* Her deal was that if she won the contest, she wouldn't have to marry the guy who won her in a contest. I mean, look. Little girls love princess stories because princess stories are about coming of age, and wedding scenes mark the symbolic end of childhood. Also, girls love princesses for the same reason that boys (and girls) love superheroes — because they're transcendent, peerless, righteous, and true; because they dwell in the supernatural. They're consoling proof of a moral universe in which goodness defeats evil. They wear fancy costumes. Both the superhero and the princess are symbols operating in the realm of perfection. But superheroes vanquish evil before finding love, whereas princesses aren't expected to fight their way out of situations. They aren't expected to want things, or fight for them, or win.

Once, when I was a teenager, my mother said to me, "The problem with you is that you don't know what you want. You only know what you don't want." This stung, and for a long time I held it within me like a secret flaw — proof of my fundamental inability to make the life I wanted for myself because of my inability to visualize it.

But it isn't easy to visualize. There is no coherent narrative that's generally regarded as the universal story line for women, in stories or in life. After a point, the plot just falls off a cliff.

17

All the Bad Guys Are Girls

SNOW WHITE AND THE SEVEN DWARFS IS THE FIRST DISNEY
princess movie Kira ever saw. It marked her lightning-bolt conver-
sion to the cult of Disney princesses. A few months before her third
birthday, she and her dad were at a friend's house when he texted
me a picture of her sitting on a couch in a nylon Snow White gown
with a big red bow on her head. Her eyes were wide, her jaw slack,
her face glowing. I'd later learn the come-to-princess moment was
common among girls whose parents had tried, vainly, to shield
them. My friend Dominique told me about the "Cinderella" sippy
cup someone gave her daughter Simone when she was eighteen
months old, and how from that moment on she refused any liquid
that did not emanate from its magical spout.

Soon after she saw the movie, Kira's grandparents gave her a
beautiful pop-up book of the Brothers Grimm version of "Snow
White," in which the deranged Evil Queen tries to assassinate her
stepdaughter three times for being prettier than she is — first with
a lethal lace corset, then with a poisoned comb, and finally, taking a tip from Satan, with her pièce de résistance: the poisoned
apple. In the movie, there's just the apple. The fruit of knowledge
knocks Snow White out cold, and the dwarves place her in a large
display case until the prince comes along and rescues her with his
reanimating Dr. Frankenstein kiss. Princesses were always getting
into trouble for not doing as they were told, for touching and tast-
ing forbidden things. Kira was used to this. Her favorite part of
"Sleeping Beauty" was when a hypnotized Aurora touches the spindle. ("Touch the spindle, I say! TOUCH IT!" she bellowed as we

read the book every night for nearly a year.) Yet she was amazed to discover that Snow White had fallen for the Queen's tricks not once but three times in the original. "She's the second-prettiest," she observed matter-of-factly. "But she's really dumb." There was a lot more anguish in her voice when she asked me why all the bad guys in movies were girls. She meant Disney villains, which, with the exception of Prince Hans, are in fact almost exclusively women, and never young. Princesses suffer at the hands of evil stepmothers, wicked queens, and malevolent fairies consumed with envy and rage. Experience makes them powerful, but exile makes them mean. Princesses must retain their innocence and helplessness, must not accrue experience. They must rely instead on magical (possibly imaginary) friends and the kindness of princes for any hope of delivery. I told Kira it was a good question. A few months after her third birthday, she decided she wanted to dress up as *Snow White*'s Evil Queen for Halloween. I made her a flowing cape with a stiff, upright white felt collar. She wore a cowl over her hair and a crown on top of the cowl. We hung a mirror around her neck and gave her red lips and withering eyebrows. She stayed in character all night as she trick-or-treated, imperiously looking down her nose at every Snow White she passed.

The year before she was the Evil Queen at Halloween, Kira was a robot princess. I stayed up all night making the costume from scratch, using a gallon-size milk jug with a tiara glued to it and spray-painted silver as a helmet. The year after the Evil Queen, when she was four, she dressed as a bride. We got that one at Target, in the girls'-costume aisle. When she was five, she was a cat. When she was six, she was a pirate, with an eye patch and a fake parrot pinned to her shoulder. By the time she was seven, her intense communion with princesses was over. She had moved on.

I went to see *Maleficent* without her. I worried it would be too scary, and I told her I'd tell her what it was about and then she could decide whether she wanted to see it. Afterward, I said, look —

it's really sad. Maleficent lives in a fairy kingdom that borders a human kingdom ruled by a bad king. She is pure and strong and kind and good. She has huge wings. She becomes friends with an orphan boy named Stefan who lives on the other side, and they love each other for years. ("Stefan, Aurora's dad?" she asked. In the story, Sleeping Beauty's father has a name, but her mother doesn't. "Yes, Stefan, Aurora's dad.") One day, the human king attacks the fairy kingdom, and Maleficent fights back and wins. The king wants Maleficent killed, so Stefan, who wants to be the next king after the old king dies, comes back to the fairy kingdom, drugs Maleficent, and cuts off her wings while she is sleeping to take back to the king. ("He's the bad guy?!" "He's the bad guy. I told you, it's sad.") Maleficent doesn't die, but she can't fly anymore, and it makes her sad and angry. She doesn't understand why her friend did this to her, and she never trusts anyone again. When Stefan becomes king, he marries Aurora's mother, and they have a baby. ("And Maleficent puts the curse on the baby because she is mad." "Right.") Then King Stefan gives the baby to the other fairies to hide her and take care of her, but the fairies are silly and careless, so Maleficent has to watch over Aurora to make sure she doesn't die. She feels bad about the curse. Aurora grows up feeling like someone is looking out for her, and one day, she sees Maleficent, and says, "I know who you are. You're my fairy godmother!" On Aurora's sixteenth birthday, she is taken back to King Stefan's castle, and he locks her up in a tower. He says it's for her protection. But Aurora is still cursed, so on her sixteenth birthday she pricks her finger on the spindle of a knitting needle, and not even Maleficent can undo the curse so that she doesn't die. ("Only true love's kiss." "Yes.") Then everybody tries to find Prince Philip, a cute guy Aurora met on her way to the castle, to give her true love's kiss, but it doesn't work. ("They just met the one time." "Exactly.") So everyone is really sad, because they think Aurora is going to die, especially Maleficent, because Aurora is like her daughter, so she sneaks into the castle and kisses her on the forehead because she loves her, and Aurora wakes up. ("True love's kiss!") And then, King Stefan's men try to kill Maleficent, and Aurora tries to help her and discovers the wings in a glass case, because everybody is putting girls and their parts in glass cases all the time in these stories, and the wings go flapping off to the edge of the tower and reattach themselves to Maleficent, just as Stefan is about to kill her. She flies up, and he falls over the edge to his death.

Maleficent is more than a retelling, it's a corrective. It changes the story completely by looking at it another way, from another perspective. Suddenly, it makes sense. The princess was never expected to succeed the king, or live her own adventures, or explore new lands. She was expected to disappear into her happy ending, where she would remain happily ever after, never to be heard from again. In exchange for obedience and playing her role, she would get love, praise, attention, support, and protection — all of which would be immediately withdrawn at the slightest hint of transgression or rebellion, at which point she would realize that the king was only ever protecting her against himself. That king wasn't a dad, he was a mob boss.

Say the princess plays the girl all her life but finds herself grown rich, experienced, wise, and powerful, with no male authority to lord over her — then what? What does she become, a wise ruler? a benevolent leader? a beloved queen? or an old witch? Will she be vilified, persecuted, and shunned? Will all the young princesses be told scary stories of her evil, wicked ways, and warned against following in her footsteps? Will they be denied their subjectivity and gaslighted into confusion? Will they be systematically taught to fear and loathe their future selves, the evil hag, the wicked witch, and then soothed by the promise of the benevolent protection of the paternalistic king? Is that what we want for them? Is that what they want?

"The fairy tales we have come to revere as classical are not ageless, universal, and beautiful in and of themselves," Jack Zipes writes in *Fairy Tales and the Art of Subversion,* "and they are not the best therapy in the world for children. They are historical prescriptions, internalized, potent, explosive, and we acknowledge the power they hold over our lives by mystifying them."[1] *Sleeping Beauty* is a mystification demystified by *Maleficent*. *Maleficent* allows the princess to reclaim her mother. It repairs the bond that the culture works so hard to sever. Still, the idea of Kira's beloved Sleeping Beauty losing the father she'd been so happy to return to — maybe it was too much. Maybe it would scare her. I braced for Kira to be upset, to be angry. But she thought about it. She considered the story from another angle. She got some critical distance. She understood how the story shaped the story, and how it might be reshaped. Then she said:

"That's sad. But he was mean."

18

Girls Love Math

1. NOBODY DISPUTES THE FACT THAT AGE IS CRUELER TO women than men. But why? Facebook, that tireless corroborator of the relentless march of time and its startling effect on people you knew in high school, backs me up on this. The girls don't transform in the same way. They hang on to their hair. They cycle from the soul. They can moisturize without inspiring someone to make a documentary about it.

We expect women to submit to this self-evident truth and for men to be gracious about it and try not to gloat. Mostly, we expect nobody to notice or question the different ways in which "primeness" is constructed for each gender; it is not based on the same criteria at all. If, as Hegel suggested, ideas are not just ideas but come wrapped in all flavors of attitudes, then this particular idea is a giant, gorgonzola-stuffed, bacon-wrapped fig of a notion — decadent, cloying, aged in a barrel of bullshit, warmed over, and served up again and again.

2. "Epigenetics means that our physical and mental tendencies were not set in stone during the Pleistocene age," Judith Shulevitz wrote in the *New York Times*. "Rather, they're shaped by the life we lead and the world we live in right now. Epigenetics proves that we are the products of history, public as well as private, in parts of us that are so intimately ours that few people ever imagined that history could reach them." Stories sink in and hybridize us, in other words.

I read another article about how older men are more likely than young ones to father autistic or schizophrenic kids because of random mutations that increase with age. "The age of mothers had no bearing on the risk for these disorders, the study found."[1]

And then there was this: scientists in Kyoto had successfully created fertile eggs from mouse stem cells, which, if or when the science is ever applied to humans, could mean the end of the biological clock. Will stories change to conform to reality? Or will we hold on?

3. I was about ten when I first discovered fashion magazines. My mom didn't buy them, but she did subscribe to *¡Hola!*, the Spanish version of the TV presenter and royalty-obsessed English tabloid *Hello!*, which produced a couple of fashion supplements a year. The way I remember them, they were mostly made up of row after row of small photos from designers' collections. There was something incredibly fierce about the monastic severity of the models and the cultured hauteur of the designers. (Saint Laurent! Lagerfeld! So strict and mean!) I was looking at a kind of abstracted ideal of adult womanhood in its most fully realized state. The models looked so deadly, deadly serious, these steely-eyed soldiers in their exquisite, artful, status-conferring garments (signaling discretionary income, power, and leisure to burn). I would have been shocked to learn they were not much older than I was at the time.

There's been much debate about the fact that runway models have been getting younger and younger. How young is too young for a girl to trudge down a glorified auction block in thousands of dollars' worth of clothes, impersonating a grown woman on her way to the fashion abattoir? I had honestly never given the question much thought until recently, when I stopped to read a series of op-eds weighing in on a proposal by the Council of Fashion Designers of America that a minimum age limit of sixteen be set for runway models. Some designers already adhere to it, and some don't. Even if they do, the girls they hire are rarely much more than kids, which is worth pausing to consider for many obvious reasons but also some not so obvious. In the not-so-obvious category, one comment in particular jumped out at me.

"Note that the gender-neutral models that need protecting here are implicitly girls, not boys," wrote Ashley Mears, a pop-culture and gender-sociology professor and the author of a book about the economics of modeling, in her op-ed. "Partly this stems from the entrenched celebration of women, not men, on display, and partly because male models in fashion tend to be older than their female counterparts. A 16-year-old boy on the catwalk would be as rare a sighting as a 35-year-old woman."

4. Of course I already knew this. Everybody knows. But we acclimate to weird things. The comment might not have caught my attention had I not also just been flipping through the September issue of *Harper's Bazaar*. I'd been looking at one of those seasonal roundups that tell you — "you" being the lucky possessor of tens of thousands of dollars in disposable income earmarked for your fall "must-haves" — what to wear in your twenties, thirties, forties, fifties, sixties, and seventies and beyond. Mostly, the guide was made up of pictures of garments laid flat against a background, unviolated by the imperfection of the human form. Each decade was also accompanied by a large photo of a professional modeling the look, and a small insert of a woman representative of the particular age group. (All but one of these were former models, but, OK, whatever.) Indeed, the whole thing seemed fairly inclusive and democratic (they went all the way to seventies and beyond!). But the discrepancy between the models and the "real people" grew more jarring as the ages advanced, so that by the time we arrived at the seventies (plus!), a small photo of Barbara Walters was dwarfed by a picture of a girl who could easily have been her thirteen-year-old great-granddaughter looking sad in her dowager costume.

Pairing pictures of adolescent girls with adult men, or of young women with middle-aged men, to suggest age parity produces a kind of cognitive dissonance on a mass scale. So does constantly reinforcing the idea that a thirty-three-year-old woman is somehow "older" than a man seven years older than her. (What's being referred to, though not in so many words, is her use-value in the sexual marketplace.) Cognitive dissonance, which is the condition of holding two or more conflicting cognitions at the same time, causes psychological discomfort, which is what makes toddlers in beauty pageants so creepy. (Two words that just don't go together: sexy baby.) The other thing that makes them creepy is that they call attention to how little we question this practice of systematically barring images of women over thirty-nine and replacing them with images of kids in grown-up drag. The narrative that is repeated again and again, visually and in stories, is that a woman's physical prime can never coincide with her intellectual, professional, or artistic prime. In this way, the aspirational ideal is placed in the past, where it can never be accessed. Youth and experience are once again pitted against each other; youth wins. As one commenter on the Room for Debate series said, however, "Looking at children as examples of my adulthood feels wrong."

5. Chicks really are crazy, though. The double bind is crazy-making. In the 1960s, it was thought that schizophrenics were schizophrenic because their mothers made them crazy. This theory was the result of research conducted by Gregory Bateson at Stanford. Bateson and his team formulated a theory that schizophrenics were not born but made by their mothers: mothers who trap their young, dependent children into impossible double binds, demanding two contradictory and irreconcilable outcomes at once (for example, "be yourself" and "hide your feelings") for extended periods of time. For a time, psychologists believed that this made people certifiably crazy. This theory was eventually discredited, when schizophrenia came to be seen as a biological disorder.

Paul Gibney, an Australian psychiatrist and author, in a paper symbolically rehabilitating Bateson's double bind theory for application in other situations, reframed it like this: "The essential hypothesis of the double bind theory is that the 'victim' — the person who becomes psychotically unwell — finds him or herself in a communicational matrix, in which messages contradict each other, the contradiction is not able to be communicated on and the unwell person is not able to leave the field of interaction."[2]

Bateson's original training, by the way, was as an anthropologist (he was married for a long time to Margaret Mead), and he focused on communications systems, systems theory, and cybernetics, which he then applied to the behavioral sciences. Cybernetics can be applied to the study of all kinds of systems — mechanical, physical, biological, cognitive, and social — so long as the system is part of a closed signal loop, in which the actions of a system cause changes in the environment that are fed back into the system and change its behavior.

6. I live in Los Angeles, where despite my best (and usually successful) efforts to avoid them, I occasionally hear a story like this. A friend knows an actress whose burglar-alarm code, 2828, serves as a reminder of the age she must never surpass, repeated twice for good measure. Another friend lives next door to a model-actress who, at twenty-seven, is considered to be so far out on the tail end of her prime that she was recently cast in a commercial as the wife of a forty-five-year-old man and mother of two teenage children. Although it is biologically possible that she could have given birth to the younger of the two children at the age of twelve, it hardly would have been considered optimal, nor would she have been considered an appropriate partner, at the age of ten, for a relatively mature guy of twenty-eight. (Of course, nobody really considers a twenty-eight-year-old man mature, but that's beside the point.)

Math interfered with my enjoyment of the first season of *Homeland*, because I couldn't get past the decorative casting of Morena Baccarin in the role of Nicholas Brody's wife. Damien Lewis, who plays Brody, is eight years older than Baccarin, and their daughter on the show was eighteen at the time of this writing, which means her mom would have been fifteen at the time of delivery, an unwed tenth-grader with a twenty-three-year-old Marine boyfriend, because she could not have legally married at that age.

In the pilot of *The Mindy Project*, Mindy Kaling — who was thirty-three at the time, playing an anxious thirty-one-year-old doctor — goes on a blind date with a guy played by Ed Helms — who was thirty-eight but playing who-cares — when she is interrupted by a call from a boy, the son of a patient, whose indigent, uninsured, non-English-speaking mother has gone into labor. Mindy does everything she can to dodge the call, finally grabbing the phone and hissing, "Do you know how hard it is for a chubby thirty-one-year-old woman to get a legit date with a guy who majored in economics at Duke?"

If Malcolm Gladwell was right about the study that found it takes ten thousand hours, or ten years, to get really good at what you do, then the Mindy character faces the depressing prospect of being over the hill before she even gets within shooting distance of the hill. Double binds make you crazy.

"What we see on broadcast television is that the majority of female characters are in their twenties and thirties," says Martha Lauzen, a professor and the executive director of the Center for the Study of Women in Television at San Diego State University, in Jennifer Seibel Newsom's documentary *Miss Representation*. "That is just a huge misrepresentation of reality, and that really skews our perceptions."

The movie offers some statistics. Women in their teens, twenties, and thirties are 39 percent of the population, yet they comprise 71 percent of the women on TV. Women forty and older are 47 percent of the population, yet comprise 26 percent of women on TV.

When I first moved to Los Angeles, in my late twenties, I remember being shocked by how readily women my own age accepted the "fact" that they had aged out of desirability; how resigned they were to their own irrelevance; how uncritically so many accepted this ideology propping up privilege and power inequality as being synonymous with reality rather than helping produce and maintain reality; how readily they mistook culture for nature. "It's like when a female reaches the age of 39 or 40 she simply needs to go away," Lauzen says. "When any group is not featured in the media they have to wonder, 'Well, what part do I play in this culture?' There's actually an academic term for that. It's called symbolic annihilation."

7. Remember when they made that talking Barbie, and what she said was "Math is hard!"? That was bullshit. Girls love math. We do it constantly. As a kid, I'd often lie awake in bed, frantically performing mental calculations in my head to help me figure out when, exactly, I would get to live the adult life I imagined was being suggested in the *¡Hola!* fashion supplements, some kind of unencumbered, sophisticated but fully inhabited adulthood. Not a broke, insecure young adulthood, nor a crabby, resentful parenthood, but the good part. I'd think, *If I finish graduate school at, say, twenty-eight, that leaves me six months to a year in which to work before I have children before the drop-dead date of thirty.*

Was it crazy to worry about being dismissed for being too young right up until I could start being dismissed for being too old? I spent a disproportionate piece of my twenties and thirties thinking it was all over. The funny thing is that I've always looked and sounded younger than my age. At twenty-three, I looked about sixteen — and not a lanky, ectomorphic sixteen that passes for thirty with the right makeup and clothes, either, but the kind that gets hit on by twelve-year-olds and gets patted on the head a lot. In job interviews, I'd clock the time it took for the look of surprise on the interviewer's face to relax into a look of fond condescension. Looking young, at least for me, never really got me much beyond getting carded a lot. It wasn't particularly advantageous, professionally or even socially. Considering, I can't believe how much of my youth I squandered on feeling old.

19

Train Wreck

The "liberated woman," like the "free world," is a fiction that obscures real power relations and defuses revolution. How can women, subordinate in every other sphere, be free and equal in bed? Men want us to be a little free — it's more exciting that way. But women who really take them at their word make them up-tight and they show it — by their jokes, their gossip, their obvious or subtle put-downs of women who seem too aggressive or too "easy."

— ELLEN WILLIS, "UP FROM RADICALISM:
A FEMINIST JOURNAL"

TO CALL A PERSON A "TRAIN WRECK" IS TO DECLARE WITHout equivocation that he or she is headed toward a foreseeable yet unavoidable disaster. There is no such thing as a minor train wreck. The phrase evokes a catastrophic pileup of mangled metal and bodies — a scene so grisly and gruesome that we can regard it only with horror and disgust. It's beyond empathy, recognition, even pity.

The phrase "train wreck" is used to describe a man or a woman who has lost control. But women are expected to keep more things under control than men are. When a man loses control over his libidinal impulses, we regard it with some measure of awe: it's a flameout. When a woman fails to contain herself, we leer. The female train wreck is needy, emotional, grotesque. There may be blood.

So what might a lighthearted comedy called *Trainwreck* whose main character is an adventurous young woman be about?

The title refers to a familiar tabloid trope: the attractive but reckless young girl who ruins her life, career, reputation, and finances by gorging herself on drugs, alcohol, food, toxic boyfriends, expensive clothes, and bad plastic surgery. You get it! But this isn't that story, which you already know how to consume and enjoy: ironically, with zero empathy. "Getting" the story means you're in on the joke, which means you're not the joke, which means the joke must be on her — the train wreck. So, the movie hasn't even started, and already it's painted itself into a narrative and moral corner. You expect to feel some sense of positive identification with the character. You expect to like her and relate to her. But you find yourself sitting in the stands, looking down as the girl stumbles around drunk and wobbly in platform shoes, stunned and blinded by flashbulbs. This doesn't feel great. You don't want to cast her out. You don't want to kill her. You are not a monster. So, what needs to happen? How can we look at her in such a way as to reconcile this problem?

Two possible ways: from inside Amy, looking out, or outside Amy, looking down on her.

The movie goes like this. Once upon a time, there were two little girls named Amy and Kim, who were sisters. Amy was the big sister, and Kim was the little sister. One day, their father sat them down on the hood of the car in the driveway and explained that he and their mother were getting divorced because he couldn't stop playing with other dolls (he was trying to make an analogy that they could understand) and their mother didn't like that. He explained to them that monogamy isn't realistic and asked them to repeat after him: Monogamy isn't realistic. Monogamy isn't realistic. Monogamy isn't realistic.

Jump ahead about twenty years, and Amy is now a successful magazine writer in New York. She works at a men's magazine called *S'Nuff*. She lives alone in a cute apartment, wears nice clothes, and suffers from what is framed as a pathological inability to pair-bond, which is further compounded by the delusion that she is happy. She has lots of one-night stands with guys who would all like to get to know her better but whom she can't get away from fast enough. Her hookups are as brisk, well-lit, and efficient as gynecology appointments, with the same dissociative I'm-going-to-pretend-this-isn't-really-happening-right-now quality. Amy fucks with her bra on and orgasms like a sneezing kitten. She makes jokes about penis size and pretends to fall asleep before reciprocating oral sex. She has rules against sleeping over. She drinks, but it doesn't appear to impact her life much. She is up for a big promotion at work. She has no female friends, except one girl she talks to at work. Her social life consists of hanging out with her dad, who has multiple sclerosis, and her sister, Kim, who is married and has a young stepson who seems to be about ten years old. This being a fairy tale, their mother is dead. Amy is sort of seeing a sensitive trainer, played by John Cena, who has unrequited feelings for her but is also gay. The possibility that she has not met the right person and fallen in love is not entertained. There is just something wrong with her.

One day at work, a colleague pitches a profile of Dr. Aaron Conners, surgeon to NBA stars. Amy says, "No offense, but I just think that sports are stupid and anyone who likes them is just a lesser person. And has a small intellect." So their editor assigns the story to Amy. After her first interview with Aaron, she gets drunk with him, jumps in a cab with him, and tells him to give the driver his address. He's taken aback but doesn't object. She doesn't meet his gaze. The whole thing is awkward. Nobody makes out in the cab. It's a scene about a drunken hookup written by someone who either has never had a drunken hookup or has blacked out every time. For a train wreck, Amy is remarkably together and composed.

Aaron is a rich New York City surgeon with front-row Knicks tickets and an enormous Manhattan penthouse with wraparound views of the city. His best friend is LeBron James. He is nice, down-to-earth, well-adjusted, and humble. He is also practically a virgin, having slept with just three women in his entire life. He's the forty-year-old practically-a-virgin. (LeBron James, meanwhile, plays himself as a frugal, sensitive, persnickety, hopelessly romantic, and naive *Downton Abbey* fan who is vicariously obsessed with his friend's romantic life.) He has all the positive attributes and fancy extras. This is meant to signal that he's a nice guy, a prince among men, but actually it's just weird. After his first interview/date/drunken hookup, he says, "I really like you, so we should be a couple." She's not interested, but he comes to her sick dad's rescue, and in this vulnerable moment she gives in. Amy's lifelong resistance to monogamy evaporates, and from that point on they are an item. But of course romantic comedies are about overcoming obstacles, and from the outset the obstacle to be overcome is Amy's "slutty past." It's not like you don't see it coming. From the moment weird Aaron enters the picture, the movie's perspective stops being Amy's, even though Schumer is credited as the sole screenwriter. To be fair, Aaron is also not a character so much as a combination of stereotypical attitudes: that is, he's a direct inversion of "the girl" stereotype (wrapped in a diversionary, toxic "nice guy" veneer) infused with a fragile (stereotypical) male ego. Aaron sees Amy entirely as an extension of himself. It bothers him that she doesn't like sports and criticizes the cheerleaders. When she yells, "You're going to lose us the right to vote!" from the bleachers, he tuts, "These girls work really hard!" At Kim's baby shower, Kim's husband, Tom, jokes that Aaron had better "keep [Amy] away from those pro athletes," and rather than tell Tom he's a dick, Aaron gets upset, and Tom has to reassure him that Amy's not really a slut, those are just the jokes she makes about herself, ha-ha. Amy tells inappropriate sexual jokes at the shower (girls never tell sexual jokes), and Kim doesn't like it. Their father dies, and Amy and Kim argue, because Kim feels that Amy is too critical of her "normal" choice to get married and raise her stepson. In an Orwellian twist, it turns out to be a movie about a liberated girl who finds happiness in conformity.

Later on in the movie, Aaron is honored by Doctors Without Borders and asked to give a speech. Beforehand, he criticizes Amy's dress for being inappropriate and asks if she doesn't have a gown or something. (Amy mocks him, but his hit was much harder.) At the dinner, Amy gets a text in the middle of his speech. It's from her crazy (female) editor telling her to answer or she is fired. She can't afford to lose the job. She goes outside to take the call, and when he is finished, Aaron comes out to find her. He is angry. He finds her smoking pot out the window and asks if she skipped his speech to get stoned. She explains that she thinks she is losing her job. He says it doesn't matter. He needs her. She is his "lifeline." Somehow, this segues into her asking him why he likes her — what's wrong with him? She's "a drinker." She's "been with a lot of guys."

"I don't care!" he says. "How many?"

"I don't know. How many women have you slept with?"

"I've slept with three women."

"Me, too," she says. "I've slept with three women, too."

Aaron doesn't like it that Amy drinks, smokes pot, or slept with a lot of guys before meeting him, because it makes him "feel unsafe." Just to reiterate, sex that she had before she met him makes him feel "unsafe." He says he loves her, but all he has done is claim her. Aaron tells Amy that it bothers him that she had a life before him. Amy says that maybe he should marry a cheerleader.

"Go be with that kind of girl. Little Texan with huge hair and big tits. But when you get married, she wants to be more conservative, so she gets smaller fake tits. But they still look amazing," she says.

"You know the thing about cheerleaders is they bring people together and make them happy," he replies. "Unlike you and your friends at your magazine, who sit there and judge people from afar, because if you don't try then you can't fail. That's why you're threatened by cheerleaders."

Amy keeps him up all night berating him, even though she knows he's performing a very important surgery on a very important basketball player the next day. Aaron, meanwhile, heroically struggles to stay awake for her tirade. The next morning, he tells his patient that he can't keep his eyes open, because "Amy was acting like a psycho last night." He doesn't know what he did wrong. He really likes her, "but she's like a fucking demon. She's like the fucking exorcist."

So, they really got through to each other.

In a 1992 article about *Seinfeld* in the *Atlantic*, Francis Davis writes,

> [Jerry Seinfeld's] specialty used to be called "observational" humor but has been renamed "recognition" humor, and the difference is more than semantic. Instead of generalizing from his own experience, as Mort Sahl, George Carlin, and Richard Pryor do and Lenny Bruce used to, Seinfeld, like most of his standup contemporaries, internalizes everybody's experience. The result is peevish bits about airports and dating and the candy we ate as children, which — timing and other tricks of the trade aside — you feel as though you could have come up with yourself . . . He said that when he wearies of doing the show, he'll write a final episode in which "my character will get a TV show and have to move to Los Angeles." In other words, *Seinfeld* isn't about "nothing" anymore. It's increasingly about itself.

What does it mean when a hugely famous and influential comedian or writer "internalizes everybody's experience"? Who, exactly, is "everybody" in this scenario? The short answer is, nobody. To internalize "everybody's experience" is to deny your own and replace it with what you assume (but can't possibly know) "everybody" is thinking. "Recognition humor" is a kind of preemptive defensive conformity; a hedge against experiencing your own experiences, and feeling your own feelings, and thinking your own thoughts. It's pandering to a presumed audience that expects their expectations to be met. It's McDonald's humor. It assigns comedic value to things "we can all agree are funny" (which explains how a movie like *Shallow Hal* even gets made). And it's really not very funny most of the time.

When I was a movie critic, I remember being struck by how reflexively people laughed at references simply because they'd caught the reference. Chuck Klosterman talked about something similar in his essay on laugh tracks: people laugh to indicate that they are in on the joke, that they are not the joke, that the joke is someone else. This is the falsest, most insidious kind of "recognition humor." On *Inside Amy Schumer*, things are funny because they're true; because the skits show things as we really see them but as they're rarely portrayed. We laugh because we've seen it before, because we've been there before, because there was some effort involved, some tension, in pretending things were otherwise, and her perspective lets us be real and let it go.

Conversely, in *Trainwreck*, things are funny because they're not true. The humor comes from thwarting expectations, but the expectations it thwarts are those created by other movies and TV shows a lot like *Trainwreck*.

For example:

- On *Inside Amy Schumer*, a woman feels so much pressure to fit in and be "cool" with her toxic work environment that she volunteers to bury the stripper that her coworker has strangled, while only making seventy cents to his dollar.
- A football town is so steeped in rape culture that when a new high school football coach bans raping, old ladies spit on him while out on their power walks.
- A medieval peasant girl learns she's actually a princess, then discovers to her surprise that being a medieval princess is less about balls and gowns and more about being a geopolitical pawn constantly under threat of execution and incubating male heirs.

- An all-female panel of highly intelligent professional women devolves into an apologyfest, where they apologize even while bleeding to death on stage as the moderator rolls his eyes.
- In a parody of a birth-control commercial, Amy talks to her doctor as a man's voice says, "Ask your doctor if birth control is right for you." Then a long gauntlet follows including, "Ask your boss if birth control is right for you. Ask your boss to ask his priest. Find a Boy Scout and see what he thinks. Ask the Supreme Court," and so on. Finally, she goes to the pharmacy and picks up her prescription. The pharmacist tells her there are no refills. She will have to ask everyone again next month. "Ask yourself why you insist on having sex for fun." After she leaves, a very young boy approaches the counter and asks the pharmacist for a gun. The pharmacist tosses one over and says, "Remember, that's your right!"

The jokes reveal the lie at the basis of everything (every law, every story): That only men have a sex drive, that only men have libidinal desires, that only men want things and can go out and get them. That "normal" women want nothing more than to take care of their kids and do all the housework. As Amy Schumer jokes later in the episode, "I think sex is just explained incorrectly, as far as genders go. It's like men love sex, and women just deal with it, right? Every movie, every TV show, the guy gets home from work and he's like, 'Honey, how about tonight?' And she's always like, 'Blech! You know I hate your dick!' (Laundry, laundry)." She mimes doing a small pile of laundry. "I don't know any girls like that, right? Also, it's always such a tiny, little pile of laundry. It's like not enough for a load, which I think should be the title of my next special. *Not Enough for a Load.*"

In *Trainwreck*, meanwhile, Amy breaks up with Aaron and, after their breakup, gets drunk with the magazine's intern and goes home with him. His mother walks in on them and freaks out, because he is sixteen. She's fired from her job, and her work friend — her only nonrelated friend in the world — takes her promotion. Amy shows up at the door of the immaculate, palatial suburban manse where her sister spends her days alone. Amy rings the doorbell, and Kim answers in an old flannel shirt and jeans, looking very young, like a teen hostage or a "mole woman" from *The Unbreakable Kimmy Schmidt*. You want to wrap her in a blanket and whisk her away to safety.

For a minute, I got confused and thought I'd wandered into *Room* by accident. Or some meta version of it; *Room* within a *Room*, in which Brie Larson plays a young girl locked up like a Stepford Wife, and Amy Schumer plays herself, trapped in a story fiendishly engineered to contain the uncontainable Amy Schumer.

20

Look at Yourself

JOAN AND PEGGY ARE STANDING SIDE BY SIDE IN AN ELE-
vator, staring ahead in tense silence. They've just come from a meeting at McCann Erickson, the agency that absorbed their agency,
and it did not go well. The meeting was to propose a partnership
between their client Topaz Pantyhose and McCann's client Mar-
shall Field's department store, but the McCann executives refused
to take them seriously. Instead, they spent the whole time harassing
Joan and ignoring Peggy. They said things like, "Why aren't you in
the brassiere business? You should be in the bra business. You're a
work of art," and suggesting they send the client rep a box of pears,
"because he likes a good pair." In the elevator on the way out, Joan
and Peggy stew in silence. Peggy asks Joan if she wants to get lunch.
"I want to burn this place down," Joan replies.

Peggy is angry, too. It doesn't matter how far they came at Sterling Cooper. In the new office, they're back where they started —
back to being girls in the office. Disempowered but still enraged,
they turn on each other.

"Joan, you've never experienced that before?"

"Have you, Peggy?"

"You can't have it both ways. You can't dress the way you do and
expect —"

"How do I dress?"

"Look, they didn't take me seriously, either."

"So what you're saying is, I don't dress the way you do because I
don't look like you, and that's very, *very* true."

Joan and Peggy are two of the three main female characters in

Mad Men, part of a triad that also includes Betty (Draper) Francis, Don's first wife. Joan is the former lone female partner at Sterling Cooper Draper Price, a former secretary who started out as the catty office bombshell whose real métier, at first, was men. Peggy is the working-class workhorse, the media martyr, the good girl who takes on extra work for free for the opportunity to prove herself again and again and again. Once Joan starts work at McCann, it becomes clear that the respect she won from her colleagues at Sterling Cooper won't translate. The men at the new company will never take her seriously. She'll have to start all over again from the ground up. A colleague makes a pass at her, and when she complains to her boss, he tells her to suck it up. After coolly purring her way through conflict her whole life, Joan finally loses it. She threatens to call her lawyers, the Equal Employment Opportunity Commission (EEOC), Betty Friedan, and the ACLU. Enraged, her boss fires her and says he will pay her only half of her buyout money. As establishment boys like Pete Campbell scamper off into the sunset with everything they ever wanted, Joan's career in advertising comes to an ignominious end. Her boyfriend, Dennis, a retired new-age business guy, isn't sad to hear it. He never really understood why Joan cared so much about her job in the first place. "Look at yourself!" he keeps saying, as if she could see herself through his eyes — as if she didn't look out and see things she wanted, too.

Among other things, *Mad Men* was an invitation to look back at the fictions that powered postwar consumer culture as authored by self-made and self-mythologizing men like Don Draper and endlessly promoted in mass media, mostly as a way to sell soap. Don was a copywriter, an author of influential, terribly persuasive ad campaigns, and an all-around creative genius. He re-created himself and the world so that his success would magically build up around him. In this world, only he looked out and saw what he wanted. The unwanted, unloved son of a prostitute, Don joined the service as Dick Whitman, stole a dead soldier's identity, and started over after the war as someone new. He made himself up and became the man he wished he were, a sophisticated adman about town; the man who had everything.

Don was the ostensible hero, but no characters on *Mad Men* traveled as far, or as elliptically, as Joan and Peggy. There was no route for them to travel. The wide-open primrose path that establishment boys like account executive Pete Campbell and agency partner Roger Sterling traveled in a clear, uninterrupted shot was off-limits to them, so they started by following the rules and hewing as closely as possible to the roles they'd been assigned. Peggy was the ingenue, Joan was the bombshell. Peggy learned to suppress her femininity for validation; Joan exploited hers in return for admiration and favors. Don's wife, Betty, was the alternative: the housewife marooned in the suburbs, stewing in resentment, shooting at pigeons with a cigarette dangling out of her mouth, like a wannabe outlaw.

Categories are useful to a point, but they don't tell us much about who someone is — just look at Don. Where his characteristics become meaningful is where they grant symbolic or literal admission (or both) to a group where most of the power, privilege, wealth, and authority to speak for everybody else resides; a group that positions itself as the universal subject, gazing out proprietarily on its domain, tuning everything to its pleasure, asking itself only what it likes, what it wants, what it thinks, how it feels to be itself, how the world looks from where it's standing; where only one person gets to fly off into the sunset happily ever after in a personal jet, like WASP golden-boy-executive Pete Campbell in the series finale, absolved of all mistakes and eternally forgiven.

This ready-made identity was available to Don because of the categories he belonged to and the felicitous way he looked. And, unlike the constricting female identities that limited his wife, girlfriends, and female coworkers, his ready-made identity was liberating. He was semiotically lucky. He stepped into the role of privilege as though it were a custom-made suit someone had tossed in a Dumpster. It put him in the subject position. It opened every door. That privilege was built on the same fictions that set the standards for Joan, Peggy, and Betty, whether they liked them or not, whether the standards applied to them or not, whether they acknowledged their existence in the real world or not, and regardless of what it took for each of them to wake up from the dream and become who they were.

Then again, look at Don. He was alienated from his outward self and lived inside an identity that didn't allow for the full expression of his humanity. He used his image and its effect on people to get what he wanted, because he knew (and he was right) that he could never have gotten it as he really was. He watched other people watch him and revised his behavior based on feedback. But whereas Joan and Peggy had to earn everything they became, as well as the context in which to be their actual selves, all Don had to do was walk in the door. To his credit, at least he was aware of the door. And he had to wait a long, sad time for an opening. Unlike Roger and Pete, who were born inside the room and weren't aware that a door existed, Don never took his eyes off his privilege. He knew exactly how valuable it was, how hard it was to get, how easy it was to lose. He knew it didn't just "happen naturally," that it wasn't just "what is." He understood that he could put on this persona like an off-the-rack suit or like one of the fur coats he used to sell before Roger rescued him.

Mad Men is not nostalgia; it's hindsight. Nostalgia obscures history's lessons, but hindsight lets us learn from the past. From a contemporary perspective, *Mad Men* looks at times like a horror movie. Joan, Peggy, and Betty were trapped inside the sealed-off, bricked-in fortresses that Don (consciously, because his privilege was borrowed) and Roger and Pete (unconsciously, because their privilege was inherited) had constructed for them: inescapable ideas about what they were, endlessly replicated. Joan, Peggy, and Betty had to find ways to push their way out and make themselves from scratch. They had to start to build a world in which they could exist. Joan created a separate space in which to do this undisturbed. Peggy claimed her space inside the system. Betty remarried someone who loved her, and eventually enrolled in a psychology program in order to understand. She died before she could become herself. (At least she was spared Freud.) In the symbolic world that Don helped create, there was no *space*—no real or imagined context—for Joan, Peggy, and Betty to exist and to act as protagonists or subjects of desire. This is what Virginia Woolf was talking about in *A Room of One's Own*. One needs not just an actual room but also symbolic space in which to exist.

Joan, Peggy, and Betty all had "that outward existence which conforms, the inward life which questions" that Kate Chopin ascribed to her heroine Edna Pontellier in *The Awakening*. Like Henrik Ibsen's *A Doll's House*, George Bernard Shaw's *Pygmalion*, and Callie Khouri's *Thelma and Louise*, *The Awakening* is the story of a heroine becoming conscious of her condition; reclaiming her identity, femininity, and independence; and then—the story goes one of two ways—walking off a cliff or out the door. Thelma, Louise, and Edna go off the cliff, into the ocean; Ibsen's Nora, Shaw's Eliza, and *Mad Men*'s Joan walk out the door.

By the end of the series, Don had traded places with the women. His outward existence, the persona of the hero, the protagonist he took on, conferred on him all the things he lacked when he was a poor, unloved, unwanted, marginalized, traumatized nobody and gave him everything he needed to be a person in the world: freedom, agency, autonomy, and the authority to shape reality with his words to serve and please himself. He stepped into the role of the male subject with ease, no matter how fraught and misdirected his own relationship to his identity was, no matter how different his inner existence, because he looked the part (unlike, say, his brother, or the unattractive young copywriter who took his advice on acting like a dick to gain the client's respect only to get himself fired.

After inviting Peggy to be her partner in a new company (Peggy is flattered but decides to put in her time at McCann), Joan gathers together the fragments of herself; calls her new company Holloway-Harris, hyphenating her maiden and married names, putting herself back together, and striking out on her own. Meanwhile, Peggy, whose defining characteristic, as she told Joan on her very first day at work, is that she "always tries to tell the truth" — "Good for you," coos Joan, who always tries not to — marches back into McCann like she owns the place, strutting down the hall with her sunglasses on, a cigarette dangling from her lips, and Bert Cooper's Japanese painting of a woman being pleasured by an octopus under her arm. "I always try to tell the truth" is a funny thing for a future copywriter to say, but she means it. Like her mentor, Don, whose success hinges on his inborn talent for locating emotional truths in the biggest deceptions, she knows that, as Virginia Woolf said in *A Room of One's Own*, "fiction here is likely to contain more truth than fact."

The scene with Joan and Peggy in the elevator takes place during the final season of *Mad Men*, set in 1970. The first season took place in 1960. Joan and Peggy were fucked from the outset: Joan by Roger, who betrayed her by finally leaving his wife and marrying his *new* secretary, Jane; and Peggy by Pete, who came over to her apartment drunk the night of his bachelor party, when she was brand-new at work and had been made to understand that part of the job was always saying yes, and got her pregnant. (Peggy had the baby and gave it up, and never told anyone about it.) But they didn't stay fucked for long. Here are some of the things that actually happened between 1960 and 1975. In 1960, the FDA approved the birth-control pill. In 1961, President Kennedy established the President's Commission on the Status of Women and appointed

Eleanor Roosevelt as its chairwoman. In 1963, the commission issued a report documenting substantial workplace discrimination against women and made specific recommendations for improved hiring practices, paid maternity leave, and affordable child care. In 1963, Betty Friedan published *The Feminine Mystique* and Congress passed the Equal Pay Act, which made it illegal to pay a woman less than what a man would make for the same job. In 1964, Title VII of the Civil Rights Act barred employment discrimination on the basis of race, religion, national origin, and sex. The EEOC was established to investigate complaints. In 1966, Friedan and others founded the National Organization for Women (NOW), which tried to end sexual discrimination, mostly in the workplace, through legislative lobbying, litigation, and public demonstrations. In 1967, President Lyndon Johnson's affirmative-action policy of 1965 was expanded to cover gender discrimination.

The Miss America protest in Atlantic City took place in 1968. That year, the EEOC ruled to end sex-segregated help-wanted ads. In 1969, California adopted no-fault divorce, and laws were passed regarding the equal division of common property. In the summer of 1970, in what turned out to be the largest protest for gender equality in U.S. history, fifty thousand women marched down Fifth Avenue in New York demanding equal employment, educational opportunities, and twenty-four-hour child-care centers to make it possible to take advantage of these opportunities. In 1972, *Ms.* magazine was published for the first time, with a picture of Wonder Woman on the cover. That year, a universal twenty-four-hour day-care bill was drafted into existence and passed by Congress. Nixon vetoed the bill in 1972. In 1973, President Johnson's affirmative-action ruling was upheld by the Supreme Court and allowed women to apply for higher-paying jobs that had previously been open only to men. A U.S. court of appeals ruled that jobs needed to be "substantially equal" but not "identical" to be protected by the Equal Pay Act, making it illegal for an employer to change a job title in order to pay women less than men. A group called WOWI (Women on Words and Images) conducted a study of children's readers called *Dick and Jane as Victims,* used in New Jersey public school districts. The group found that boy-centered stories outnumbered girl-centered stories 5 to 2; adult male main characters outnumbered adult female main characters 3 to 1; male biographies outnumbered female biographies 6 to 1; male animal stories outnumbered female animal stories 2 to 1; and male folk or fantasy stories outnumbered female folk or fantasy stories 4 to 1. By the age of eight, 99 percent of children of both sexes were in basic agreement about "which sex does which job, what kind of person a girl or boy should be, and what the role limitations and expectations are."[1] WOWI pushed for revising the curriculum.

The Ms. Foundation released Marlo Thomas's 1972 book and album *Free to Be . . . You and Me,* which featured celebrities singing songs about celebrating individuality, tolerance, and being happy with who you were. (I got the *Free to Be . . . You and Me* album in 1973, when I was in kindergarten in New Jersey, where I learned to read using *Dick and Jane* books.) In 1972, Title IX of the Civil Rights Act was passed, prohibiting discrimination on the basis of sex in any federally funded education program or activity. In 1973, the Supreme Court ruled on *Roe v. Wade,* making abortion legal, and Nixon endorsed the Equal Rights Amendment, which later failed to be ratified by the requisite number of states. The Equal Credit Opportunity Act passed in 1974. Before that, a single, widowed, or divorced woman couldn't get a bank loan, credit card, or mortgage, regardless of income, unless a man cosigned the loan with her. The vice president of public relations for NOW testified before the National Association of Broadcasters Television Code Review Board and the Radio Code Review Board on the representation of women and the women's movement in the media and advertising.

I had no idea that any of these things were happening, or what they meant. I was listening to *Free to Be . . . You and Me* tell me I could do anything. It wasn't true yet, but I didn't know that. I didn't know how close to the edge I was, and have been all this time. It gives me vertigo to think about this now.

It's no coincidence that *Mad Men* ended when Joan and Peggy began, or that Joan and Peggy began when *Mad Men* ended. Don's true secret identity — bigger than his Dick Whitman secret, which turned out not to be a big deal in the end — was that he was a girl, too. He was hiding inside a performance that he was able to pull off because of the way he looked. He knew he was lucky. He understood what it was like not to be seen, to live in the wrong story. Who had a better view of the disconnect between the feminine ideal of the happy homemaker and mother, and reality? Don lived with Betty for years. He helped make her into the woman she was: sad, lost, angry, and mean. He understood better than anyone what it was to be trapped in a story, and how a story could set you free. He knew that transforming oneself into a strict category prototype, into the platonic ideal of a happy housewife, a *Playboy* mad-man-about-town, a bombshell, or a single career girl in the big city, was not only impossible but undesirable, inhuman: that it was to turn yourself into a robot.

As Roger's African American secretary, Dawn, tells him when she quits to take another job, in insurance, "Advertising is not a very comfortable place for everyone." And it's not. This polarized, highly unequal, antagonistic, symbolic place where everybody is the opposite of somebody else is dangerous. And then the whole thing gets called art, or, worse, human nature, instead of being recognized as the capitalist glory hole it really is.

21

Phantombusters; or, I Want
a Feminist Dance Number

A COUPLE OF YEARS AFTER PUBLISHING *A ROOM OF ONE'S Own*, Virginia Woolf was asked to give a speech at the National Society for Women's Service on the topic of professions for women. The day before giving the speech, while taking a bath, she'd had an idea for a whole new book. It would be, she wrote in her journal, "a sequel to *A Room of One's Own* — about the sexual life of women: to be called *Professions for Women*."[1]

Woolf started her speech by thanking the women writers who had come before her, and acknowledged that she'd had "very few material obstacles" to overcome in choosing writing as a profession. In fact, writing had historically been one of the few professions available to middle-class women. The reason for this, she said, was that writing as a woman posed few threats to the established order. It was "reputable and harmless," and "the family peace was not broken by the scratching of a pen." It required no capital investments or costly equipment. Paper was cheap, so "no demand was made upon the family purse" by women writers. The fact that writers didn't need "pianos and models, Paris, Vienna and Berlin, masters and mistresses" was probably the biggest reason that "women have succeeded as writers before they have succeeded in the other professions." In other words, writing was something a woman could do without raising eyebrows, ruffling feathers, making demands, taking up space, spending money, promoting herself, flaunting her success, or drawing any attention to herself. That's what made it, on the one hand, a good profession for a woman.[2]

What made it a difficult profession for women, on the other

hand, was that it required a degree of candor and freedom to speak and behave as one liked. It required a level of disinhibition and unconscious privilege that few women in 1930s England possessed. Woolf herself had been unaware of her own internalized inhibitions until she sat down to write her second piece of journalism. She wrote her first piece on spec, sold it, and bought herself a Persian cat with the proceeds. What could be easier, she thought, than to keep selling pieces and buying cats? Then she got her first assignment: a review of a book by a male author, a great man of letters. As she sat down to write, she heard a rustle of skirts and noticed that a "phantom" had cast a shadow on her paper.[3]

The "phantom" was a woman, but she was not a real woman. She was the Victorian ideal of femininity made famous by the poem "The Angel in the House." Woolf recognized her at once:

> She was intensely sympathetic. She was immensely charming. She was utterly unselfish. She excelled in the difficult arts of family life. She sacrificed herself daily. If there was chicken, she took the leg; if there was a draught she sat in it — in short she was so constituted that she never had a mind or a wish of her own, but preferred to sympathize always with the minds and wishes of others. Above all — I need not say it — she was pure. Her purity was supposed to be her chief beauty — her blushes, her great grace. In those days — the last of Queen Victoria — every house had its Angel.

Woolf recognized the phantom as her internalized Angel, the Angel she was brought up to be, who often came between her and her paper when she sat down to write. The Angel whispered to Woolf to remember her place: she was a young woman writing a review of a book by a famous man. The Angel cautioned her to be tender, to flatter and deceive her subject, to watch what she said. The Angel so bothered her, wasted her time, and tormented her that at last, in her imagination, Woolf attacked: "I turned upon her and caught her by the throat. I did my best to kill her." Her excuse in a court of law would be that she acted in self-defense: "Had I not killed her she would have killed me. She would have plucked the heart out of my writing." Because you can't write, you can't even review a novel, without a mind of your own, she explained, "without expressing what you think to be the truth about human relations, morality, sex . . . freely and openly" — and the Angel said women couldn't do this. Women must charm, conciliate, and lie to succeed. "Thus, whenever I felt the shadow of her wing or the radiance of her halo upon my page, I took up the inkpot and flung it at her. She died hard. Her fictitious nature was of great assistance to her. It is far harder to kill a phantom than a reality."[4]

If this doesn't prove unequivocally that Virginia Woolf predicted not just the all-female *Ghostbusters* reboot but also the insane prebacklash — forelash? — against it, then I don't know what does. The woman was an incandescent (her favorite word) genius. The speech dramatized the internal conflicts and problems that women who are women artists confront. It reworked the conflict between the Victorian "angel in the house," or the internalized voice of her mother and Mrs. Ramsay of *To the Lighthouse,* and herself and Lily Briscoe, as artists. Woolf wrote her death-match with the Angel as a comic battle between the author-heroine and the invisible forces that haunted her, as Julia Briggs wrote, "to show how the Victorian idealization of motherhood had also been a source of restraint and oppression, and, in particular, of sexual repression."[5] A woman who writes (or speaks, or directs, or makes anything, or leads) "has still many ghosts to fight, many prejudices to overcome," Woolf said. "Indeed, it will be a long time still, I think, before a woman can sit down to write a book without finding a phantom to be slain, a rock to be dashed against."[6]

Since the moment director Paul Feig announced his all-girl remake of *Ghostbusters* in the summer of 2014, he and the movie's leads were subjected to a sustained campaign of abuse. Feig called it "some of the most vile, misogynistic shit I've ever seen in my life." Rabid middle-age fanboys accused Feig of ruining their childhoods, threatened to boycott the movie, and tweeted sexist and racist abuse at the cast. Trolls banded together to make the movie trailer the most disliked video in the history of YouTube. They insisted, demanded, that the film not exist. When it stubbornly came into being despite their objections, they did their best to sabotage it.

This is not a new phenomenon, but in its current form it's not that old, either. When I was growing up, the assumption was that as older generations were replaced by younger generations, sexism would fade. This narrative was not only rarely challenged but remains popular to this day. It is hard to reconcile where we are with these obsessive, persistent, psychotically virulent attacks on anyone who refuses to conform to gender stereotypes, this insistence that certain fondly held ideas not be sullied by empirical reality.

Trolls are made, not born. Men in groups—like Telemachus and his buddies sending Penelope to her room, like the husbands of Stepford—bond by excluding women from power, by silencing them and policing their speech. Men who would never act this way individually change their behavior in a dominant group. This is what patriarchy is—a virtual Stepford.

A Room of One's Own was written a decade after women gained the vote. A backlash was in full swing. Woolf anticipated the criticism she would get in the essay, guessing that readers would object to the fact that she failed to compare the relative merits of men and women as writers. Even if it were possible to quantify talent in this way, if talent could be weighed "like sugar and butter," it would be counterproductive or, worse, would persist in framing the desire to redress pernicious and systemic gender inequality as a competition. In this, as in most things, she was prescient. For some reason, all these years later, the arguments are still essentialist, still personal. We still talk about what women can and can't have, or how much of it they can have. "All this pitting of sex against sex," Woolf wrote, "of quality against quality; all this claiming of superiority and imputing of inferiority, belong to the private-school stage of human existence where there are 'sides,' and it is necessary for one side to beat another side, and of the utmost importance to walk up to the platform and receive from the Headmaster himself a highly ornamental pot."

Just as Katharine Hepburn would later, Woolf attributed her freedom to pursue her art to family money and to the independence it gave her. She did not need to live by her charm, so she didn't. Even so, a writer must tell the truth about her own experiences as a body, and the obstacles against women doing this "are still immensely powerful — and yet they are very difficult to define." They are not obvious, or even visible to most. They are invisible forces, social conditioning, unspoken interdictions, ectoplasmic pop-culture slime. Woolf worried that people would object to her money, but "500 [pounds] a year stands for the power to contemplate, [and] a lock on the door stands for the power to think for oneself." She was prepared for even her intimate friends to dislike the "shrill feminine tone" of *A Room of One's Own*, and sure she would be "attacked for a feminist" and "hinted at for a sapphist" in the press. And this was decades before *Fox & Friends* and Twitter trolls.

I saw *Ghostbusters* with Kira, Darby, and Sydney. The girls loved it. They talked about it for hours and acted out scenes. Abby (Melissa McCarthy) and Erin (Kristen Wiig) are reunited after confronting the ghost of a Victorian lady, an "angel in the house" with the face and annihilating force of a demon. Sydney said it wasn't scary except for the anticipation before the first ghost appeared. Darby said she knew how Sydney felt: it reminded her of the dread she'd felt as a little girl in Connecticut in the seventies, terrified of growing up to be trapped in a beautiful house. Kira decided to be Kate McKinnon's Jillian for Halloween, and asked if it was too soon to start working on a costume. (It was July.)

The second-best thing about *Ghostbusters*, for me, was that it was good but not great; an enjoyable summer comedy. The best thing about it was that the four main characters were women playing people, not people playing "girls." The ordinariness of the characters was what made it thrilling.

If the *Ghostbusters* backlash proved anything, it's that the phantom that Virginia Woolf thought she killed is still alive. That Victorian lady ghost still needs to be busted.

Strange things happened to me while I was working on this book: fortuitous encounters, bizarre coincidences, unexpected turns of events, happy reunions, unlucky breaks that turned into lucky ones. Themes and motifs and patterns appeared in stories and in real life. For a while, I felt like I was writing in circles. Then, one day, I ran into a friend at the farmers' market who asked how it was going, and I told her I was writing in circles. She said I was not, I was writing in spirals, which is how the heroine's journey progresses. If the hero's journey of Joseph Campbell's oversimplified myth, the bane of folklorists' existence, is a money-shot parabola, then the heroine's journey is a corkscrew, a recursive journey inward to discover the authentic self.

She told me not to judge my spirals.

The next day, I went to the bookstore where I'd bought the copy of *Alice's Adventures in Wonderland,* to buy a book she had recommended. While there, I was overcome with the urge to buy a copy of *A Room of One's Own,* which I hadn't read since college. I barely remembered anything about it except that I loved it. All I recalled was something about how a woman needs an income of five hundred pounds a year and her own room if she is ever going to be a serious writer of fiction or poetry. Woolf was being literal about the money and the room with a door that locked, but she was also talking symbolically.

A Room of One's Own is Virginia Woolf's semifictional quest to prepare a lecture on the subject of women and fiction. At first, it seems simple enough, but the more she thinks about it, the more complicated it seems: "The title women and fiction might mean . . .

women and what they are like; or it might mean women and the fiction they write; or it might mean women and the fiction that is written about them; or it might mean that somehow all three are inextricably mixed together and you want me to consider them in that light."

Woolf decides to walk along the river at the fictional Oxbridge College to ponder the topic, but when she sits on the grass, she is shooed off by the beadle, who tells her the grass is for men only. Women must stay on the gravel path. She enjoys a sumptuous lunch as a guest at King's College, then a sad one with no wine at the women's college, Newnham. She wonders why women are so poor in relation to men, and decides to go to the British Museum to find out the truth about women — because where but the British Museum, she wonders drily, could such a truth be found?

Looking under the letter *W* in the catalog, she finds hundreds of books written by men about "women and their effect on whatever it may be" — about their character, their natural inclinations, their relative weakness, their moral, intellectual, and physical inferiority — a number of books so overwhelming that she can't bring herself to open them. The titles feel so hostile and dismissive and dehumanizing that it makes her cheeks flush and her pulse quicken. They all seem to be written in anger. This puzzles her — compared to women, men have everything. What are they so angry about? Why are they so determined to write about women, to make it hard for them to write, and then to refuse to read them?

She reads a fictional novel by a fictional contemporary woman novelist, and is amazed to encounter two female characters who like each other. "Chloe liked Olivia," she reads. And then it strikes her that it is perhaps the first time in literature that such a thing has happened. Until now, she's come across only fictional women who were jealous of each other or otherwise shown in relation to men. "Hence, perhaps, the peculiar nature of women in fiction;" she wrote, "the astonishing extremes of her beauty and horror; her alternations between heavenly goodness and hellish depravity."

Not to mention that every time she reads the newspaper, she is reminded "that when a woman speaks to women she should have something very unpleasant up her sleeve. Women are hard on women. Women dislike women. Women — but are you not sick to death of the word?"

I was still reading *A Room of One's Own* when the second season of *Doll and Em* premiered. The first shot of the first episode of the second season is a shot of a lighthouse. I thought, *That's weird*, because I'd forgotten that in the last scene of the first season, Em suggested to Doll that they go someplace to write something together as equals. They wind up in a lighthouse by the sea writing a play loosely based on themselves, and their friendship, and how they see each other's lives. The creators and stars of *Doll and Em* use their own lives and real families to produce a metanarrative that explores "their place," as artists and as women, in the world and in the entertainment industry. Wells's real-life husband and two kids play Em's husband and kids on the show. Mortimer's actual husband, Alessandro Nivola (who also produces), and her real-life son play husband and son to the character based on her, Lily, in the play. Doll and Em are loosely based on Virginia Woolf's characters in *To the Lighthouse*, the married Mrs. Ramsay and the single artist Lily Briscoe. The whole thing is a hall of mirrors in which it becomes impossible to tell when life is imitating art, and when art is shaping life. In fact, it's pointless to make the distinction. It's an eternally recurring loop; a infinite echo of diminishing — not ever-biggering — scale.

Doll and Em get off to a slightly bumpy start, because Em has vertigo and the lighthouse is one hundred feet high, but she recovers and they have an incredible time writing a surreal, allegorical play that "holds up a mirror to their lives." At first, they are exhilarated. "It's just so cool to finally be saying something for ourselves!" Em enthuses. The play is called *Joanna's Gift* (although there is no Joanna) and is inspired by the comedies of Shakespeare, so it is full of cross-dressing and mistaken identities and people falling in love with the wrong people. It's about them, but also not about them. Back in New York, where Em lives with her family, they pitch the play to Harvey Weinstein as being about "tiny moments that we don't feel other people see"; it is also "a metaphor . . . for . . . women . . . at this time." The pitch is so bad, so meandering and diffuse, that Weinstein gets up and walks out in the middle of it without a word.

Not long after that, Em gets an audition for a big-budget movie set in space (it sounds a lot like *Gravity*) starring Ewan McGregor, and directed by a first-timer (a Belgian chef) who has been given a budget of $60 million. They decide that if a Belgian chef can make a $60 million movie, then certainly they can direct their own play. Buddy, the English producer Dolly hooked up with in season 1, introduces them to his godfather, Mikhail Baryshnikov, who owns a theater and lets his friends use it for free. Because Em's movie schedule might conflict with the play, they decide to cast two younger, American actors — Olivia Wilde and Evan Rachel Wood, as themselves. Olivia is Lily, who is sort of Em, and Evan is Grace, who is sort of Doll, though they both insist they are not writing about themselves or each other.

Tensions escalate. The more Doll uses Em's real life as material, making Em feel hurt, resentful, and exposed, the more Em withdraws from Doll into her family and her movie career, making Doll feel abandoned, lost, and alone. Em gets cast in the Ewan McGregor movie, but then Doll meets McGregor in a bar and tells him that his character sounds "kind of like a giant iPhone charger," because he transfers his powers to his wife at the end so that she can save the world. Doll then proceeds to have sex with Ewan McGregor in the bathroom. Meanwhile, Em and her husband, Noah, are at a standoff. He has grown an Old Testament beard to protest her controlling nature, and she feels like Olivia is horning in on her actual life. Ewan drops out of the movie after thinking about what Doll said, and never calls her back. The movie financing falls apart.

Meanwhile, Evan and Olivia don't get the play. They don't understand what Doll and Em are trying to say, or it doesn't ring true. Doll and Em's stereotypically feminine traits — their vulnerability, openness to showing their feelings and sharing their thoughts, no matter how insensitive, insecure, or crazy-sounding — are what make them artists, and brave. They are also what make people impatient with them. Doll and Em can't stop rewriting the play, using it as a way to comment on each other and each other's lives without saying so directly. Evan and Olivia feel like they are caught in the middle of a private psychodrama, which they are. Evan and Olivia are ten years younger than Doll and Em, and American, and confident in that American way that equates self-deprecation with low self-esteem.

Evan and Olivia appear to live entirely inside the bubble of what things are supposed to be like. They are so committed to the narrative of the "strong female character" that they pretend not to know what Doll and Em are talking about when they say women have a harder time saying how they really feel and stating what they want — and that they aren't entirely free.

"This is set in 2015, right?" Evan asks with a note of contempt, as if to say, Haven't we moved on? Haven't *you* moved on? *Because we have, old ladies.*

So they say.

Yet Evan and Olivia's slick, impenetrable emotional carapace makes them better suited for Hollywood, where self-deprecating humor is met with horror. When the four of them have dinner at Em's house one night and Em says something about the disappointing way her dessert turned out, Evan and Olivia are amazed.

"You don't give a shit, do you?" Evan exclaims in delighted shock. What she means is, *You don't give a shit about what people think of you. You don't manage your image. You don't perform your self for others to admire and envy and long for. You are a liability to your own brand.* The inversion is strange. Evan and Olivia are enslaved to appearances, aggressively performing their freedom to say and be anything. As long as it's not, you know, old, weak, indecisive, afraid.

Olivia gets into it, though. She studies Em's life, slips on her robe, tests out her bed, chats with her husband, takes her kids to dinner. She's the younger, easier, less neurotic version, the version with the kinks worked out — she's the Stepford Wife.

In an interview, the real Emily Mortimer told a story about meeting a producer at a party once. When he asked what she did for a living, she found herself in the clichéd scenario of having to tell him that she was an actress. So she tacked on, "Not a very good one," and he looked at her like she'd just admitted she ate out of Dumpsters.

Near the end of the episode, as Emily is walking down the street, Virginia Woolf shows up and gives Emily permission to be herself, to say what she wants.

The next day, Em tells Doll: "I want a feminist dance number."
Evan and Olivia quit, so Doll and Em take the stage.

When I was a kid, I assumed I could be anything, because I was everything, and anything could happen. When we learn, in ambient, subconscious ways, that some people belong to categories that are more important than others, we start to apply these values to ourselves. As girls, we're born into a world that directs our subjectivity away from us all the time, that tells us not to trust our own eyes, that tells us to deny our feelings, that makes it nearly impossible to know who we are. What makes you feel seen? How much of your self-concept have you absorbed from the world around you? Is it possible to remove that self-concept from your mind? To remove all of that information from your brain and re-create a self and walk around in it? Women do this work daily. Before the heroine can set out on her journey, she has to free herself from the tower like Rapunzel, or from the lunatic reverend's suburban-backyard bunker. She has to liberate herself from the oppressive fairy tale, the fearmongering tabloid story. She has to refuse and to write her own way out. She can do it, because she's unbreakable, like *The Unbreakable Kimmy Schmidt* theme song says. She's alive, dammit.

Near the start of *The Heroine's Text,* Nancy K. Miller observes that the orphaned ingenue heroine — the young princess — is not "a sophisticated decoder" of the story she has grown up in. None of us are experienced decoders at first. It takes a long time to wake up. And even then, the snooze button is always at hand. Sleeping Beauty wakes up and is delivered by her prince into the house of her father and her nameless mother. Alice wakes up, runs home for tea, and is dreamed again by her sleeping sister as a young mother, telling stories to children about adventures that never happened.

Six months later, when Alice steps through the looking glass, she finds the countryside is laid out in squares like a chessboard, and her moves are determined by rigid rules that guide her toward one conclusion. Alice starts out as a pawn with very little control over the direction of her life or even where she is headed. Her choices and movements are constrained by a bigger system, and her actions are not really free. She becomes a queen despite herself, involuntarily. She has no power to influence outcomes. Even as she moves toward her goals, she senses that she's being acted upon, that the story is happening to her, including her rescue by the White Knight. Language, meanwhile, has the power to make things happen.

For me, the experience of going back through the looking glass of pop culture was transformative. It remade my relationship with myself. It changed my understanding of my marriage, of marriage in general. It helped me renegotiate it, like Tracy and Dexter did, though a series of long, open-ended conversations, and try again, with clearer eyes. The heroine's journey starts with the realization that she is trapped inside the illusion of a perfect world where she has no power. She employs coping strategies at first, or tries to deny reality, but eventually she is betrayed, or loses everything, and can no longer lie to herself. She wakes up. She gathers her courage. She finds the willingness to go it alone. She faces her own symbolic death. (The hero, conversely, chooses outer exploration over inner exploration, questions authority, and becomes his true self. Neither journey is gender-specific.) The heroine's journey is circular. It moves forward in spirals and burrows inward, to understanding. It can be undertaken by anyone, male or female, who is ready to move past the illusion of a perfect world and a straight shot to selfhood. The path is treacherous. The territory is hostile. But the heroine is brave. She knows what she wants. She's determined to get it. Isn't that how all good stories start?

Acknowledgments

I thank my agent, the incomparable Sarah Burnes, for her friendship, encouragement, enthusiasm, and support. I'm grateful to have had not one but two of my brilliant, funny, insightful, and patient editors, Jenna Johnson and Pilar Garcia-Brown, the latter of whom shepherded the book to completion with such humor and spot-on instincts. Thanks so much to Rachael DeShano, Tammy Zambo, and the production team for putting up with last-minute changes. A million thanks to Kathy Daneman, Lori Glazer, Stephanie Kim, and everyone on the marketing and publicity team for their enthusiasm and great ideas. I'm also so grateful to Logan Garrison, Rebecca Gardner, and everyone at the Gernert Company for being unfailingly great at all times.

I could not have written this book without the overwhelming love, free therapy, wire transfers, plane tickets, hot meals, impromptu retreats, feedback, and emotional, domestic, tech, and all-around life support of my amazing family and friends. I'm especially grateful to my mom, Olga María Penny; my parents-in-law, Linda and Ken Wadlin; my siblings, Gonzalo Chocano and Magaly Chocano; my brother-in-law, Tirso Sigg; my friends, Darby Maloney, Janelle Brown, Dawn MacKeen, Erica Rothschild, Annabelle Gurwitch, and Christine Beebe; and my husband, Craig Wadlin, for their generosity, patience, and perseverance in keeping me alive.

I'd like to thank Meghan Daum, Heather Havrilesky, Tula Jeng, Adam Sternbergh, Rachel Abramowitz, Rachel Samuels, Lisa Hamilton-Daly, Kimberly Burns, Andy Young, Kathleen A. Laughlin, Billy Mernit, Martha Lauzen, Titia Vermeer, Dana Simmons, Jillian Lauren, Keshni Kashyap, Marian Belgray, Emily Ryan Lerner, Tracy McMillan, Gina Fattore, Strawberry Saroyan, Ramune Nagisetty, Anne-Marie O'Connor, Jade Chang, Stella Oh, Miranda Thompson, Danielle Parsons, Kristina Lear, Josh Zetumer, Tim

Kirkman, and everyone at Suite 8 for their input, feedback, advice, support, and political inspiration.

Special thanks to Jill Soloway for magically appearing to douse the flame with lighter fluid just when it was down to a flicker and in imminent danger of being extinguished by a discreet, ladylike yawn. Thank you for the conflagration.

And to my amazing daughter, Kira, for being ever curious, always insisting on presenting her evidence, and never holding her tongue.

And to Hillary Clinton, for inspiring us both.

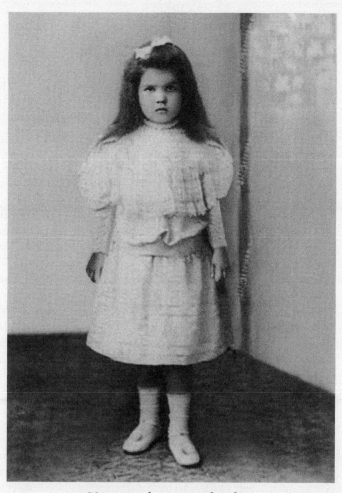

My maternal great-grandmother,
Rosa María Montenegro de la Fuente, age six.
Chiclayo, Peru, 1906.

Notes

Introduction

1. Lewis Carroll, *Alice's Adventures in Wonderland* (Mineola, NY: Dover Publications, 2011), 120.
2. Barbara Welter, *Dimity Convictions: The American Woman in the Nineteenth Century* (Athens: Ohio University Press, 1976).
3. Gerda Lerner, *The Creation of Patriarchy* (New York: Oxford University Press, 1986).
4. Lori Anne Loeb, *Consuming Angels: Advertising and Victorian Women* (New York: Oxford University Press, 1994), 21.
5. "Notes on New Womanhood," Professor Catherine Lavender, prepared for students in HST 386: Women in the City, 1998, https://csivc.csi.cuny.edu/history/files/lavender/386/newwoman.pdf.
6. Lerner, *The Creation of Patriarchy*.
7. Barbara Welter, "The Cult of True Womanhood: 1820–1860," *American Quarterly* 18, no. 2, part 1 (Summer 1966): 151–74.
8. Renata Adler, *A Year in the Dark: A Year in the Life of a Film Critic, 1968–1969* (New York: Berkeley, 1971).
9. "Borat's Babe Plans a Hollywood Sex Revolution," *New Zealand Herald*, October 9, 2007, http://www.stuff.co.nz/entertainment/25788/Borats-babe-Isla-plans-sex-revolution.
10. Ibid.

1. Bunnies

1. "Hugh Hefner: 'I Am in the Center of the World,'" interview by Oriana Fallaci, *Look*, January 10, 1967.
2. Carlye Adler, "Hugh Hefner Playboy Enterprises: 'In 1953 I Didn't Fully Appreciate What I Had Created. It Was the First Successful Magazine for Young, Single Men,'" CNNMoney.com, September 1, 2003.
3. Susan Braudy, "Up Against the Centerfold: What It Was Like to Report on Feminism for *Playboy* in 1969," *Pictorial*, March 18, 2016, posted on *Jezebel*, accessed January 29, 2017.
4. Hefner, interview by Fallaci.

5. Judith Butler, *Gender Trouble: Feminism and the Subversion of Identity*, 2nd ed. (New York: Routledge, 2006).

6. Katha Pollitt, "Hers; The Smurfette Principle," *New York Times Magazine*, April 7, 1991.

2. Can This Marriage Be Saved?

1. Judy Klemesrud, "Feminists Recoil at Film Designed to Relate to Them," *New York Times*, February 26, 1975, http://query.nytimes.com/gst/abstract.html?res=9f04e2d71e3de034bc4e51dfb466838e669ede.

2. Ibid.

3. Jane Elliott, "Stepford U.S.A.: Second-Wave Feminism, Domestic Labor, and the Representation of National Time," *Cultural Critique* 70, no. 1 (2008): 32–62, doi:10.1353/cul.0.0022.

4. Susan Brownmiller, *In Our Time: Memoir of a Revolution* (New York: Dial Press, 1999), 84.

5. Roger Ebert, review of *The Stepford Wives*, screenplay by William Goldman, directed by Bryan Forbes, RogerEbert.com, January 1, 1975, http://www.rogerebert.com/reviews/the-stepford-wives-1975.

6. Betty Friedan, *The Feminine Mystique* (New York: Norton, 1963).

7. Stephanie Coontz, *A Strange Stirring: "The Feminine Mystique" and American Women at the Dawn of the 1960s* (New York: Basic Books, 2011).

8. Friedan, *The Feminine Mystique*.

9. Ibid.

10. Kathleen A. Laughlin, Julie Gallagher, Dorothy Sue Cobble, Eileen Boris, Premilla Nadasen, Stephanie Gilmore, and Leandra Zarnow, "Is It Time to Jump Ship? Historians Rethink the Waves Metaphor," *Feminist Formations* 22, no. 1 (Spring 2010): 76–135.

11. Kate Millett, *Sexual Politics* (Urbana: University of Illinois Press, 2000).

12. Nancy K. Miller, *The Heroine's Text: Readings in the French and English Novel, 1722–1782* (New York: Columbia University Press, 1980), x.

13. Elliott, "Stepford U.S.A."

14. Ibid.

15. Coontz, *A Strange Stirring*.

16. Ibid., xxii.

17. Charlotte Perkins Gilman, *Women and Economics: A Study of the Eco-*

nomic Relation Between Men and Women as a Factor in Social Evolution (Berkeley: University of California Press, 1998).

18. Wednesday Martin, "Poor Little Rich Women," *New York Times*, May 16, 2015.

19. Rebecca Onion, "Lock Up Your Wives!," *Aeon*, September 8, 2014, https://aeon.co/essays/the-warped-world-of-marriage-advice-before -feminism.

20. Ibid.

21. Alexandra Stern, *Eugenic Nation: Faults and Frontiers of Better Breeding in Modern America* (Berkeley: University of California Press, 2005), 189–90.

22. Onion, "Lock Up Your Wives!"

23. Frank Kermode, *The Sense of an Ending: Studies in the Theory of Fiction,* new ed. (Oxford: Oxford University Press, 2000).

3. The Bronze Statue of the Virgin Slut
Ice Queen Bitch Goddess

1. Ana Salzberg, *Beyond the Looking Glass: Narcissism and Female Stardom in Studio-Era Hollywood* (New York: Berghahn, 2014), 35–53.

2. Oliver O. Jensen, "The Hepburns," *Life*, January 22, 1940, 48.

4. What a Feeling

1. Mick LaSalle, "Replay: 'Flashdance,'" *SFGate* (blog), March 22, 2014, http://blog.sfgate.com/mlasalle/2014/03/22/replay-flashdance.

2. Teresa de Lauretis, *Alice Doesn't: Feminism, Semiotics, Cinema* (Bloomington: Indiana University Press, 1984).

3. Mary Ann Doane, *The Desire to Desire: The Woman's Film of the 1940s* (Bloomington: Indiana University Press, 1987).

4. Molly Haskell, *From Reverence to Rape: The Treatment of Women in the Movies* (New York: Holt, Rinehart & Winston, 1974), 30.

5. Linda Seger, *When Women Call the Shots: The Developing Power and Influence of Women in Television and Film* (New York: Henry Holt & Co., 1996).

6. Ibid.

7. "Meta Wilde, 86, Faulkner's Lover," *New York Times*, October 21,

1994, http://www.nytimes.com/1994/10/21/obituaries/meta-wilde-86 -faulkner-s-lover.html.

5. The Eternal Allure of the Basket Case

1. Alex Beam, "The Mad Poets Society," *Atlantic*, July 2001, http://www .theatlantic.com/magazine/archive/2001/07/the-mad-poets-society /302257/.
2. James Dearden, "*Fatal Attraction* writer: Why My Stage Version Has a Different Ending," *Guardian*, March 9, 2014.
3. Nancy Jo Sales, "Love in a Cold Climate," *Vanity Fair*, November 2011.

6. The Ingenue Chooses Marriage or Death

1. Julia V. Douthwaite, *Exotic Women: Literary Heroines and Cultural Strategies in Ancien Régime France* (Philadelphia: University of Pennsylvania Press, 1992).
2. Rebecca Walker, "Becoming the Third Wave," *Ms.*, January 1992.

7. Thoroughly Modern Lily

1. Adam Gopnik, "Metamoney," *The New Yorker*, November 9, 1998.
2. Ernest Jones, Lionel Trilling, and Steven Marcus, *The Life and Work of Sigmund Freud* (New York: Basic Books, 1961).
3. Sigmund Freud, "Some Psychical Consequences of the Anatomical Distinction Between the Sexes" (1925), index of Sigmund Freud files, accessed August 11, 2016, http://aquestionofexistence.com/Aquestionof existence/Problems_of_Gender/Entries/2011/8/28_Sigmund_Freud .html.

9. The Kick-Ass

1. Slavoj Žižek, *The Sublime Object of Ideology* (London: Verso, 1989).

10. Surreal Housewives

1. Charlotte Brunsdon, *The Feminist, the Housewife, and the Soap Opera* (Oxford: Clarendon Press, 2000).

2. Robin J. Ely, Pamela Stone, and Colleen Ammerman, "Rethink What You 'Know' about High-Achieving Women," *Harvard Business Review,* December 1, 2014, https://hbr.org/2014/12/rethink-what-you-know -about-high-achieving-women.

11. Real Girls

1. Julie Beck, "Married to a Doll: Why One Man Advocates Synthetic Love," *Atlantic,* September 6, 2013, http://www.theatlantic.com /health/archive/2013/09/married-to-a-doll-why-one-man-advocates -synthetic-love/279361/.

12. Celebrity Gothic

1. Fred Botting, *Gothic* (New York: Routledge, 2014).
2. Jim Rutenberg, "The Gossip Machine, Churning Out Cash," *New York Times,* May 21, 2011, http://www.nytimes.com/2011/05/22/us/22 gossip.html?_r=0.
3. Jonathan L. Fischer, "Shocking! The Proto-TMZ," *T* magazine, January 20, 2010, http://tmagazine.blogs.nytimes.com/2010/01/20/shocking -the-proto-tmz/.
4. Rutenberg, "The Gossip Machine."

13. Big Mouth Strikes Again

1. Michel Foucault, *Fearless Speech,* ed. Joseph Pearson (Los Angeles: Semiotext(e), 2001).
2. David Denby, "A Fine Romance," *The New Yorker,* July 23, 2007.
3. Ibid.

14. The Redemptive Journey

1. Jack Zipes, *Fairy Tales and the Art of Subversion: The Classical Genre for Children and the Process of Civilization* (New York: Wildman, 1983).
2. Steve Almond, "Eat, Pray, Love, Get Rich, Write a Novel No One Expects," *New York Times Magazine,* September 21, 2013, http://www .nytimes.com/2013/09/22/magazine/eat-pray-love-get-rich-write-a -novel-no-one-expects.html.
3. Zipes, *Fairy Tales.*

15. A Modest Proposal for More Backstabbing in Preschool

1. Alison Gopnik, "A Manifesto Against 'Parenting,'" *Wall Street Journal*, July 8, 2016, http://www.wsj.com/articles/a-manifesto-against-parenting-1467991745.
2. Rhaina Cohen, "Who Took Care of Rosie the Riveter's Kids?," *Atlantic*, November 18, 2015, http://www.theatlantic.com/business/archive/2015/11/daycare-world-war-rosie-riveter/415650/.
3. Sonya Michel, *Children's Interests/Mothers' Rights: The Shaping of America's Child Care Policy* (New Haven, Conn.: Yale University Press, 1999); Chris M. Herbst, "Universal Child Care, Maternal Employment, and Children's Long-Run Outcomes: Evidence from the U.S. Lanham Act of 1940" (PhD diss., Arizona State University, 2013).
4. Susan J. Douglas and Meredith W. Michaels, *The Mommy Myth: The Idealization of Motherhood and How It Has Undermined All Women* (New York: Free Press, 2004), 34.
5. Nancy L. Cohen, "Why America Never Had Universal Child Care," *New Republic*, April 23, 2013, https://newrepublic.com/article/113009/child-care-america-was-very-close-universal-day-care.
6. R. Cohen, "Who Took Care?"

16. Let It Go

1. Jack Zipes, *Fairy Tales and the Art of Subversion: The Classical Genre for Children and the Process of Civilization* (New York: Wildman, 1983).
2. Ibid.
3. Marina Warner, *From the Beast to the Blonde: On Fairy Tales and Their Tellers* (New York: Farrar, Straus & Giroux, 1995).
4. "Scriptnotes, Ep 128: Frozen with Jennifer Lee—Transcript," John August, last modified February 1, 2014, http://johnaugust.com/2014/scriptnotes-ep-128-frozen-with-jennifer-lee-transcript.

17. All the Bad Guys Are Girls

1. Jack Zipes, *Fairy Tales and the Art of Subversion: The Classical Genre for Children and the Process of Civilization* (New York: Wildman, 1983).

18. Girls Love Math

1. Benedict Carey, "Father's Age Is Linked to Risk of Autism and Schizophrenia," *New York Times*, August 22, 2012.
2. Paul Gibney, "The Double Bind Theory: Still Crazy-Making after All These Years," *Psychotherapy in Australia* 12, no. 3 (May 2006): 48–50.

20. Look at Yourself

1. Jenny McPhee, "Cordelia Fine, Neurosexism, and My Mother (Again)," *Bookslut*, October 2010, http://www.bookslut.com/the_bombshell/20 10_10_016690.php.

21. Phantombusters; or, I Want a Feminist Dance Number

1. Julia Briggs, *Virginia Woolf: An Inner Life* (Orlando: Harcourt, 2005).
2. Virginia Woolf, *Selected Essays*, ed. David Bradshaw (Oxford: Oxford University Press, 2008).
3. Ibid.
4. Ibid.
5. Briggs, *Virginia Woolf.*
6. Ibid.

Works Consulted

Books/Recommended Reading

Beauvoir, Simone de. *The Second Sex*. New York: Knopf, 1953.

Brownmiller, Susan. *In Our Time: Memoir of a Revolution*. New York: Dial Press, 1999.

Brunsdon, Charlotte. *Screen Tastes: Soap Opera to Satellite Dishes*. London: Routledge, 1997.

Butler, Judith. *Gender Trouble: Feminism and the Subversion of Identity*. 2nd ed. New York: Routledge, 2006.

Carroll, Lewis. *Alice's Adventures in Wonderland*. Illustrated by Alison Jay. New York: Dial Books for Young Readers, 2006.

Coontz, Stephanie. *A Strange Stirring: "The Feminine Mystique" and American Women at the Dawn of the 1960s*. New York: Basic Books, 2011.

Crosby, Christina. *The Ends of History: Victorians and "the Woman Question."* New York: Routledge, 1990.

de Lauretis, Teresa. *Alice Doesn't: Feminism, Semiotics, Cinema*. Bloomington: Indiana University Press, 1984.

Doane, Mary Ann. *The Desire to Desire: The Woman's Film of the 1940s*. Bloomington: Indiana University Press, 1987.

Douglas, Susan J. *Where the Girls Are: Growing Up Female with the Mass Media*. New York: Times Books, 1994.

———. *Enlightened Sexism: The Seductive Message that Feminism's Work Is Done*. New York: Times Books, 2010.

Friedan, Betty. *The Feminine Mystique*. New York: Norton, 1963.

Gilbert, Sandra M., and Susan Gubar. *The Madwoman in the Attic: The Woman Writer and the Nineteenth-Century Literary Imagination*. New Haven: Yale University Press, 1979.

Gilman, Charlotte Perkins. *Women and Economics: A Study of the Economic Relation Between Men and Women as a Factor in Social Evolution*. Berkeley: University of California Press, 1998.

———. *The Yellow Wallpaper and Selected Writings*. London: Virago, 2009.

Gilman, Charlotte Perkins, and Ann J. Lane. *Herland*. New York: Pantheon Books, 1979.

Haskell, Molly. *From Reverence to Rape: The Treatment of Women in the Movies.* New York: Holt, Rinehart & Winston, 1974.

Heilbrun, Carolyn G. *Writing a Woman's Life.* New York: Ballantine, 1989.

Henry, Astrid. *Not My Mother's Sister: Generational Conflict and Third-Wave Feminism.* Bloomington: Indiana University Press, 2004.

Holmes, Su, and Diane Negra. *In the Limelight and Under the Microscope: Forms and Functions of Female Celebrity.* New York: Continuum, 2011.

hooks, bell. *Feminist Theory from Margin to Center.* Boston: South End Press, 1984.

Lerner, Gerda. *The Creation of Patriarchy.* New York: Oxford University Press, 1986.

Levin, Ira. *The Stepford Wives: A Novel.* New York: Random House, 1972.

Loeb, Lori Anne. *Consuming Angels: Advertising and Victorian Women.* New York: Oxford University Press, 1994.

Mann, William J. *Kate: The Woman Who Was Hepburn.* New York: Henry Holt & Co., 2006.

Mill, John Stuart. *The Subjection of Women.* London: Electric Book Co., 2001.

Miller, Nancy K. *The Heroine's Text: Readings in the French and English Novel, 1722–1782.* New York: Columbia University Press, 1980.

Millett, Kate. *Sexual Politics.* Urbana: University of Illinois Press, 2000.

Ryan, Christopher, and Cacilda Jethá. *Sex at Dawn: How We Mate, Why We Stray, and What It Means for Modern Relationships.* New York: Harper, 2011.

Schubart, Rikke. *Super Bitches and Action Babes: The Female Hero in Popular Cinema, 1970–2006.* Jefferson, N.C.: McFarland, 2007.

Seger, Linda. *When Women Call the Shots: The Developing Power and Influence of Women in Television and Film.* New York: Henry Holt & Co., 1996.

Showalter, Elaine. *The Female Malady: Women, Madness, and English Culture, 1830–1980.* New York: Pantheon, 1985.

———. *Sexual Anarchy: Gender and Culture at the Fin de Siècle.* New York: Penguin, 1991.

Warner, Marina. *From the Beast to the Blonde: On Fairy Tales and Their Tellers.* New York: Farrar, Straus & Giroux, 1995.

Welter, Barbara. *Dimity Convictions: The American Woman in the Nineteenth Century.* Athens: Ohio University Press, 1976.

Wollstonecraft, Mary. *A Vindication of the Rights of Woman.* 2nd ed. Edited by Eileen Hunt Botting. New Haven, Conn.: Yale University Press, 2014.

Woolf, Virginia. *A Room of One's Own.* San Diego: Harcourt Brace Jovanovich, 1989.

Yalom, Marilyn. *A History of the Wife.* New York: HarperCollins, 2001.

Zeisler, Andi. *Feminism and Pop Culture.* Berkeley: Seal Press, 2008.

Zipes, Jack. *Fairy Tales and the Art of Subversion: The Classical Genre for Children and the Process of Civilization.* New York: Wildman, 1983.

———. *The Irresistible Fairy Tale: The Cultural and Social History of a Genre.* Princeton: Princeton University Press, 2012.

Articles/Chapters

Elliott, Jane. "Stepford U.S.A.: Second-Wave Feminism, Domestic Labor, and the Representation of National Time." *Cultural Critique* 70 (2008): 32–62.

Goodlad, Lauren M. E. "The *Mad Men* in the Attic: Seriality and Identity in the Narrative of Capitalist Globalization." *Modern Language Quarterly* 73 no. 2 (June 2012): 201–34.

Salzberg, Ana. "Katharine Hepburn and a Hollywood Story." In *Beyond the Looking Glass: Narcissism and Female Stardom in Studio-Era Hollywood,* 35–54. 1st ed. New York: Berghahn Books, 2014.

Studies

"The Status of Women in the U.S. Media 2015." Women's Media Center. Accessed November 4, 2016. http://www.womensmediacenter.com/pages/2015-statistics.

Lauzen, Martha. "It's a Man's (Celluloid) World: Portrayals of Female Characters in the Top 100 Films of 2015." Center for the Study of Women in Television & Film. Accessed November 4, 2016. http://womenintvfilm.sdsu.edu/research/.

———. "Boxed In 2015–16: Women On Screen and Behind the Scenes in Television." Center for the Study of Women in Television & Film. Accessed November 4, 2016. http://womenintvfilm.sdsu.edu/research/.

———. "Thumbs Down 2016: Top Film Critics and Gender." Center for the

Study of Women in Television & Film. Accessed November 4, 2016. http://womenintvfilm.sdsu.edu/research/.

———. "Women in Independent Film, 2015–16." Center for the Study of Women in Television & Film. Accessed November 4, 2016. http://womenintvfilm.sdsu.edu/research/.

Films/Recommended Viewing (or Not!)

Camille Claudel. Directed by Bruno Nuytten. France: MGM, 1988.

Camille Claudel 1915. Directed by Bruno Dumont. France: 3B Productions, 2013.

Cinderella. Directed by Clyde Geronimi, Wilfred Jackson. Hollywood: Walt Disney Pictures, 1950.

Desperately Seeking Susan. Directed by Susan Seidelman. Hollywood: Orion Pictures, 1985.

Diary of a Mad Housewife. Directed by Frank Perry. Hollywood: Universal Pictures, 1970.

L'Eclisse. Directed by Michelangelo Antonioni. Rome: Cineriz, 1962.

Entre Nous. Directed by Diane Kurys. France: Partner's Pictures, 1983.

Fast Times at Ridgemont High. Directed by Amy Heckerling. Hollywood: Universal. 1982.

Fatal Attraction. Directed by Adrian Lyne. Hollywood: Paramount Pictures, 1987.

Flashdance. Directed by Adrian Lyne. Hollywood: Paramount Pictures, 1983.

Maleficent. Directed by Robert Stromberg. US/UK: Walt Disney Pictures, 2014.

My Brilliant Career. Directed by Gillian Armstrong. Australia: GUO, 1979.

The Philadelphia Story. Directed by George Cukor. Hollywood: MGM, 1940.

Pretty Baby. Directed by Louis Malle. Hollywood: Paramount, 1978.

Private Benjamin. Directed by Howard Zieff. Hollywood: Warner Bros., 1980.

Snow White. Directed by Clyde Geronimi. Hollywood: Walt Disney Pictures, 1959.

Snow White and the Seven Dwarfs. Directed by William Cottrell and David Hand. Hollywood: Walt Disney Pictures, 1937.

The Stepford Wives. Directed by Frank Oz. Hollywood: Columbia Pictures, 1975.

The Stepford Wives. Directed by Bryan Forbes. Hollywood: Paramount Pictures, 2004.

The Story of Adele H. Directed by François Truffaut. France: Les Artistes Associés, 1975.

An Unmarried Woman. Directed by Paul Mazursky. Hollywood: Twentieth Century Fox, 1978.